TRAUMA, SPIRITUALITY, AND POSTTRAUMATIC GROWTH IN CLINICAL SOCIAL WORK PRACTICE

Edited by Heather M. Boynton and Jo-Ann Vis

Trauma and the exposure to traumatic events is part of life, making the need for current and informed social work research and training in this area essential. *Trauma, Spirituality, and Posttraumatic Growth in Clinical Social Work Practice* highlights unique and diverse circumstances throughout a client's lifecycle where trauma is experienced, how one's spirituality is awakened or activated, and how this experience can intersect with interventions toward posttraumatic growth (PTG). More than just a primer on trauma effects, the book offers social workers insights into how to properly assess current resources and individual levels of distress. It also provides practical strategies on how spirituality and spiritual practices can be integrated into psychotherapeutic interventions at various levels of social work practice.

Addressing the impact of trauma-related events and emphasizing the importance of spirituality, the book will inspire and provide transferable knowledge that social workers can use to meet the unique needs of the clients, families, and communities they serve.

HEATHER M. BOYNTON is an assistant professor in the Faculty of Social Work at the University of Calgary, an adjunct professor of Kinesiology at Lakehead University, a faculty member at the Northern Ontario School of Medicine, and Vice President of the Canadian Society for Spirituality and Social Work.

JO-ANN VIS is an associate professor in the School of Social Work at Lakehead University.

Trauma, Spirituality, and Posttraumatic Growth in Clinical Social Work Practice

EDITED BY HEATHER M. BOYNTON
AND JO-ANN VIS

UNIVERSITY OF TORONTO PRESS
Toronto Buffalo London

ISBN 978-1-4875-4394-5 (cloth)   ISBN 978-1-4875-4396-9 (EPUB)
ISBN 978-1-4875-4395-2 (paper)   ISBN 978-1-4875-4397-6 (PDF)

Library and Archives Canada Cataloguing in Publication

Title: Trauma, spirituality, and posttraumatic growth in clinical social
    work practice / edited by Heather M. Boynton and Jo-Ann Vis.
Names: Boynton, Heather M., editor. | Vis, Jo-Ann, editor.
Identifiers: Canadiana (print) 20210346442 | Canadiana (ebook)
    20210346566 | ISBN 9781487543945 (hardcover) | ISBN 9781487543952
    (softcover) | ISBN 9781487543969 (EPUB) | ISBN 9781487543976 (PDF)
Subjects: LCSH: Social service – Religious aspects. | LCSH: Psychic trauma –
    Treatment. | LCSH: Post-traumatic stress disorder – Treatment. |
    LCSH: Spirituality.
Classification: LCC RC552.T7 T73 2022 | DDC 362.2/5 – dc23

We wish to acknowledge the land on which the University of Toronto Press
operates. This land is the traditional territory of the Wendat, the Anishnaabeg, the
Haudenosaunee, the Métis, and the Mississaugas of the Credit First Nation.

University of Toronto Press acknowledges the financial support of the Government
of Canada, the Canada Council for the Arts, and the Ontario Arts Council, an agency
of the Government of Ontario, for its publishing activities.

Canada Council   Conseil des Arts
for the Arts   du Canada

ONTARIO ARTS COUNCIL
CONSEIL DES ARTS DE L'ONTARIO
an Ontario government agency
un organisme du gouvernement de l'Ontario

Funded by the   Financé par le
Government   gouvernement
of Canada   du Canada

Canada

Contents

TRAUMA, SPIRITUALITY, AND POSTTRAUMATIC GROWTH IN CLINICAL SOCIAL WORK PRACTICE

Introduction

HEATHER BOYNTON AND JO-ANN VIS

There now appears to be consensus that there is a role for including spirituality in social work, and its necessity for working holistically with individuals, families, and communities (Carrington, 2017; Gardner, 2017). Yet, there is a gap in the area of spirituality and social work and its essential role in trauma and posttraumatic growth (PTG), especially within the Canadian context. Crisp (2017) posed a very critical question regarding spirituality: "Does the local spiritual/religious culture have implications for social work practice, and if so, how?" (p. 376). We believe that this book demonstrates that in Canada, given its multicultural nature, there are various local spiritual/religious cultures and cultural practices that have considerable implications for practice, as well as for education and research.

Social workers are well positioned to facilitate PTG through attending to spirituality. Looking at the broader literature across disciplines assists in thinking about spirituality from a social work lens. Swinton (2001) described spirituality as an "outward expression of the inner workings of the human spirit" (p. 20). He viewed spirituality as a personal and social process where one interprets the experiences of the spirit. This also comprises our inner processes involving ideas, concepts, values, attitudes, and behaviours. He included the process of *becoming* as part of spirituality, a process which involves reflecting on who one is, and how one comes to know. He saw these experiences and processes as core features of spirituality, and explains that spirituality is "an intra, inter and transpersonal experience that is shaped and directed by the experiences of individuals and the communities within which they live out their lives. It is *intrapersonal* in that it refers to the quest for inner connectivity … it is *interpersonal* in that it relates to the relationships between people and within communities. It is *transpersonal* in so far as it reaches beyond self and others into the transcendent realms of experience that move beyond that which is available at a mundane level" (p. 20). His conceptualization signifies the multidimensional relationships involved which one should be mindful of in research.

Some spiritual concepts and methods can be applied at the individual level and address local and personal aspects, and others can be adopted more broadly across the lifespan and at the community level. Spirituality and PTG share mutual views in the sense that they often include a search for connection, meaning-making and a sense of purpose. Furthermore, the practice of social work deals with supporting connections, facilitating meaning and the integration of re-storying, as well as assisting with finding purpose.

Research has emerged supporting the relationships between spirituality, trauma, resilience, recovery, and PTG. Individuals may encounter a spiritual emergency, crisis, or distress and engage in existential rumination and questioning (Vis & Boynton, 2008). Spiritual struggles, including a loss of faith or distrust or anger at a higher power, can stimulate spiritual tasks of meaning reconstruction and processing that can potentially lead to spiritual growth. Grief and bereavement can be catalysts for spiritual connection, contemplation, and PTG. Individuals may feel stronger, develop greater empathy and compassion, have a greater appreciation for life and renewed life priorities, and deepen their spirituality through trauma. Suffering and trauma can play a significant role in transformation and transcendence, spiritual development, and a deepening of spiritual understandings.

Many studies across the lifespan indicate that individuals turn to their spirituality, including their spiritual beliefs, rituals, traditions, and activities, and they engage in spiritual coping when they encounter traumatic events. They also rely on spiritual resources, support, and community. Spiritual growth and development are linked to processes of reconstruction of values, beliefs, self-concept and identity, roles, relationships, philosophy of life and world view. Therefore, social workers need to develop an awareness and understanding of these complex, interrelated aspects of trauma, spirituality and PTG and their importance for treatment and interventions. In her guidebook on PTG, Schwartz (2020) conveyed that "traumatic life experiences can be devastating, they can also become a powerful force that awakens us to an undercurrent of our aliveness. Painful events inevitably shape who we are, but it is essential that we learn to look beyond the blackened trees of our internal landscape and trust in our capacity for new growth. The work of trauma recovery is a difficulty, but this same work can uncover the wisdom and awaken the heart" (p. xvii). Social workers can assist clients through the suffering from trauma and facilitate PTG and transcendence through understanding the spiritual dimension and the ability to tap into spiritual strengths and resources for clients. Social workers are encouraged to adopt a sensitive spiritual approach in this effort.

Canda and Furman (2010) asserted that spiritually sensitive practice is part of a strengths-oriented practice. They present five core principles of a spiritually sensitive practice, which are consistent with social work values and ethics. The first principle involves value clarity and ongoing self-reflectivity with the intent of self-growth and deeper self-understanding. This practice requires a process of acknowledging personal strengths, feelings, beliefs, religious and spiritual views, as well as opinions, biases, prejudices, and negative attitudes that could impact clients. It involves challenging one's personal historical, cultural, political, and spiritual ideologies. The second principle of respect not only affirms the inherent dignity and worth of others, but it also recognizes their spiritual essence and their right to achieve spiritual transcendence.

Adopting a client centredness approach that regards the client's own cultural and spiritual contexts is the third principle. The social worker aims to value and honour the spiritual world view, spiritual experiences, aspirations, values and beliefs, and self-understandings of the client. Judging the client's spiritual ideologies or proselytizing is not appropriate or ethical. The fourth principle is inclusivity, which is more than tolerating spiritual diversity. It involves appreciating and advocating for the client's religious and spiritual freedoms, spiritual expressions, and their spiritual self-determination and self-transcendence. The personal safety and regard for the rights of others remain central. The final principle is creativity, which recognizes the capacity of resilience and creative possibilities in situations. Pain and suffering are viewed as potentially leading to opportunity and creative transformation. Creativity within the client is encouraged while the social worker facilitates the "birthing" of a renewed self for the client. The social worker is creative, spontaneous, flexible, intuitive, and remains in the moment with the client.

Within a spiritually sensitive approach, social workers view themselves as co-collaborators, co-creators, and co-authors in the treatment process with clients. The client is the expert of his or her own life and experiences. A spiritually sensitive therapist is respectful, humble, caring, curious, and is an interested partner who brings theoretical and practical expertise into the therapeutic relationship (Clark, 2006; Corey, 2005). "Spiritually sensitive practice is a way of being and relating throughout the helping process" (Canda & Furman, 2010, p. 214). We believe that in working in the area of trauma and facilitating PTG, a spiritually sensitive approach is not only required but is a best practice for social work. Social workers require knowledge of the interconnect-edness of the areas of trauma, spirituality, and PTG.

Trauma

Traumatic events can include a range of abuses, including sexual, phys-ical, and emotional abuse, exposure to violence, catastrophes and disas-ters including natural disasters, wars and terrorism, accidents, illnesses and disease, separation, loss and death, and various other dangers or life-threatening events. Terr (1991) classified traumas into Type I (sin-gle events) and Type II (multiple, ongoing, or recurring events, or an extreme or horrific single trauma). A traumatic event is one that is stress related, producing intense feelings of fear, anxiety, or helplessness and it is unexpected, sudden, and beyond the norm of everyday life, which goes beyond an individual's perceived ability to meet its demands and disrupts one's frame of reference and world view (McCann & Pearlman, 1990). Trauma experienced in childhood that is severe or prolonged can lead to toxic stress and impeded development and brain architecture (Alberta Family Wellness Initiative, 2020). Trauma can lead to a myriad of distressing symptoms such as anxiety and panic attacks, nightmares and sleep issues, flashbacks, dissociation, rumination, irritability, depression etc. Increasing and repeated traumatic incidents can add to a person's trauma load and compromise one's ability to manage. Vari-ous conditions are linked with experiencing, witnessing, or exposure to trauma, including acute stress disorder, posttraumatic stress disorder (PTSD), vicarious trauma, compassion fatigue, secondary traumatic stress, and occupational stress injury.

Traumatic experiences can trigger an existential and spiritual crisis, create a sense of vulnerability, helplessness, or even shame and humili-ation. Maladaptive appraisals, even in children, can lead to the devel-opment of PTSD; however, those who engage in healthy and spiritual meaning-making and constructive processing seem to have improved outcomes (Meiser-Stedman et al., 2009; Simon et al., 2010). Conversely, many individuals do not develop stress-related disorders but find spiri-tual growth, a renewed sense of identity, better quality of life, and life satisfaction. Park and Halifax (2011) impart that death, grief, spiritu-ality, and religion are intertwined and play fundamental roles in life. Spirituality, when positively accessed through trauma, can be support-ive and a resource for individuals in making sense of suffering through meaning-making processes, in re-storying of the traumatic events, memories, and beliefs, and in benevolent reappraisal and reconstruct-ing a revised spiritual world view.

Spirituality

Spirituality in Social Work in Canada

Graham et al. (2006) discussed the early origins of spirituality and religion in social work and its early leaders in Canada, and provided an overview of spirituality in social work, including how spirituality has seen a re-emergence in social work. They illuminated how Ed Canda, a professor in the United States, brought spirituality forth through his research and writing since the mid-1980s, and collaborated with Canadian Scholars to promote this important area of social work. This stimulated a renaissance in the area since the 1990s in Canada (Graham et al., 2006). In 2001, the Canadian Society for Spirituality and Social Work (CSSSW) was developed by several professors across Canada. The board of directors began to work closely with the Society for Spirituality in Social Work in the United States, with conferences in alternate years, to promote and disseminate research, theory, and practice-related aspects. Proceedings from these conferences have been published in several special edition journals. Some of the leaders on the CSSSW board published a book on spirituality and social work with selected Canadian readings (see Coates et al., 2007).

Since the article written by Graham et al. (2006), there has been a significant increase in scholars across Canada recognizing and attending to the area of spirituality as a critical and central aspect of social work. Spirituality is now being viewed as a vital component in social work practice across the lifespan, and within research and scholarship, and it has become a social justice concern. As organizers of the *Seventh Annual North American Conference on Spirituality & Social Work: "The Evolution of Spirituality across the Lifespan; Embracing spiritual diversity from Northern Communities to Global Localities"* in 2012, we also were guest editors of a special edition based for the conference proceedings published in the *International Journal of Religion and Spirituality: Social Thought*. Several of the authors in this book have or currently sit on the board of directors for the CSSSW. Diana Coholic is a past member, and Heather Boynton, Susan Cadell, and Indrani Margolin are current members.

Defining Spirituality

In the social work literature, there are many attempts at defining spirituality and definitions range from elaborate to succinct. Tensions and ongoing processes in developing a common definition and delineating the various constructs of spirituality have been apparent across many of the helping professions (see Canda & Furman, 1999; Chiu et al., 2004; Helminiak, 2008; Hill & Pargament, 2003; MacDonald, 2009; Meraviglia, 1999; Roehlkepartain et al., 2006). This is due to the fact that spirituality is a multidimensional construct, as it is experienced by individuals in different ways, is uniquely expressed, and it overlaps with religion and religiosity, and it develops across the lifespan (Canda & Furman, 1999; Crisp, 2010; MacDonald, 2009; Senreich, 2013). Canda and Furman have continued to expand on the definition and description of spirituality in their texts (Canda & Furman, 1999, 2010; Canda et al., 2020). The definitions in the literature range from succinct to robust with many aspects and attributes involved (see Canda et al., 2020; Crisp, 2010).

Often spirituality and religion are used interchangeably within the literature which makes it confounding. Sheldrake (2012) highlighted how spirituality is central to all religions and, in recent times, it has risen in numerous non-religious environments. He stated that it is a broad term which is aspirational in relation to how humans engage in life, and "stands for lifestyles and practices that embody a vision of human existence and of how the human spirit is to achieve its full potential" (p. 1). Sheldrake (2012) further noted how humans are seeking deeper levels of life fulfilment and meaning, and not only has spirituality arisen in many of the helping professions and health sciences, it also has been a topic of focus in education, business, sports, architecture, engineering, and sciences.

The core aspects in most descriptions include a search for meaning, purpose, and connection to the deepest aspects or core of oneself, connections to others, nature, and beyond the human realm such as a higher power of one's belief, or other spiritual entities. Spirituality relates to identity and sense of self, and it also encompasses aspects such as hope, faith, empathy, compassion, peace, wonder, awe, mystery, creativity, transformation, and transcendence. It is experienced through the mind, and the body and our felt sense, and through our senses and the intuitive dimension. It involves our values, beliefs, morals, and cognitive processes. It also is experienced via emotions, and through hope and faith. It includes virtues such as kindness, respect, fairness, honesty, loyalty, integrity, and love. There is a process of self-discovery and development throughout life. We experience spirituality intra-personally, as well as interpersonally through connection to others, and transpersonal or transcendentally through experiences beyond the human realm.

Spirituality is deemed to be socially and culturally constructed yet unique to each individual, and may or may not involve faith, religion, or religious activities, practices, and communities. Spiritual world views are created and transformed through cognitive and emotional processes of spiritual searching and meaning-making related to purpose in life (Ai et al., 2005; Vis & Boynton, 2008). Canda and Furman (2010) contend that "*Spirituality* is the Gestalt of the total process of human life and development, encompassing biological, mental, social, and spiritual aspects. It is not reducible to any of these components; rather, it is the wholeness of what it is to be human" (p. 66). Senreich (2013) also asserted that spirituality includes an individual's cognitive, emotional, and intuitive relationship to that which cannot be fully known in terms of life and existence, and that the spiritual component of social work needs to honour each individual's belief system and way of conceptualizing the universe.

Sheldrake (2012) states that spirituality "is chameleon-like in that it takes on the shape and priorities of the different contexts in which it is used" (pp. 1–2). We recognize the wide spectrum of spiritual beliefs and expressions, the multiple perspectives of ways of being and knowing, and the interconnectedness of life, and how spirituality is a strength and a resource for many individuals. Therefore, we believe that spirituality should be defined contextually. You will note that the authors in this book do use similar and different definitions of spirituality based on their context. They speak to the differing dimensions and as such demonstrate its diversity and the uniqueness in different contexts.

Spirituality in Social Work Practice

Various researchers have identified that spirituality is being encountered in practice with individuals across the lifespan as clients are bringing up spiritual topics, experiencing spiritual struggles and that social workers are incorporating spiritually based interventions, practices, and activities into their work with clients (Canda & Furman, 1999, 2010; Coholic, 2010, 2011; Kvarfordt & Sheridan, 2007). There is evidence that social work research, education, and training have not kept up to date with the importance of spirituality in practice and developed a thorough theoretical framework for practice. Oxhandler and Pargament (2014) found in their study that two-thirds of social workers believed they had a lack of skills and knowledge for effectively addressing spirituality in practice. Kimball (2008) contended that for those working with youth "there is a crisis of confidence among social workers when it comes to engaging the spiritual experience of young people" (p. i). There is a great need for further training and education on spirituality in social work, as issues with self-efficacy and competence for social workers, as well as ethical concerns may arise as workers may not have the knowledge and skills to address this critical area.

Spirituality plays a critical role in major life traumas and can generate enormous existential and metaphysical challenges that need to be managed, processed, and integrated into a new world view. Social workers therefore may need to navigate spiritually related issues in working with individuals experiencing trauma. They may need to include it in psychotherapy, assess for spiritual strengths and struggles, facilitate spiritual activities and practices, access spiritual supports, or make referrals. They also need to be aware of their own spirituality as a first step in developing spiritually sensitive practice. In the past decade there have been several texts that have emerged that address spirituality in counselling and psychotherapy. This literature provides theoretical and practice frameworks and discusses how to integrate spirituality into practice, especially for when talk therapy is insufficient or requires an alternate approach (see Béres, 2014, 2017; Canda & Furman 2010; Canda et al., 2020; Crisp, 2010, 2017; Dudley, 2016; Land, 2015).

Spiritual Strengths, Activities, and Practices

Research has indicated that spirituality can be a pathway to decline or growth (Pargament et al., 2006; Sheldrake, 2012). By attending to spiritual strengths and the spiritual processes of individuals, social workers can assist in guiding them on the pathway to PTG. Spiritual processes involving narratives, rituals, and coping bridge the past and assist in adjusting to the present and in discovering a path into the future (Angell et al., 1998). Social workers should garner an understanding of the spiritual processes and beliefs that may be halted, disrupted, or ruminated upon, as well as those that may be activated or strengthened for the individual through questioning and listening for spiritual and existential qualities. Calhoun and Tedeschi (1999) provided spiritual themes to probe and attend to such as "issues related to mortality, life's purpose and meaning, one's life priorities, fundamental choices about how to live, issues related to traditional religious beliefs and expressions, and broad spiritual themes" (p. 119). Other themes include client values, morals, existential outlook on life, or questions of this regard. Client comments can be somewhat masked, necessitating social workers to be genuinely present and attentive. Social workers should also listen for spiritual engagement activities and practices.

PTG

PTG is conceptualized as both a process and an outcome. Calhoun and Tedeschi (2006) discuss the paradox of trauma and loss leading to positive gains, and that individuals often experience growth through the trauma trajectory. According to Shaw et al. (2005), spirituality can be a springboard for increased personal growth and development, the development of wisdom, connectedness to a higher power, and a deepening of spirituality, faith, values, and beliefs. They also found that "positive religious coping, religious openness, readiness to face existential questions, religious participation and intrinsic religiousness are typically associated with posttraumantic growth" (p. 1). Thus, a spiritual framework can assist with interpreting challenges and providing resolution.

The five domains of PTG outlined by Calhoun and Tedeschi (2006) include: (1) new possibilities, (2) relating to others, (3) personal strength, (4) appreciation of life, and (5) spiritual change. Further opportunities include finding meaning in new or existing activities and interests and new avenues of pursuit in life. Relating to others in more meaningful ways and an ability to understand and have empathy and compassion for others who are suffering is increased. Individuals describe improved and stronger relationships or focusing on associations that are more meaningful, positive, and supportive. Individuals also express recognition of strengths, skills and abilities and their life purpose. They often go through a process of reordering their priorities to include engagement in meaningful activities that bring a quality of life and overall satisfaction. These aspects also contribute to existential and spiritual change, growth, and development. These domains are attributed to transformations and are advanced for new levels of functioning.

Processing traumatic memories and cognitive restructuring play a crucial role in the processes of healing, recovery, positive growth, and personal change (Tedeschi & Calhoun, 1995; Wright et al., 2007). Processing allows individuals to tolerate adverse emotional reactions and to construct renewed and adaptive meanings (Simon et al., 2010). Developing new meanings is also known as reappraisal, and it involves a global meaning system of core schemas in a revised world view (Park & Ai, 2006). Positive reappraisal and spirituality are significant factors contributing to PTG and transcendence (Neimeyer, 2004; Prati & Pietrantoni, 2009). Clay et al. (2009) purport that children's schemas are more malleable; therefore, with care, they may be able to incorporate positive meanings more readily. By introducing PTG in treatment with youth, it may also assist caregivers in viewing the future in a positive light, offering promising alternatives. For adolescents and adults who engage in abstract and complex thinking, it may take more time and attention to facilitate the integration of positive meanings.

Calhoun and Tedeschi (1999) stated that for PTG to be more likely, "the clinician must be knowledgeable about, comfortable with, alert to, and active in working with the client's spiritual issues" and that the therapist must "develop some degree of comfort in the roles of philosopher and spiritual guide," adding that this is be done "in the service of the client's wellbeing and growth" (p. 120). Tedeschi et al. (2015) state that "the clinician must be well attuned to the client when the client may be in the process of reconstructing schemas, thinking dialectically, recognizing paradox, and generating a revised life narrative" (p. 509). They advocate for embracing an existential, cognitive, narrative healing process listening for and labelling posttraumatic growth.

As we increase our understanding of spirituality and its role in PTG, the chapters in this book offer further insights into various levels of practice. Focusing on strengths, encouraging collaboration, and believing in the inherent resiliency and potential for growth in the individual, group, community, or organization are fundamental concepts in social work goal-setting and change. Equally, social workers are familiar with generalist education and training, espousing transferable skills at the micro, mezzo, and macro levels of practice. These core concepts place social workers in a unique position pertaining to trauma recovery. Gardner (2017) asserted that "the influence of context needs to be recognized for individuals, families and communities in exploring spirituality" (p. 305) and the various chapters in this book explore multiple contexts of practice and approaches to PTG.

This book was created by Canadian social workers to address the impact of trauma-related events on individuals, families, and organizations, emphasizing the importance of spirituality and PTG. While it addresses specific needs within Canadian context, many of the issues addressed are of concern to social workers in many other countries.

It has been established in the literature that exposure to a traumatic event throughout one's lifetime is probable and that social workers will more than likely encounter trauma survivors many times within one's career. This book, however, is more than a primer on trauma effects. It seeks out unique circumstances throughout a client's life cycle where trauma is experienced, how one's spirituality is awakened or activated, and how this experience can intersect with interventions towards growth. It offers social workers insights into how to assess for spirituality. It also provides practical strategies on how spirituality and spiritual practices can be integrated into psychotherapeutic interventions at various levels of social work practice with diversity across the lifespan.

The chapters offered in this book present unique client circumstances in which trauma has infiltrated lives. Likewise, the sections are introduced to capture realistic social work roles at the micro, mezzo, and macro levels. While some chapters in this book do discuss specific client populations and related cultural and spiritual concerns, others offer information that can be applied across populations and clinical scenarios. Overall, it is anticipated that these chapters will inspire and provide transferable knowledge that social workers can use to meet the unique needs of the clients they serve. And it is hoped that it may stimulate further research and dialogue in this critical area of social work. It also can aid in educating students, academics, and new workers as well as those who have been in practice longer. It can further promote global dialogue and collaborations.

The book begins with chapters dedicated to the youngest of our clients, children. The initial chapter by Heather Boynton, "Spirituality and Possibilities for Posttraumatic Growth in Children," enhances our understanding of how children who experience trauma, grief, and loss rely on their spirituality and turn to spiritual relationships and practices for support. There have been advancements in the area of children's spirituality and PTG, where it is understood that children experience spiritual struggles and engage in spiritual coping. Focusing on spiritual aspects can assist with emotional regulation and feelings of self-control and self-mastery. Spirituality and facilitating positive spiritual rumination in children can be an avenue for supporting PTG and spiritual development.

Joey Wark, Boynton, and Jo-Ann Vis's chapter, "Spirituality and Child Welfare Practice with Indigenous Families: Fostering a 'Culture of Strengths,'" provides a timely discussion concerning the distressing absence of the role of spirituality in child welfare literature. Considering the impact of historical trauma and the importance many Indigenous peoples place on spirituality, this topic is of great significance for all Canadian social workers at the micro, mezzo, and macro levels. The vast overrepresentation of Indigenous children in the child welfare system in Canada demands a review of the available research in this area. While the role of spirituality as a strength for children and families involved with child welfare services has been established for Indigenous populations, these findings seem to have little influence on contemporary child welfare practices. This chapter offers social workers a thorough understanding of the strength of spirituality and growth among Indigenous families and makes recommendations for spiritually informed cultural child welfare practice

Boynton, Vis, and Taylor Smith's chapter, "Spiritual-Trauma-Informed Schools: Supporting Children Exposed to Interpersonal Trauma," builds on the conversation that child school communities are important intervention avenues within which children can experience support from institutions that are trauma-informed and appreciate opportunities for growth. The chapter explores the effects of chronic trauma exposure on a child's development and how social workers can assist in the creation of trauma-informed schools that hold powerful avenues for potential posttraumatic growth and improved child development. Utilizing a systems perspective, social workers can provide education and policy recommendations to create interventions informed by awareness and offer growth opportunities at the cognitive, emotional, and social levels. Advocating for a collaborative approach to include children, parents, educators, and school administrators serves as a response to the growing number of suffering families.

The next selection of chapters moves towards issues for clients in the adult life stage. Joanne Smit and Vis start this section with "Body-Mind Oriented Trauma Therapy with Childhood Sexual Abuse Survivors: Benefits and Challenges." This chapter discusses the inclusion of body-mind approaches with adult female survivors of childhood sexual abuse. The chapter offers information for social workers who provide support with this adult population. These authors describe implications for treatment based on a brief theoretical overview of the effects of childhood complex trauma on the bio-psycho-social-spiritual lives of survivors. The section on consequences for treatment offers social workers, both at the entry and experienced level, an understanding of the benefits and challenges that they face in their work when they include spirituality and growth as part of the treatment process.

In the next chapter, Vis shifts focus to an area where many adults spend most of their waking hours at work. In "Exploring Meaning and Purpose: Underpinnings to Posttraumatic Growth for Front Line Professionals," the emphasis is placed on the post-trauma impact on one's meaning and on the purpose of their work. The chapter offers information concerning the psychological and spiritual stressors following trauma exposure for front line workers. Vis advocates that social workers often meet and work with these front line professionals throughout the micro-to-macro continuum. The author proposes that issues about spirituality are often left unchecked for front line workers, leading to the diminishment of one's sense of professional meaning and purpose in the workplace. The chapter concludes with information to assist social workers to enhance the perception of meaningful work in efforts to promote PTG for these professional working groups while increasing organizational health and well-being.

Susan Cadell, the author of the next chapter, "Grief and Loss: A Shifting Landscape," writes about another life stage certainty: providing care for someone who is seriously ill. The author suggests that identities shift as the ill person, no matter what their age, becomes a patient and the other person, regardless of the relationship, becomes a caregiver. When someone dies, identities and links are also transformed. Caregiving and bereavement are often isolating and stigmatized activities. In this unique chapter, Cadell draws on decades of research in posttraumatic growth, addressing caregiving and grief. Populations presented in the chapter range from bereaved HIV/AIDS carers, to parents caring for a child with a life-limiting illness, to those who memorialize someone with a tattoo. She offers essential ideas and concepts that can be transferable to a variety of client situations social workers will encounter throughout their careers.

Shelley Poluchowicz and Boynton discuss results from a program evaluation on a spiritually focused group with adult women in their chapter, "The Soulful Journey: A Spiritual-Based Group for Treatment." They review the inclusion of spirituality in group work that incorporates a variety of other therapies (i.e. cognitive and acceptance approaches) as a recovery intervention for individuals with complex grief and trauma. The concepts of spirituality including connection, meaning, empathy, compassion, gratitude, hope, and appreciation facilitated transcendence and transformation are key elements of the group work. The evaluation of the group includes results from John Fisher's (2010) SHALOM questionnaire, which demonstrated improvements in personal, communal, environmental, and transcendent dimensions of spirituality, as well as dimensions of quality of life. Qualitative themes are highlighted with responses from participants which speak to the posttraumatic growth in their lives.

Kathy Kortes-Miller's chapter, "Offering Social Work Care for Spiritual Needs at the End of Life," reminds us that social workers encounter dying, death, loss, and grief in all settings of practice. This chapter will examine the need for social workers to have a level of spiritual competence in their interactions with people who are dying and emphasize the need for interprofessional collaboration to enhance this form of care. Practice examples and tools are offered across the support continuum, showcasing methods for assessing spiritual needs and demonstrating competent spiritual support. Examples of religious and spiritual practices that individuals, families, and communities may utilize to strengthen their spiritual coping at the end of life are provided.

The final selection of chapters concentrates primarily on interventions that can apply to client groups across the lifespan. Diana Coholic's chapter, "Addressing the Effects of Trauma Using Holistic and Creative Mindfulness-Based Practices and Concepts," discusses how the holistic philosophy and practice of mindfulness can assist people in addressing trauma. The exercise of mindfulness, the understanding and application of its ideas, can help with the effects of trauma. Mindfulness concepts, which are also known as the attitudinal foundation of mindfulness, can help people process trauma. For one example, negative self-judgment and the need to develop self-compassion is of paramount importance. Coholic reminds us that when we tell ourselves that we should not feel something, it creates a roadblock, and the feeling remains repressed or suppressed, creating further problems. Self-compassion includes the idea that self-kindness helps us to tolerate and understand our challenges without judging our pain and suffering.

Indrani Margolin and Tulshi Sen contribute further to interventions that can apply across one's lifetime in their chapter, "Posttraumatic Growth: Discovery of Identity and Deep Driving Desire with Mahavakyam Meditation in Clinical Social Work." The authors note that the psyche has an incredible capacity to protect individuals during traumatic exposure. Within the context of micro-level social work, the authors argue for holistic approaches that work to realign the body, mind, and spirit in safe and supportive ways when assisting with trauma. This chapter discusses the importance of spirituality across the lifespan in assessment and intervention, providing examples incorporated into work as a professor, researcher, and counsellor promoting PTG. A meditation system called Proclamation (Mahavakyam) Meditation is highlighted. Inclusion of spirituality, along with these modalities, can be viable options to empower trauma sufferers to safely, slowly, and consciously reconnect previously severed sensations, feelings, and thoughts to re-experience self-awareness, self-compassion, memory, creativity, as well as self-other and self-world connection.

David Nicolas and Christopher Kilmer build on the intervention section with a mezzo focus on community. Their chapter, "Spirituality and Faith Communities Relative to Developmental Disability and Health Issues: Considerations in Disability, Illness, and End of Life Care," encourages social workers to remember the significance of one's system as a strength-based resource for clients exposed to trauma. The authors discuss that for many individuals, spirituality and faith are essential contributors to their well-being. They go on to suggest that engagement in spirituality and faith communities represents a significant component of meaning and a broader community of support for many individuals. The authors also share research findings concluding that support from a faith community provides a source of hope and guidance. Compelling case examples are provided to illustrate a range of experiences along with practice implications for social workers.

This book is intended to provide a greater understanding of trauma, spirituality, and PTG in its diversity and complexity. It will provide social workers with some knowledge and frameworks for intervention and facilitation of PTG through attending to spirituality in trauma. Equally, it is anticipated that this book will stimulate further dialogue, research, and development of theoretical aspects in this crucial area of social work education and practice.

REFERENCES

Ai, A.L., Cascio, T., Santangelo, L.K., & Evans-Campbell, T. (2005). Hope, meaning and growth following the September 11, 2001, terrorist attacks. *Journal of Interpersonal Violence, 20*(5), 523–48. https://doi.org/10.1177 /0886260504272896. Medline: 15788553

Alberta Family Wellness Initiative. (2020). *The foundations of lifelong health: The brain story.* https://www.albertafamilywellness.org/what-we-know/the -brain-story

Angell, G.B., Dennis, B.C., & Dumain, L.E. (1998). Spirituality, resilience, and narrative: Coping with parental death. Families in Society: *The Journal of Contemporary Social Services, 79*(6), 615–30. https://doi.org/10.1606/1044-3894.865

Béres, L. (2014). *The narrative practitioner: Practice theory in context* (J. Fook, Ed.). Palgrave MacMillan.

– (Ed.) (2017). *Practising spirituality: Reflections on meaning-making in personal and professional contexts (practice theory in context).* Palgrave MacMillan.

Calhoun, L.G., & Tedeschi, R.G. (1999). *Facilitating posttraumatic growth: A clinician's guide* (I.B. Weiner, Ed.). Lawrence Erlbaum Associates.

– (2006). The foundations of posttraumatic growth: An expanded framework. In L.G. Calhoun & R.G. Tedeschi (Eds.), *Handbook of posttraumatic growth: Research and practice* (pp. 1–23). Lawrence Erlbaum Associates.

Canda, E.R., & Furman, L.D. (1999). *Spiritual diversity in social work practice: The heart of helping.* The Free Press.

– (2010). *Spiritual diversity in social work practice: The heart of helping* (2nd ed.). Oxford University Press.

Canda, E.R., Furman, L.D., & Canda, H. (2020). *Spiritual diversity in social work practice: The heart of helping* (3rd ed). Oxford University Press. https://doi.org /10.1080/15426432.2020.1739388

Carrington, A.M. (2017). A spiritual approach to social work practice. In B.R. Crisp (Ed.), *The Routledge handbook of religion, spirituality and social work* (pp. 291–9). Routledge.

Chiu, L., Emblen, J.D., Van Hofwegen, L., Sawatzky, R., & Meyerhoff, H. (2004). An integrative review of the concept of spirituality in the health sciences. *Western Journal of Nursing Research, 26*(4), 405–28. https://doi .org/10.1177/0193945904263411. Medline: 15155026

Clark, J.L. (2006). Listening for meaning: A research-based model for attending to spirituality, culture and worldview in social work practice. *Critical Social Work, 7*(1), 1–25. https://ojs.uwindsor.ca/index.php/csw/article /download/5771/4710 https://doi.org/10.22329/csw.v7i1.5771

Clay, R., Knibbs, J, & Joseph, S. (2009). Measurement of posttraumatic growth in young people: A review. *Clinical Child Psychology and Psychiatry, 14*(3), 411–22. https://doi.org/10.1177/1359104509104049. Medline: 19515756

Coates, J., Graham, J.R., Swartzentruber, B., & Ouellette, B. (Eds.). (2007). *Spirituality and social work: Selected Canadian readings.* Canadian Scholars Press Inc.

Coholic, D. (2010). *Arts activities for children and young people in need: Helping children to develop mindfulness, spiritual awareness and self-esteem.* Jessica Kingsley Publishers.

– (2011). Exploring how young people living in foster care discuss spiritually sensitive themes in a holistic arts-based group program. *Journal of Religion & Spirituality in Social Work: Social Thought, 30*(3), 193–211. https://doi.org /10.1080/15426432.2011.587379

Corey, G. (2005). *Case Approach to Counseling and Psychotherapy* (6th ed.). Thomson.

Crisp, B.R. (2010). *Spirituality and social work.* Ashgate Publishing.

– (Ed.) (2017). *The Routledge handbook of religion, spirituality and social work.* Routledge.

Dudley, J.R. (2016). *Spirituality matters in social work: Connecting spirituality, religion, and practice.* Routledge.

Fisher, J. (2010). Development and application of a spiritual well-being questionnaire called SHALOM. *Religions, 1*(1), 105–21. https://doi .org/10.3390/rel1010105

Gardner, F. (2017). Critical spirituality and social work practice. In B.R. Crisp (Ed.), *The Routledge handbook of religion, spirituality and social work* (pp. 300–8). Routledge.

Graham, J., Coholic, D., & Coates, J. (2006). Spirituality as a guiding construct in the development of Canadian social work: Past and present considerations. *Critical Social Work, 7*(1), 1–17. https://doi.org/10.22329/csw.v7i1.5774

Helminiak, D.A. (2008). Confounding the divine and the spiritual: Challenges to a psychology of spirituality. *Pastoral Psychology, 57,* 161–82. https://doi .org/10.1007/s11089-008-0163-9

Hill, P.C., & Pargament, K.I. (2003). Advances in the conceptualization and measurement of religion and spirituality: Implications for physical and

mental health research. *American Psychologist, 58*(1), 64–74. https://doi
.org/10.1037/0003-066x.58.1.64. Medline: 12674819

Kimball, E.M. (2008, June). *Developing spirituality in adolescents: Research-
informed practice and practice-inspired research* [Paper presentation].
Third North American Conference on Spirituality and Social Work,
University of Minnesota. https://www.spiritualityandsocialwork.ca
/uploads/2/5/8/0/25806130/lisakimball-developingspiritualityinadolescents
.pdf

Kvarfordt, C.L., & Sheridan, M.J. (2007). The role of religion and spirituality in
working with children and adolescents: Results of a national survey. *Journal
of Religion & Spirituality in Social Work: Social Thought, 26*(3), 1–23. https://
doi.org/10.1300/j377v26n03_01

Land, H. (2015). *Spirituality, religion, and faith in psychotherapy: Evidence-based
expressive methods for the mind, brain, and body.* Lyceum Books Inc.

MacDonald, D.A. (2009). Identity and spirituality: Conventional and
transpersonal perspectives. *International Journal of Transpersonal Studies,
28*(1), 86–106. https://doi.org/10.24972/ijts.2009.28.1.86

McCann, I.L., & Pearlman, L.A. (1990). Vicarious traumatization: A framework
for understanding the psychological effects of working with victims. *Journal
of Traumatic Stress, 3*, 131–49. https://doi.org/10.1002/jts.2490030110

Meiser-Stedman, R., Dalgleish, T., Glucksman, E., Yule, W., & Smith P. (2009).
Maladaptive cognitive appraisals mediate the evolution of posttraumatic
stress reactions: A 6-month follow up of child and adolescent assault and
motor vehicle accident survivors. *Journal of Abnormal Psychology, 118*(4),
778–87. https://doi.org/10.1037/a0016945. Medline: 19899847

Meraviglia, M.G. (1999). Critical analysis of spirituality and its empirical
indicators: Prayer and meaning in life. *Journal of Holistic Nursing, 17*(1),
18–33. https://doi.org/10.1177/089801019901700103. Medline: 10373840

Neimeyer, R.A. (2004). Research on grief and bereavement: Evolution
and revolution. *Death Studies, 28*(6), 489–90. https://doi.org/10.1080
/07481180490461179

Oxhandler, H.K., & Pargament, K.I. (2014). Social work practitioners'
integration of clients' religion and spirituality in practice: A literature
review. *Social Work, 59*(3), 271–9. https://doi.org/10.1093/sw/swu018.
Medline: 25076651

Pargament, K.I., Desai, K.M., & McConnell, K.M. (2006). Spirituality: A
pathway to posttraumatic growth or decline? In L.G. Calhoun & R.G.
Tedeschi (Eds.), *Handbook of posttraumatic growth* (pp. 127–37). Lawrence
Erlbaum Associates.

Pargament, K.I., Koenig, H.G., Tarakeshwar, N., & Hahn, J. (2004). Religious
coping methods as predictors of psychological, physical and spiritual
outcomes among medically ill elderly patients: A two-year longitudinal

study. *Journal of Health Psychology, 9*(6), 713–30. https://doi.org/10.1177
/1359105304045366. Medline: 15367751

Park, C.L., & Ai, A.L. (2006). Meaning making and growth: New directions for
research on survivors of trauma. *Journal of Loss and Trauma, 11*(5), 389–407.
https://doi.org/10.1080/15325020600685295

Park, C.L., & Halifax, R.J. (2011). Religion and spirituality in adjusting
to bereavement: Grief as burden, grief as gift. In R.A. Neimeyer, D.L.
Harris, H.R. Winokuer, & G.F. Thornton (Eds.), *Grief and Bereavement in
Contemporary Society* (pp. 355–64). Routledge.

Prati, G., & Pietrantoni, L. (2009). Optimism, social support, and coping
strategies as factors contributing to posttraumatic growth: A meta-analysis.
Journal of Loss and Trauma, 14(5), 364–88. https://doi.org/10.1080
/15325020902724271

Roehlkepartain, E.C., Benson, P.L., King, P.E., & Wagener, L.M. (2006).
Spiritual development in childhood and adolescence: Moving to the
scientific mainstream. In E.C. Roehlkepartain, P.L. Benson, P.E. King, &
L.M. Wagener (Eds.), *The handbook of spiritual development in childhood and
adolescence* (pp. 1–15). Sage Publications.

Schwartz, A. (2020). *The posttraumatic growth guidebook: Practical mind-body tools
to heal trauma, foster resilience, and awaken your potential.* PESI Publishing and
Media.

Senreich, E. (2013). An inclusive definition of spirituality for social work
education and practice. *Journal of Social Work Education, 49*(4), 548–63.
https://doi.org/10.1080/10437797.2013.812460

Shaw, A., Joseph, S., & Linley, P.A. (2005). Religion, spirituality, and
posttraumatic growth: A systematic review. *Mental Health, Religion and
Culture, 8*(1), 1–11. https://doi.org/10.1080/1367467032000157981

Sheldrake, P. (2012). *Spirituality: A very short introduction.* Oxford.

Simon, V.A., Feiring, C., & McElroy, S.K. (2010). Making meaning of traumatic
events: Youths' strategies for processing childhood sexual abuse are
associated with psychosocial adjustment. *Child Maltreatment, 15*(3), 229–41.
https://doi.org/10.1177/1077559510370365. Medline: 20498128

Swinton, J. (2001). *Spirituality and mental health care: Rediscovering a 'forgotten'
dimension.* Jessica Kingsley Publishers.

Tedeschi, R.G., & Calhoun, L.G. (1995). *Trauma and transformation: Growing in
the aftermath of suffering.* Sage Publications.

Tedeschi, R.G., Calhoun, L.G., & Groleau, J.M. (2015). Clinical applications
of posttraumatic growth. In S. Joseph (Ed.), *Positive psychology in practice:
Promoting human flourishing in work, health, education and everyday life*
(2nd ed., pp. 503–18). Wiley. https://doi.org/10.1002/9781118996874.ch30

Terr, L.C. (1991). Childhood traumas: An outline and overview. *The American
Journal of Psychiatry, 148*(1), 10–20. https://doi.org/10.1176/ajp.148.1.10.
Medline: 1824611

Vis, J., & Boynton, H.M. (2008). Spirituality and transcendent meaning making: Possibilities for enhancing posttraumatic growth. *Journal of Religion and Spirituality in Social Work: Social Thought*, 27(1–2), 69–86. https://doi.org/10.1080/15426430802113814

Wright, M.O., Crawford, E., & Sebastian, K. (2007). Positive resolution of childhood sexual abuse experiences: The role of coping, benefit-finding and meaning-making. *Journal of Family Violence*, 22, 597–608. https://doi.org/10.1007/s10896-007-9111-1

1 Spirituality and Possibilities for Posttraumatic Growth in Children

HEATHER BOYNTON

There is an emergence of literature and research demonstrating that spirituality is an important and critical aspect for navigating trauma, grief, and loss (TGL) for children, and it is linked with posttraumatic growth (PTG). Calhoun and Tedeschi (2006) outlined five core domains of PTG: personal strengths and a renewed self-perception; changes to relationships with others and a sense of greater connections with others, and feeling compassion and a greater understanding for others who are suffering; appreciating life more fully, and changes to priorities and meaningful activities; new possibilities, new interests and activities; and existential and spiritual change, which can be the most significant in PTG. Studies with children in the areas of spirituality and in PTG are lagging in relation to research with adults and adolescents (Kilmer, 2006). However, initial studies are providing valuable data and information especially in the domain of spiritual change. Given the high prevalence of trauma for children, social workers need to develop the knowledge, attitudes, and skills for developing spiritually sensitive practice and attend to children's spirituality while integrating it into therapeutic interventions that can promote and facilitate posttraumatic growth.

According to van Der Kolk et al. (2019), over one billion children worldwide experience trauma, and cumulative exposure to trauma creates significant negative biopsychosocial outcomes. The well-known Adverse Childhood Event study (Felitti et al., 1998) found that experiencing a childhood traumatic event created significant mental health concerns, disease and severe health risks and potential for early death. In a study of 701 children, those who experienced one adverse event were ten times more likely to have mental health concerns, and children experiencing four or more adverse events were 30 per cent more likely to suffer from both mental and physical health concerns (Burke et al.,

2011). Thompson and Cui (2000) highlighted an increase in childhood trauma in Canada including abuses, fearful experiences, and separation from significant others, although this increase could be due to more reporting of abuse and violence. Coleman (2015) asserted that trauma affects all ethnicities and demographics and children's mental health and wellbeing is a significant policy concern for Canadian children. She stated that those who experience trauma often have significant behavioural and mental health difficulties, have higher rates of suicide attempts, have lower educational attainment, lower paying work, and misuse substances more often, and it can lead to intergenerational transmission of trauma. Therefore, she professed a great need to "heal the personal and social ills of trauma as well as promoting individual and community resilience in the face of it" (p. 2). Attending to the spiritual domain is an important path in this endeavour.

This chapter aims to convey that spirituality is a critical aspect of TGL and PTG growth. It will briefly describe TGL and its effects, present pertinent aspects of spirituality, and discuss how it is a resiliency factor and component that contributes to PTG. The chapter will highlight how spirituality can be included in TGL interventions, and by including spirituality in treatment social workers may be able to facilitate PTG.

Trauma, Grief, and Loss

A trauma event is something that is sudden or beyond the norm where the individual perceives an inability to meet the related demands of the trauma (McCann & Pearlman, 1990). Childhood traumas can include abuse, victimization, loss, family pathology, catastrophes and natural disasters, violence, terrorism and wars, animal attacks, accidents, illness, death, infectious disease outbreaks, and other life threatening or dangerous events. TGL invoke intense feelings of distress, anxiety, helplessness, fear, or disorientation that challenge one's cognitive structures and perceptions regarding one's world view, meanings, and purpose in life (Janoff-Bulman, 2006; Park & Ai, 2006; Tedeschi & Calhoun, 2006). Aspects of disorganization and disintegration result from the psychological unpreparedness of a new disrupted altered reality (Janoff-Bulman, 2006). TGL have interrelated processes as grief and loss are important aspects of traumatic experiences that can create overwhelming feelings of sadness and despair, especially for children. The age of a child, and their social developmental level, temperament, cognitive and emotional expressive abilities, language, and communication styles are important factors that can create differences in TGL responses (Hooyman & Kramer, 2006; Paris et al., 2009).

A TGL response can include overwhelming, intrusive, and disturbing thoughts, images, and memories. These can stimulate arousal, confusion, dysphoria, and loneliness, and can be triggered by situations, people, places, and sensory information such as smells, sounds, tastes, sights, and physical sensations that remind the child of the event and are recalled as powerful reminders and flashbacks of the TGL experience (Cohen et al., 2006, 2010; Monahon, 1993; Tedeschi et al., 1998). Some children may experience more emotional and behavioural difficulties due to fewer personal capacities for coping, and some may exhibit irritability, reactivity, sleep disturbances, and nightmares, and somatic aches and pains. Children may display abnormal or exaggerated behaviours, hypervigilance, or hyperarousal, demonstrate disrupted or clingy behaviour, have an exaggerated startle response, or demonstrate a lack of engagement, withdrawal, avoidance, numbing, and restricted or blunted affect. Detachment and dissociation are more serious symptoms. Retelling and replaying of aspects of the event are common reactions (Johnson, 1989; Monahon, 1993; Nader, 2008).

Traumatic events can cause adverse effects on development. They can cause psychiatric symptoms, affect neurobiology and brain functioning, disrupt attachment processes, and contribute to future problems and difficulties and engagement in high risk behaviours (Briere, 2006; Cohen et al., 2006; Decker, 1993; Johnson, 1989; Nader 2008). Neurochemical changes resulting from trauma can affect personality, mental processes and skill development (Nader, 2008). TGL events can shatter a child's spiritual confidence creating challenges to spiritual world view, spiritual disconnection, and spiritual crisis (Angell et al., 1998; Tedeschi & Calhoun, 2006). Spiritual struggles, questions and concerns can stimulate spiritual reflection and rumination. Children rely on their spiritual relationships, activities, practices, and rituals to navigate TGL and to bring them hope, comfort, and support (Boynton, 2016).

Spirituality, Resilience, and PTG

Various definitions of spirituality exist in the social work literature. The core themes include a search for meaning and purpose, connectedness to self, others, nature, or a higher power, and ultimate reality, and it may or may not include religion. Spirituality also includes aspects of transcendence, joy, empathy, passion, compassion, hope, and faith. A Canadian study of 51 adolescents identified that religion was related to spirituality, and spirituality included a personal philosophy/world view and search for meaning, an internal element related to identity, development of a belief system, self-discovery and awareness, and the existence of a soul, spirit, or conscience (Sveidqvist et al., 2003).

Research with children demonstrates that spirituality is normal and important to them, is part of their narratives, it is related to their health, happiness, and well-being, and is part of transcending TGL (Boynton, 2016; Bosacki & Ota, 2000; Holder et al., 2008; Houskamp et al., 2004). Trauma can disrupt our sense of rootedness and normality creating soul pain, as well as create suffering and loss of our sense of joy, hope and transcendence causing spiritual pain (Attig, 2004). However, children who have stronger spiritual resources and a sense of spirituality exhibit fewer negative symptoms as spirituality has been deemed to be a resilience factor and can contribute to greater PTG (Cheon & Canda, 2010; Jackson et al., 2010; Kilmer et al, 2014).

PTG has been defined as an "individual's experience of a significant positive change arising from the struggle with a major life crisis" that is transformative (Calhoun et al., 2000, p. 521). Whereas resilience is described by Lepore and Revenson (2006) as "dynamic processes that lead to adaptive outcomes in the face of adversity," the "capacity to recover from stressors over time," and the "capacity to change oneself to adapt to a stressor" (p. 29). Resilience may or may not manifest as part of PTG (Lepore & Revenson, 2006). As noted above, PTG involves emerging from trauma feeling stronger, enriched, and better equipped to deal with future challenges (Thompson & Walsh, 2010). Existential and spiritual change can be the most significant in PTG, especially for children who are experiencing significant spiritual development processes.

Children experiencing TGL often seem to move beyond their expected level of development with advances in empathy and maturity, and they value the depth of relationships compared to peers who have not experienced a major loss (Boynton, 2016; Hooyman & Kramer, 2006). Coholic et al. (2009) maintain PTG in children is characterized by personal strengths, awareness of new possibilities, appreciating life, and spiritual change. Cryder et al. (2006) found that transformative PTG was correlated with competency beliefs within the child.

Kilmer et al. (2014) developed a conceptual model of PTG and asserted that some children go through productive rumination which involves constructive cognitive processing of the trauma and integrating it into a new way of living. Supportive adults can facilitate this process that is beyond normative growth through guidance and support in coping. They also illuminated that context and culture play a role in trauma responses and that PTG trajectories may differ. They indicated research demonstrating that children who are more religious or spiritual have significantly higher levels of PTG. Laceulle et al. (2015) found that stress reactions in preadolescents were positively related to overall PTG, that girls experienced more PTG than boys, and younger children had greater PTG than older children. Social support from peers was related to greater PTG, and children who identified with a religion reported more PTG. A Canadian study by Yaskowich (2002) found that children with cancer not only experienced PTG but their PTG was correlated with support from teachers, an awareness of parental PTG, and female gender. Children were found to have improved relationships and spiritual awareness correlated with cancer related impairments. They asserted that an existential focus in cognitive therapy could provide opportunities for spiritual growth and meaning-making. Vloet et al. (2017) reviewed the literature on PTG and the measures that have been used in studies with children. They surmised that more research is required in the area to determine factors that influence PTG and treatment approaches. In a study investigating results of the revised *Posttraumatic Growth Inventory for Children* and correlates of PTG by Kilmer et al. (2009), spirituality items were found to be ones in which children reported the most total growth. It is important to note that the spiritual growth aspects in the PTG measures related to aspects of religion and God versus a broader conceptualization of spirituality.

Interventions

Duncan et al. (2010) convey that the heart and soul of change lies in relationship factors, an explanation of presenting issues and healing rituals or plans to resolve these, and engagement of the client and therapist with hope and expectancy of improvement. Given that spirituality involves a sense of connectedness, hope and faith, rituals, and meaning-making of life events, it is sagacious that focusing on these aspects would improve outcomes and the potential for facilitating PTG. Components of various trauma interventions for children include psychoeducation, parenting skills, stress reduction and relaxation skills, affective modulation skills, cognitive coping skills and monitoring of thoughts, talking through trauma narratives, processing and meaning-making, in vivo mastery of trauma reminders, conjoint child-parent sessions, and enhancing safety and future development (Cohen et al., 2006, 2010; Nader, 2008). However, many interventions do not include attending to the spiritual strengths and resources of the child that also include spiritual rituals, practices, and activities, and facilitating strengthening of spiritual relationships for the child.

Models that do include spirituality, meaning and purpose, and transcending adversity are beginning to emerge. Spiritual aspects can be readily integrated into trauma interventions and may provide an opportunity to enhance PTG. Supportive therapeutic, social, and familial connections, and connections to nature and a higher power of one's belief are significant in spiritually focused TGL interventions. Relationships that are spiritual in nature can make the child feel cared for, worthy, offer hope and comfort, and are transformative (Boynton, 2016; Cohen et al., 2006, 2010; Nader, 2008; Walton, 1996). Lutz et al. (2007) contended that open communication and the ability to talk about feelings and meanings associated with trauma events can improve functioning and wellbeing. Relationships and spiritual community resources help to re-establish trust, provide hope and faith, and support identity within a wider sociological context in the trauma journey (Boynton, 2016; Thompson & Walsh, 2010).

Walker et al. (2010) advanced the evidence supporting the trauma-focused cognitive behavioural therapy model by applying a spiritual paradigm offering case examples of spiritual issues and struggles. They stress the necessity of addressing spirituality within trauma treatment. Aspects such as parental spirituality, how spirituality can aid in healing, and the effects of TGL on personal spiritual functioning are highlighted. Children may require support in maintaining, redeveloping, or reconnecting to their spirituality.

Children engage in a variety of coping strategies, many of which include spiritual activities, rituals, practices, prayer, and communicating with spiritual entities when going through the trauma journey. High numbers of youth believe that spending time in nature, praying, sharing problems with others, journaling, creative activities, and exercise are spiritual activities that assist in coping with TGL (Boynton, 2016; Jackson et al., 2010). Staples et al. (2011) found that incorporating meditation, guided imagery, breathing techniques, and self-expression through words, drawings, and movement reduced symptoms of posttraumatic stress and improved hope. Boynton and Vis (2011) highlighted that meaningful relationships, spiritual coping and meaning-making are important for TGL and PTG. They discuss a variety of spiritual and creative expressive therapies for TGL treatment including rituals, play, art, storytelling, and music as transformational pathways. Spiritual methods of coping can contribute to a sense of control, mastery and hope.

The complex and interwoven processes of meaning-making and spirituality, contribute to our sense of self, and our world view (Bray, 2010; Vis & Boynton, 2008). Spiritual world views are created and transformed through cognitive and emotional processes of spiritual searching and meaning-making related to purpose in life (Vis & Boynton, 2008). Spiritual narratives and positive meaning-making can bridge the past, assist in adjusting to the present and discovering a path into the future (Angell et al., 1998). Kilmer et al. (2014) maintained that positive guidance for positive reappraisal, reframing, and constructive rumination, coping advice, and fostering hope, optimism, and positive future expectations held clinical relevance. Positive reappraisal and spirituality are significant factors contributing to PTG and transcendence, and including these in treatment may help children and caregivers view the future in a positive light and think in solution focused ways (Clay et al., 2009; Neimeyer, 2004; Prati & Pietrantoni, 2009). Skogrand et al. (2007) illuminated that the stages of transcendence from TGL for children include awareness, resilience, acceptance, forgiveness, care and compassion, and spirituality. A spiritually integrative framework that highlights spiritual strengths, resources, coping, relationships, and meaning-making as important aspects for transcending TGL holds promise for spiritually sensitive trauma interventions for PTG in social work.

Conclusion

It is evident that TGL can have detrimental effects on psychosocial and overall development and adaptation, however, some children fare better than others and experience PTG. This chapter has demonstrated that there are advancements in knowledge regarding children's spirituality and its importance in PTG. Spiritual struggles and concerns can arise and occur for children during a TGL event, and children often engage in spiritual coping and spiritual resources. Spiritual resources can assist the child in emotional regulation and in feeling self-control, competency, and self-mastery. Positive and constructive rumination may assist children in PTG. Spirituality can assist in meaning-making of the TGL and creating a renewed spiritual world view. Reappraisal, finding benefit and new possibilities, new spiritual meanings, and spiritual gains are related to PTG. Further research is required to assist in developing a more comprehensive theoretical spiritual framework for treating TGL and facilitating PTG. Social workers should continue to explore the PTG and spiritual domain for children.

REFERENCES

Angell, G.B., Dennis, B.C., & Dumain, L.E. (1998). Spirituality, resilience, and narrative: Coping with parental death. *Families in Society: The Journal of Contemporary Social Services*, 79(6), 615–30. https://doi.org/10.1606 /1044-3894.865

Attig, T. (2004). Disenfranchised grief revisited: Discounting hope and love. OMEGA: *Journal of Death and Dying, 49*(3), 197–215. https://doi.org/10.2190/p4tt-j3bf-kfdr-5jb1

Bosacki, S., & Ota, C. (2000). Preadolescents' voices: A consideration of British and Canadian children's reflections on religion, spirituality, and their sense of self. *International Journal of Children's Spirituality, 5*(2), 203–19. https://doi.org/10.1080/713670922

Boynton, H.M. (2016). *Navigating in seclusion: The complicated terrain of children's spirituality in trauma, grief, and loss* [Unpublished doctoral thesis]. Department of Social Work, University of Calgary. https://doi.org/10.11575/PRISM/27063

Boynton, H.M., & Vis, J. (2011). Meaning making, spirituality, and creative expressive therapies: Pathways to processing grief with children. *Counselling and Spirituality, 30*(2), 137–59.

Bray, P. (2010). A broader framework for exploring the influence of spiritual experience in the wake of stressful life events: Examining connections between posttraumatic growth and psycho-spiritual transformation. *Mental Health, Religion & Culture, 13*(3), 293–308. https://doi.org/10.1080/13674670903367199

Briere, J. (2006). Dissociative symptoms and trauma exposure: Specificity, affect dysregulation, and posttraumatic stress. *The Journal of Nervous and Mental Disease, 194*(2), 78–82. https://doi.org/10.1097/01.nmd.0000198139.47371.54. Medline: 16477184

Burke, N.J., Hellman, J.L., Scott, B.G., Weems, C.F., & Carrion, V.G. (2011). The impact of adverse childhood experiences on an urban pediatric population. *Child Abuse & Neglect, 35*(6), 408–13. https://doi.org/10.1016/j.chiabu.2011.02.006. Medline: 21652073

Calhoun, L.G., Cann, A., Tedeschi, R.G., & McMillan, J. (2000). A correlational test of the relationship between posttraumatic growth, religion, and cognitive processing. *Journal of Traumatic Stress, 13*(3), 521–7. https://doi.org/10.1023/a:1007745627077

Calhoun, L.G., & Tedeschi, R.G. (2006). The foundations of posttraumatic growth: An expanded framework. In L.G. Calhoun & R.G. Tedeschi (Eds.), *Handbook of posttraumatic growth: Research and practice* (pp. 1–23). Lawrence Erlbaum Associates.

Cheon, J.W., & Canda, E.R. (2010). The meaning and engagement of spirituality for positive youth development in social work. *Families in Society: The Journal of Contemporary Social Services, 91*(2), 121–6. https://doi.org/10.1606/1044-3894.3981

Clay, R., Knibbs, J., & Joseph, S. (2009). Measurement of posttraumatic growth in young people: A review. *Clinical Child Psychology and Psychiatry, 14*(3), 411–22. https://doi.org/10.1177/1359104509104049. Medline: 19515756

Cohen, J.A., Mannarino, A.P., & Deblinger, E. (2006). *Treating trauma and traumatic grief in children and adolescents*. The Guildford Press.

– (2010). Trauma-focused cognitive-behavioral therapy for traumatized children. In J.R. Weisz & A.E. Kazdin (Eds.), *Evidence-based psychotherapies for children and adolescents* (3rd ed., pp. 295–311). The Guilford Press.

Coholic, D., Lougheed, S., & Cadell, S. (2009). Exploring the helpfulness of arts-based methods with children living in foster care. *Traumatology, 15*(3), 64–71. https://doi.org/10.1177/1534765609341590

Coleman, K. (2015). *Coping with childhood trauma: Art as a policy strategy.* Institute for the Study of International Development. https://www.mcgill.ca/isid/files/isid/pb_2012_05_coleman.pdf

Cryder, C.H., Kilmer, R.P., Tedeschi, R.G., & Calhoun, L.G. (2006). An exploratory study of posttraumatic growth in children following a natural disaster. *American Journal of Orthopsychiatry, 76*(1), 65–9. https://doi.org/10.1037/0002-9432.76.1.65. Medline: 16569128

Decker, L.R. (1993). The role of trauma in spiritual development. *Journal of Humanistic Psychology, 33*(4), 33–46. https://doi.org/10.1177/00221678930334004

Duncan, B.L., Miller, S.D., Wampold, B.E., & Hubble, M.A. (Eds.). (2010). *The heart and soul of change: Delivering what works in therapy* (2nd ed.). American Psychological Association. https://doi.org/10.1037/12075-000

Felitti, V.J., Anda, R.F., Nordenberg, D., Williamson, D.F., Spitz, A.M., Edwards, V., Koss, M.P., & Marks, J.S. (1998). Relationship of childhood abuse and household dysfunction to many of the leading causes of death in adults: The Adverse Childhood Experiences (ACE) Study. *American Journal of Preventive Medicine, 14*(4), 245–58. https://doi.org/10.1016/s0749-3797(98)00017-8

Holder, M.D., Coleman, B., & Wallace, J. (2008). Spirituality, religiousness, and happiness in children aged 8–12 years. *Journal of Happiness Studies, 11*, 131–50. https://doi.org/10.1007/s10902-008-9126-1

Hooyman, N.R., & Kramer, B.J. (2006). *Living through loss: Interventions across the life span.* Columbia University Press.

Houskamp, B.M., Fisher, L.A., & Stuber, M.L. (2004). Spirituality in children and adolescents: Research findings and implications for clinicians and researchers. *Child and Adolescent Psychiatric Clinics of North America, 13*(1), 221–30. https://doi.org/10.1016/s1056-4993(03)00072-5

Jackson, L.J., White, C.R., O'Brien, K., DiLorenzo, P., Cathcart, E., Wolf, M., Bruskas, D., Pecora, P.J., Nix-Early, V., & Cabrera, J. (2010). Exploring spirituality among youth in foster care: Findings from the Casey Field Office Mental Health Study. *Child and Family Social Work, 15*(1), 107–17. https://doi.org/10.1111/j.1365-2206.2009.00649.x. Medline: 25057258

Janoff-Bulman, R. (2006). Schema-change perspectives on posttraumatic growth. In L.G. Calhoun & R.G. Tedeschi (Eds.), *Handbook of posttraumatic growth: Research and practice* (pp. 81–99). Lawrence Erlbaum Associates.

Johnson, K. (1989). *Trauma in the lives of children: Crisis and stress management techniques for counselors and other professionals.* Hunter House Inc.

Kilmer, R.P. (2006). Resilience and posttraumatic growth in children. In L.G. Calhoun & R.G. Tedeschi (Eds.), *Handbook of posttraumatic growth: Research and practice* (pp. 264–88). Psychology Press.

Kilmer, R.P., Gil-Rivas, V., Griese, B., Hardy, S.J., Hafstad, G.S., & Alisic, E. (2014). Posttraumatic growth in children and youth: Clinical implications of an emerging research literature. *American Journal of Orthopsychiatry, 84*(5), 506–18. https://doi.org/10.1037/ort0000016. Medline: 25110973

Kilmer, R.P., Gil-Rivas, V., Tedeschi, R.G., Cann, A., Calhoun, L.G., Buchanan, T., & Taku, K. (2009). Use of the revised posttraumatic growth inventory for children. *Journal of Traumatic Stress, 22*(3), 248–53. https://doi.org/10.1002/jts.20410

Laceulle, O.M., Kleber, R.J., & Alisic, E. (2015). Children's experience of posttraumatic growth: Distinguishing general from domain-specific correlates. *PLoS One, 10*(12), e0145736. https://doi.org/10.1371/journal.pone.0145736. Medline: 26714193

Lepore, S., & Revenson, T. (2006). Relationships between posttraumatic growth and resilience: Recovery, resistance and reconfiguration. In L.G. Calhoun & R.G. Tedeschi (Eds.), *Handbook of posttraumatic growth: Research and practice* (pp. 24–46). Lawrence Erlbaum Associates.

Lutz, W.J., Hock, E., & Kang, M.J. (2007). Children's communication about distressing events: The role of emotional openness and psychological attributes of family members. *American Journal of Orthopsychiatry, 77*(1), 86–94. https://doi.org/10.1037/0002-9432.77.1.86. Medline: 17352589

McCann, L., & Pearlman, L. (1990). *Psychological trauma and the adult survivor: Theory, therapy, and transformation.* Brunner/Hazel.

Monahon, C. (1993). *Children and trauma: A guide for parents and professionals.* Jossey-Bass Publishers.

Nader, K. (2008). *Understanding and assessing trauma in children and adolescents: Measures, methods, and youth in context.* Routledge.

Neimeyer, R.A. (2004). Research on grief and bereavement: Evolution and revolution. *Death Studies, 28*(6), 489–90. https://doi.org/10.1080/07481180490461179

Paris, M.M., Carter, B.L., Day, S.X., & Armsworth, M.W. (2009). Grief and trauma in children after the death of a sibling. *Journal of Child & Adolescent Trauma, 2,* 71–80. https://doi.org/10.1080/19361520902861913

Park, C.L., & Ai, A.L. (2006). Meaning making and growth: New directions for research on survivors of trauma. *Journal of Loss and Trauma, 11*(5), 389–407. https://doi.org/10.1080/15325020600685295

Prati, G., & Pietrantoni, L. (2009). Optimism, social support, and coping strategies as factors contributing to posttraumatic growth: A meta-analysis. *Journal of Loss and Trauma, 14*(5), 364–88. https://doi.org/10.1080/15325020902724271

Skogrand, L., Singh, A., Allgood, S., DeFrain, J., DeFrain, N., & Jones, J.E. (2007). The process of transcending a traumatic childhood. *Contemporary Family Therapy, 29*, 253–70. https://doi.org/10.1007/s10591-007-9049-8

Staples, J.K., Abdel Atti, J.A., & Gordon, J.S. (2011). Mind-body skills groups for posttraumatic stress disorder and depression symptoms in Palestinian children and adolescents in Gaza. *International Journal of Stress Management, 18*(3), 246–62. https://doi.org/10.1037/a0024015

Sveidqvist, V., Joubert, N., Greene, J., & Manion, I. (2003). Who am I, and why am I here? Young people's perspectives on the role of spirituality in the promotion of their mental health. *International Journal of Mental Health Promotion, 5*(3), 36–44. https://doi.org/10.1080/14623730.2003.9721911

Tedeschi, R.G., & Calhoun, L.G. (2006). Time of change? The spiritual challenges of bereavement and loss. *OMEGA: Journal of Death and Dying, 53*(1), 105–16. https://doi.org/10.2190/7mbu-ufv9-6tj6-dp83

Tedeschi, R.G., Park, C.L., & Calhoun L.G. (1998). Posttraumatic growth: Conceptual issues. In R.G. Tedeschi, C.L. Park, & L.G. Calhoun (Eds.), *Posttraumatic growth: Positive changes in the aftermath of crisis* (pp. 1–22). Lawrence Erlbaum Associates.

Thompson, A.H., & Cui, X. (2000). Increasing childhood trauma in Canada: Findings from the National Population Health Survey, 1994/95. *Canadian Journal of Public Health, 91*(3), 197–200. https://doi.org/10.1007/bf03404271

Thompson, N., & Walsh, M. (2010). The existential basis of trauma. *Journal of Social Work Practice, 24*(4), 377–89. https://doi.org/10.1080/02650531003638163

van Der Kolk, B., Ford, J.D., & Spinazzola, J. (2019). Comorbidity of developmental trauma disorder (DTD) and posttraumatic stress disorder: Findings from the DTD field trial. *European Journal of Psychotraumatology, 10*(1), 1–13. https://doi.org/10.1080/20008198.2018.1562841. Medline: 30728917

Vis, J., & Boynton, H.M. (2008). Spirituality and transcendent meaning making: Possibilities for enhancing posttraumatic growth. *Journal of Religion and Spirituality in Social Work: Social Thought, 27*(1–2), 69–86. https://doi.org/10.1080/15426430802113814

Vloet, T.D., Vloet, A., Bürger, A., & Romanos, M. (2017). Posttraumatic growth in children and adolescents. *Journal of Traumatic Stress Disorders & Treatment, 6*(4). https://doi.org/10.4172/2324-8947.1000178

Walker, D.F., Reese, J.B., Hughes, J.P., & Troskie, M.J. (2010). Addressing religious and spiritual issues in trauma-focused cognitive behavior therapy for children and adolescents. *Professional Psychology Research and Practice, 41*(2), 174–80. https://doi.org/10.1037/a0017782

Walton, J. (1996). Spiritual relationships: A concept analysis. *Journal of Holistic Nursing, 14*(3), 237–50. https://doi.org/10.1177/089801019601400306. Medline: 8900616

Yaskowich, K.M. (2002). *Posttraumatic growth in children and adolescents with cancer* [Unpublished doctoral thesis]. Department of Psychology, University of Calgary. https://doi.org/10.11575/PRISM/20242

2 Spirituality and Child Welfare Practice with Indigenous Families: Fostering a "Culture of Strengths"

JOEY WARK, HEATHER BOYNTON, AND JO-ANN VIS

Discussion of the role of spirituality in the lives of Indigenous peoples has been largely absent in the child welfare literature. This is concerning given that spirituality is a central aspect of traditional healing models and it is one of the three major domains of posttraumatic growth (Ai et al., 2013; Tedeschi & Calhoun 1995, 2004). According to Shaw et al. (2005), spirituality can be deepened and can contribute to posttraumatic growth in the aftermath and processing of trauma. In a systematic review of literature on posttraumatic growth and children, Meyerson et al. (2011) found that spiritual change and appreciation of life were significant factors that may be context-specific, and that spirituality could be of benefit to children who are in care in regard to coping with trauma, meaning-making, acceptance, and forgiveness. Weiss and Berger (2010) compiled research on posttraumatic growth and culture across the lifespan from around the globe. They found, however, that there was no literature on the Canadian context and very little regarding Indigenous people.

Considering the importance many Indigenous peoples place on spirituality (Baskin, 2016) and the vast over-representation of Indigenous children in the child welfare system in Canada (Trocmé et al., 2004), it appears a review of the available research in this area is in order. For the purposes of this chapter, we will not focus on a specific Indigenous nation or geographic region but will instead use the term "Indigenous" as a collective designation to refer to the descendants of the original inhabitants of North America. The pitfalls of referring to Indigenous peoples as a single, monolithic culture have been documented (Waldram, 2004), and, considering the limited literature in this area of inquiry, it should be cautioned that data that emerges from one community may not be representative for all Indigenous Canadians. When summarizing the research, the terms "Aboriginal," "First Nation," and

"Native" will be maintained if these were the terms used in the original study. The first section imparts some important history of political aspects in relation to Indigenous spirituality and effects of colonization. The second section describes Indigenous spirituality and its importance in life, health, and well-being, and in *mino-pimatisiwin*, how separation for children is damaging, and how spirituality is a strength that needs to be addressed in child welfare practice. The next section highlights research and the gaps and the importance of Elders in the care of children and their spiritual growth. Implications for practice are highlighted in closing the chapter.

Indigenous Peoples and Child Welfare in Canada

Any discussion of spirituality and child welfare interventions with Indigenous peoples would be remiss without a summary of the historical relationship between the nation-state now called Canada and Indigenous peoples. From the beginning, this relationship was founded on an assimilation agenda that viewed European culture as superior and Indigenous culture, including spiritual beliefs and practices, as having no value (Ryan, 1996). Miller (1996) maintained that for many Indigenous nations, the first contact with Europeans involved missionaries focused on saving so-called heathen souls by religious conversion to Christianity. By the late nineteenth century, changes to the Indian Act legally prohibited traditional spiritual practices and extinguished the rights of Indigenous parents to raise their children (Chansonneuve, 2005; Robbins & Dewar, 2011). To assimilate Indigenous peoples into European society, the government of what is now Canada began removing children from their families and placing them in residential schools run by various churches and missionary groups (Miller, 1996; Milloy, 1999).

In the residential school system, Indigenous children were not only separated from their families but also from their communities, cultures, and languages (Haig-Brown, 1988; Ryan, 1996). For students who attended these schools, the experience was characterized by poor instruction, cultural oppression, inadequate care, overwork, severe discipline, and gross abuse (Miller, 1996). Longboat (1987) indicated that the primary goal of the religious organizations that ran the schools was to provide training in Christian religion while reading, writing, and other skills took a secondary role. Children were forbidden to speak their own languages or practice their spiritual traditions (Milloy, 1999). Moreover, students in residential schools did not encounter healthy parental role models and, consequently as adults, frequently had diminished capacity to care for their own children (Bennett & Blackstock, 2002). Furthermore, as the residential schools declined, the Canadian government extended its assimilation setting into the realm of child welfare (Milloy, 1999).

Richardson and Nelson (2007) highlighted how changes in the Indian Act in 1951 allowed provincial child welfare agencies to administer child protection services on Indian reserves. Timpson (1995) related that this set in motion a large-scale removal of Indigenous children from their families and communities that has since been termed the Sixties Scoop. In the mid-1980s, many provincial and territorial child welfare policies were forced to acknowledge the importance of children's Indigenous heritage, and political pressure forced governments to transfer control of child welfare services to Aboriginal organizations (Timpson, 1995; Trocmé et al., 2004). And yet, the number of Indigenous children being placed in out-of-home care continues to rise, with more children in care today than at the height of the residential school era.

Indigenous Peoples and Spirituality

Despite state-sponsored efforts to eradicate Indigenous spiritual practices, spirituality remains a large component of Indigenous values and world views and is important to wellness and healing. Many nations subscribe to holistic understandings of health that recognize the physical, emotional, cognitive, and spiritual aspects of a person (Hart, 2002; Sterling-Collins, 2009). Hart (2002) described spirituality as including the concepts of "wholeness, balance, relationships, harmony, growth, healing, and *mino-pimatisiwin* [the good life]" (p. 35). Healing and health begin from the perspectives of the interconnectedness of all things in the universe and interdependence, and well-being occurs with balance and harmony among all the personal and collective life elements (The Royal Commission on Aboriginal Peoples, 2010). There is a strong connection between individuals and their communities, ancestors, descendants, plants, animals, and creatures. A sacred relationship with the land further characterizes Indigenous spirituality (Greenwood & de Leeuw, 2007; Wilson, 2003). For many Indigenous peoples, spirituality is demonstrated in activities such as meditation, prayers, ceremonies, offerings, purifications, dancing, hunting, and fishing (Hart, 2009; Isaak & Marchessault, 2008). Research had suggested that a revitalization of traditional spiritual practices can play a crucial role in healing and positive identity formation for Indigenous peoples (Anderson, 2000; McCormick, 1994). These are important aspects requiring consideration in child welfare.

Spirituality is a valued aspect in the lives of Indigenous peoples through-out the lifespan (Hart, 2002), and children and Elders are especially promi-nent in Indigenous spiritual beliefs and practices. Many Indigenous world views emphasize that children are gifts from the Creator and therefore sacred and are to be treated with reverence and nurtured (Boynton, 2015; Simpson, 2006). Blackstock (2003) imparted that children are viewed as full participants in the community as well as in the interdependent web of life. From an Indigenous perspective, a healthy sense of spirituality is said to be integral to the well-being of children (Greenwood & de Leeuw, 2007). In many Indigenous nations, Elders also hold esteemed positions, and are recognized as the transmitters of spiritual knowledge to the younger generations (Anderson, 2011; Baskin, 2016). For example, among the Anishinabek, old age marks a kind of spiritual attainment and prestige as a result of having led a good life and having honoured the responsibilities associated with earlier life stages (Anderson, 2011). Canadian Indigenous people deem traditional healing, in promoting psychological and spiri-tual well-being, to include activities such as traditional medicines, healing circles and traditional ceremonies, smudging, sweat lodges, drumming, dancing and songs, counselling, storytelling, and Elders' accumulated wisdom (Manahan & Ball, 2007; The Royal Commission on Aboriginal Peoples, 2010). It is important to note that spiritual practices are diverse and differ between communities and families.

While there is a considerable knowledge gap in the research regard-ing the use of spirituality in child welfare practices with Indigenous families (Boynton, 2015), some studies are available. In consideration of the historical and legislative variations in child welfare services in the United States, this review of the research is limited to peer-reviewed studies of Canadian Indigenous populations. The reviewed studies can be summarized along three distinct themes. First, there is empiri-cal support for the idea that the permanent separation of Indigenous children from their families, communities, and nations is spiritually harmful to these children and can produce deleterious and traumatic effects that remain present in adulthood. Second, research indicates that spirituality can be a source of strength and resilience not just for Indigenous children involved in child welfare services, but also for Indigenous mothers, kinship caregivers, and foster parents. The third theme to emerge from the research suggests that Elders play a crucial role in passing on spiritual practices to Indigenous children in the child welfare system and in applying these spiritual teachings towards the development of culturally safe child welfare services. What is missing is the role of spirituality as a strength for fathers, as well as a focus on spirituality and posttraumatic growth.

Separation as Spiritually Damaging

In her exploration of the relationship among connectedness, health, and adoption, Carriere (2005, 2008) interviewed 18 adult First Nations adoptees from British Columbia, Alberta, Manitoba, and Ontario, many of whom were adopted during the Sixties Scoop. Most of the participants reported spiritual loss and spiritual confusion throughout their lives as a result of their adoption experience. This loss and confusion manifested itself in many ways including suicidal ideation, running away from home, and feeling lost, detached, or unwanted (Carriere, 2005). Additionally, Carriere (2005) maintained that remaining connected with community or nation can be a protective factor for First Nations youth and children. Based on her findings, Carriere (2008) proposed that the spiritual development of children adopted or in care outside of their community can be supported by working with respected Elders from the child's community to preserve cultural identity.

Spirituality as a Strength

Using two case studies of Aboriginal youth involved in child welfare services, Brownlee et al. (2010) described a strengths-based intervention employed at an inner city elementary school in Thunder Bay, Ontario. The Strengths Assessment Inventory (SAI; Rawana & Brownlee, 2009) was used to identify a wide range of student strengths, including cultural and spiritual strengths, which informed interventions that enhanced the child's chances of successfully navigating his/her way through the child welfare system. Unfortunately, the case studies did not mention how spiritual strengths were tapped to enhance resilience or posttraumatic growth. It is not clear if the tool to assess spirituality includes the various aspects of Indigenous spirituality, or if it is based more on religious aspects as other tools assessing spirituality do not embrace culturally specific or address spirituality outside of religious domains. However, the authors stated that a comprehensive evaluation of strengths provided an opportunity for Aboriginal children in the child welfare system to name and identify their strengths, have these strengths recognized by caring adults, and fostered a culture of strengths within the helping systems in the child's life. They asserted that including spirituality is essential in ensuring that client needs are met through culturally appropriate social work practice. This study emphasized the importance of assessing the spiritual strengths of children. Again, the actual indicators of spiritual strengths are not clear and this is an area that needs to be better understood. It also does not speak to the role spirituality can play in the lives of adults involved with child welfare services.

Anderson (1998) interviewed six female caregivers (four mothers and two grandmothers) that were clients of an Indigenous-specific child welfare agency in Metropolitan Toronto and found spirituality to be a strength for Indigenous caregivers. Through participation in the program, the participants discovered aspects of Native spirituality, some for the first time, and the involvement in this aspect of their culture facilitated their healing process. This finding of spirituality as a strength was also echoed in a longitudinal evaluation of a parenting program for parents whose children were considered to be at risk of abuse or neglect in Vancouver, British Columbia (Harris et al., 2007). A sub-sample consisting of six Aboriginal mothers reported that access to spiritual teachings and ceremony through the program assisted them in their own wellness and healing. Besides gaining strength from traditional spiritual practices, these mothers also indicated a strong desire to pass these teachings on to their own children. This speaks to the importance of spirituality in intergenerational healing and posttraumatic growth.

Mothers are not the only caregivers of Indigenous children who are important in their lives and who draw on their spirituality as a source of strength. Manahan and Ball (2007) presented research on fathers who felt that engaging their spirituality allowed them to heal and gain confidence in preparation for fatherhood and their parenting journey. Their spirituality regenerated, reinforced, and connected them with their cultural identity, nourished family relationships, and promoted their spiritual wellness. Fathers felt that traditional practices and their indigenous spirituality allowed them to break the cycle of trauma and effects of colonialism and processes of assimilation. Practices such as traditional drumming, dancing, ceremonies, smudging, hunting, and healing circles were just some of the many suggestions offered. There appears to be a significant gap in the literature on fathers, spirituality and posttraumatic growth and further study in this area should be addressed.

According to Manahan and Ball (2007), indigenous families are cohesive multigenerational arrangements of extended kinships that encompass the various responsibilities and roles in raising children in the community. In a qualitative investigation of the experiences and needs of 16 kinship caregivers in northern British Columbia, six of whom cited Aboriginal ancestry, some of the participants cited traditional Aboriginal spirituality as a source of support in their caregiving efforts (Burke & Schmidt, 2009). In another study, Thompson et al. (2013) explored the experiences of 15 First Nations grandparents from two distinct

Canadian cities. These authors urged child welfare agencies to consider grandparents when a need for foster care arises based on the responsibility many of these grandparents felt towards passing on spiritual knowledge to the younger generations. Many of the grandparents felt rewarded by the sense of cultural healing and cultural continuity that being involved with their grandchildren afforded them. In encouraging a proud First Nations identity in their grandchildren, many of these grandparents appeared to be redefining and reclaiming historical roles that placed much importance on the role of grandparents.

Regarding caregivers from outside of the extended family, Brown et al. (2014) interviewed 82 Aboriginal foster parents about their mental health needs. The participants were from an unnamed Central Canadian province and most were Métis (65 per cent). Using concept mapping, the data suggested that the participants believed that spiritually based optimism was required to be a good foster parent for Aboriginal children. Optimism was conceptualized as an underlying belief that all would work out well; a belief founded on Aboriginal spirituality and trust in the Creator. For these foster parents, this optimism provided clarity and confidence in their understandings of self, family, and community. Accordingly, the participants' spirituality cultivated a clear sense of identity and recognition of their role in promoting a healthy sense of Aboriginal identity in the children that they fostered.

Elders as Spiritual Teachers

While some of the previously mentioned studies touched on the role that Elders play in the spiritual continuity of adopted Indigenous children (Carriere, 2008) and grandchildren in their care (Thompson et al., 2013), research suggests that Elders may also serve an essential function in shaping the vision, objectives, policies, and practices of culturally safe child welfare agencies for Indigenous families and communities. LaFrance and Bastien (2007) employed appreciative inquiry to collect data from approximately 170 participants from the Blood Reserve in Southern Alberta and concluded that community empowered approaches to child welfare in Alberta would require collaboration with Elders and ceremonialists. In another study, Simard (2009) used secondary data analysis to examine ten historical videos which described the foundational practices of Weechi-it-te-win Family Services in Fort Frances, Ontario. From this data, the author surmised that culturally restorative child welfare practices are guided by Elders' knowledge of cultural rites, ceremony, clan membership, and teachings on the role of spirituality in identity formation and childrearing.

Elders can play a significant role in the family and may have a very important role in the spirituality and posttraumatic growth of the family. Spirituality can be deepened through trauma, and positive spiritual coping can be part of family healing. In a study with indigenous people in a Pacific Island Community, Maratita (2017) found that posttraumatic growth was evident alongside historical intergenerational trauma. Storytelling, an oral family tradition, was viewed as a means of persevering history and increased posttraumatic growth. Participants shared thoughts and feelings of greater values and engagement, finding new interests, positive changes to relationships, personal strengths, appreciation of life, and growth in spirituality. No similar studies were found on Canadian populations.

Discussion

The notion that spirituality can serve as a source of strength for children and caregivers involved in the child welfare system has been well documented outside of Indigenous populations. Research has indicated that spiritual activities and spiritual support can cultivate competence and resilience and can facilitate posttraumatic growth for young persons involved in foster care (Ai et al., 2013; Daining & DePanfilis, 2007; Jackson et al., 2010). Studies have also demonstrated spirituality to be an incredible source of strength for families who have achieved reunification after child removal (Lietz & Hodge, 2011; Lietz & Strength, 2011). Furthermore, while the role of spirituality as a strength for children and families involved with child welfare services has been established for Indigenous populations (Carriere & Richardson, 2009; Coleman et al., 2001) and non-Indigenous populations (DiLorenzo et al., 2001; Seita, 2000; Van Hook, 2008), it has little influence on contemporary child welfare practices which do not fully integrate spirituality.

Furthermore, what has not been documented in the mainstream child welfare literature is the damage that the separation of children from their families and communities might have on spiritual health in adulthood. The findings by Carriere (2005, 2008) may be the result of a methodology that favours an Indigenous-based holistic view of health. Another probable contributor to this unique effect is the vast divergence between Western and Indigenous spiritual traditions, and meanings of spirituality. The spiritual damage to children separated from their families and communities is likely the result of an Indigenous conceptualization of spirituality that is highly interconnected with health and well-being (Baskin, 2016), the land of home territories (Greenwood & de Leeuw, 2007; Hart, 2009; Wilson, 2003), and relationships with relatives, ancestors (Carriere & Richardson, 2009), and community members (Cajete, 2000). Moreover, as many Indigenous children were adopted by Christian families, an enforced monotheistic upbringing could potentially have detrimental effects on one's spiritual health if Indigenous spiritual traditions are demeaned or devalued (Richardson & Nelson, 2007).

Another peculiar aspect of spirituality in child welfare services for Indigenous peoples that has not been observed in mainstream services is the role that spiritual leaders, in this case Elders, play in shaping and developing culturally safe child welfare organizations. Esteemed Elders and the spiritual knowledge they hold have been recognized as the guiding force in the formation of Indigenous child welfare services in Alberta (Carriere, 2010) and Ontario (Ferris et al., 2005). Throughout Canada, Elders play meaningful roles in Indigenous child welfare agencies in the form of consultations (di Tomasso & de Finney, 2015; Pintarics & Sveinunggaard, 2005), Elders' councils (Ferris et al., 2005), and the provision of spiritual guidance to organizations overall (Carriere, 2010; Ferris et al., 2005). Elders also play an essential role in embedding spirituality into child welfare agencies by incorporating ceremony into administrative functions, gifting sacred items to the organization (Ferris et al., 2005), and facilitating custom adoption, homecoming, and transition ceremonies for children in care (Bennett, 2015; Carriere, 2010; di Tomasso & de Finney, 2015).

Research Gaps

Colonial history, cultural heterogeneity, and fundamental differences between Indigenous and Western world views ensure that research involving spirituality among Indigenous peoples is a difficult undertaking. Indigenous spirituality is a complex phenomenon that is closely intertwined with culture and ways of living (Fleming & Ledogar, 2008). While Western science favours separating components into their smallest parts for analysis and quantification (Ermine, 1995), any examination of Indigenous spirituality cannot be separated from other aspects of culture like identity, language, cultural practices, and ways of being. Empirical inquiries in this area are also complicated by the spiritual diversity among Indigenous peoples in Canada. Child welfare services cannot assume that all members of designated populations share similar religious and spiritual views (Van Hook, 2008). Many remote Indigenous communities have strong Christian followings (Brubacher, 2006) while urban areas can be home to Indigenous peoples from many disparate nations and spiritual traditions (Fleming & Ledogar, 2008).

While Indigenous motherhood has been described as a spiritual process and responsibility (Bedard, 2006; Graveline, 1998; Simpson, 2006), this critical spiritual aspect is not fully integrated into services. Additionally, the literature reviewed in this chapter does not offer any insight into the role of spirituality for Indigenous fathers in the child welfare system. This is not surprising given that Indigenous fathers have received inadequate attention in research (Muir & Bohr, 2014) and are given little, if any, consideration in child welfare practices (Strega et al., 2008). Moreover, given the preoccupation with risk and risk management in child welfare (Strega, 2009), it has been recommended that child welfare agencies purposefully assess the spirituality of service users (Jackson et al., 2010; Lietz & Hodge, 2011; Lietz & Strength, 2011). However, apart from a study conducted with American Indian populations (Limb & Hodge, 2010), formal tools that exclusively assess the spiritual values and beliefs of Indigenous service users from an Indigenous perspective are noticeably absent in the literature.

Implications for Practice

In Canada, Indigenous child welfare has been viewed by some as an extension of the residential school system (Greenwood & de Leeuw, 2006; Richardson & Nelson, 2007). Indigenous families continue to be subjected to policies based on the colonial foundations that structure many White-Indigenous relationships (Richardson & Nelson, 2007; Wade, 1995). Implementing a "culture is treatment" stance (Green, 2010) challenges child welfare workers and agencies to incorporate culture as a vital component of intervention. Placing culture at the forefront of child welfare intervention requires "the realization that ritual, myth, vision, art and learning the art of relationships in particular environments all facilitate the health and wholeness of individuals, families, and communities" (p. 31). Prevailing historical and contemporary discourses in Canada have constructed Indigenous peoples as deficient and, consequently, in want of Euro-Canadian intervention (Greenwood & de Leeuw, 2006). In contrast, child welfare practices that recognize spirituality as integral to Indigenous well-being can foster the "culture of strengths" described by Brownlee and colleagues (2010), wherein Indigenous children and families are valued and respected and their spirituality is part of daily life, and service provision at all levels including policies, procedures, and practices. Adopting this strengths-based (Saleebey, 2006) spiritual approach can result in a paradigm shift that moves away from correcting Indigenous "deficiencies" and towards building respectful relationships between child welfare agencies and

Indigenous families and communities and addresses the whole person (Green & Thomas, 2009).

Family Preservation

While it has been argued that Indigenous child welfare agencies should provide services in the best interests of the community rather than in the best interests of the child (Baskin, 2016), the reviewed research implies that the removal of Indigenous children from their families and communities is not in the best interests of either. Placing Indigenous children in foster care may be simply replacing one set of risk factors with another set (Blackstock et al., 2007). While family separation is purported to be a last resort in child welfare, this is not always the case for Indigenous families (Richardson & Nelson, 2007). In practice, cultivating a "culture of strengths" means advocating for strengths-based processes that keep children with their families and within their communities. This may include advocating for fostering arrangements that are temporary and inclusive of the child's family, financial and clinical support for kinship caregivers (Richardson & Nelson, 2007), family group conferencing (Burford & Hudson, 2000; Chandler & Giovannucci, 2004; van Wormer, 2003), custom adoptions (di Tomasso & de Finney, 2015; Carriere, 2010), or family mediation (Pintarics & Sveinunggaard, 2005), and inclusion of spiritual connections, rituals, customs, and traditions, while also creating a strong circle of support. These considerations may contribute to greater posttraumatic growth.

Assessing Spirituality

Recognizing strengths in the assessment stage can help child welfare professionals move from "fixing" Indigenous problems to valuing and honouring the relationship with the family (Green & Thomas, 2009). By asking spiritually pertinent questions that address Indigenous spirituality and gathering information through the use of culturally and spiritually sensitive assessment tools, children, caregivers, and community members are invited to identify, ruminate, and explore strengths related to spirituality (Vis & Boynton, 2008). Spiritual strengths that are identified can be applied to interventions that work towards family preservation, reunification, and connectedness (Brownlee et al., 2010). Indigenous children and families who identify spirituality as a strength or potential strength should be provided access to spiritual teachings, ceremonies, and Elders or other spiritual leaders in their preferred spiritual tradition. It is essential that spiritual assessments include multiple sources, including fathers, grandparents, extended family members, foster parents, Elders, and traditional knowledge keepers from the family's community of origin. In light of the importance many Indigenous grandparents and foster parents place on cultural continuity, spiritual assessments can also be used to provide support and endorsement for these caregivers.

Meaningful Involvement of Elders

Creating culturally safe child welfare agencies will require significant roles for Elders in guiding and informing policy and practices involving Indigenous families. While Elders are sometimes used in a tokenistic fashion in social service agencies to gain social capital and demonstrate diversity (Baskin, 2016), respectful practitioners ensure that these spiritual leaders have meaningful involvement within the agency and defer to them in spiritual matters. Hodge and colleagues (2009) state that non-Indigenous child welfare service providers can play a role in fostering spiritual strengths that does not include delivering spiritual practices. These practices belong to the rightful spiritual helpers who are the Elders, medicine people, healers, and traditional people (Lavallée, 2010). For Indigenous peoples, ceremony for every aspect of life has been used to promote wellness, belonging, and connectedness (Anderson, 2011; Bennett, 2015; McCormick, 2009; Peacock & Morin, 2010). A context of respect and appreciation necessitates that child welfare professionals understand the value of ceremony in raising healthy children while concurrently recognizing who are the most appropriate people to facilitate these ceremonies. Given that the spiritual dimension is important in posttraumatic growth and has been found to be of benefit for children in other cultures, further research is required in this area for Indigenous children (Kiliç, 2010), especially in healing from intergenerational trauma and to ensure positive spiritual development.

Conclusion

A review of the research on the use of spirituality in child welfare services with Indigenous families and communities in Canada reveals what Indigenous peoples have long known, namely, that spirituality is essential to well-being and a source of strength and resilience. It is not separate from other aspects of life and development. The role of Elders as the keepers and transmitters of these sacred knowledges to younger generations is identified as critical. The complexity of Indigenous spirituality emphasizes the need for further research that explores the role of Indigenous fathers in cultural continuity and holistic care. There is a need for strengths-based assessment tools that can incorporate the diversity of Indigenous spiritual beliefs, traditions, customs, rituals, and ways of being. For child welfare service providers, a recognition and appreciation of the importance Indigenous peoples place on spirituality in childrearing is a rejection of historical conventions that have devalued Indigenous world views. Fostering a culture of strengths that includes spirituality in child welfare practice will depend upon professionals who work to keep Indigenous children with their families and communities, assess and nurture the spiritual strengths of the families with whom they work, and are involved in meaningful and respectful relationships with Elders and other traditional knowledge keepers.

REFERENCES

Ai, A., Foster, L.J.J., Pecora, P.J., Delaney, N., & Rodriguez, W. (2013). Reshaping child welfare's response to trauma: Assessment, evidence-based intervention, and new research perspectives. *Research on Social Work Practice*, 23(6), 651–68. https://doi.org/10.1177/1049731513491835

Anderson, K. (1998). A Canadian child welfare agency for urban Natives: The clients speak. *Child Welfare*, 77(4), 441–60.

– (2000). *A recognition of being: Reconstructing Native womanhood*. Sumach Press.

– (2011). *Life stages and native women: Memory, teachings, and story medicine*. University of Manitoba Press.

Baskin, C. (2016). *Strong helpers' teachings: The value of Indigenous knowledges in the helping professions* (2nd ed.). Canadian Scholars' Press.

Bedard, R.E.M. (2006). An Anishinaabe-kwe ideology on mothering and motherhood. In D.M. Lavell-Harvard & J.C. Lavell (Eds.), *Until our hearts are on the ground: Aboriginal mothering, oppression, resistance and rebirth* (pp. 65–75). Demeter Press.

Bennett, K. (2015). Cultural permanence for Indigenous children and youth: Reflections from a delegated Aboriginal agency in British Columbia. *First Peoples Child & Family Review*, 10(1), 99–115. http://journals.sfu.ca/fpcfr/index.php/FPCFR/article/view/243/232

Bennett, M., & Blackstock, C. (2002). *A literature review and annotated bibliography focusing on aspects of Aboriginal child welfare in Canada*. First Nations Child & Family Caring Society of Canada Inc. https://fncaringsociety.com/sites/default/files/17LitReviewEntire.pdf

Blackstock, C. (2003). First Nations child and family services: Restoring peace and harmony in First Nations communities. In K. Kufeldt & B. McKenzie

(Eds.), *Child welfare: Connecting research policy and practice* (pp. 331–42). Wilfrid Laurier University Press.

Blackstock, C., Brown, I., & Bennett, M. (2007). Reconciliation: Rebuilding the Canadian child welfare system to better serve Aboriginal children and youth. In I. Brown, F. Chaze, D. Fuchs, J. Lafrance, S. McKay, & S. Thomas-Prokop (Eds.), *Putting a human face on child welfare: Voices from the prairies* (pp. 59–87). Prairie Child Welfare Consortium. https://cwrp.ca/sites/default/files/publications/prairiebook/Putting_a_Human_Face_on_Child_Welfare.pdf

Boynton, H. (2015). Children's spirituality: A component of holistic care in child welfare. In R. Neckoway & K. Brownlee (Eds.), *Child welfare in rural remote areas with Canada's First-Nations peoples: Selected readings* (pp. 165–89). Hignell Book Printing.

Brown, J.D., Rodgers, J., Ivanova, V., Mehta, N., & Skrodzki, D. (2014). Mental needs of Aboriginal foster parents. *Child and Adolescent Social Work Journal, 31*, 539–57. https://doi.org/10.1007/s10560-014-0335-7

Brownlee, K., Rawana, E., MacArthur, J., & Probizanski, M. (2010). The culture of strengths makes them valued and competent: Aboriginal children, child welfare, and a school strengths intervention. *First Peoples Child & Family Review, 5*(1), 106–13. https://doi.org/10.7202/1069067ar

Brubacher, M. (2006). *Coming home: The story of Tikinagan Child and Family Services*. Tikinagan Child and Family Services.

Burford, G., & Hudson, J. (Eds.) (2000). *Family group conferencing: New directions in community-centered child and family practice*. Taylor & Francis.

Burke, S., & Schmidt, G.G. (2009). Kinship care in northern British Columbia. *Child Welfare, 88*(6), 123–38.

Cajete, G. (2000). *Native science: Natural laws of interdependence*. Clear Light.

Carriere, J. (2005). Connectedness and health for First Nations adoptees. *Paediatrics & Child Health, 10*(9), 545–8. https://doi.org/10.1093/pch/10.9.545. Medline: 19668687

– (2008). Maintaining identities: The soul work of adoption and Aboriginal children. *Pimatisiwin: A Journal of Aboriginal and Indigenous Community Health, 6*(1), 61–80. http://www.pimatisiwin.com/uploads/1917536646.pdf

– (Ed.) (2010). *Aski awasis/Children of the earth: First Peoples speaking on adoption*. Fernwood.

Carriere, J., & Richardson, C. (2009). From longing to belonging: Attachment theory, connectedness, and Indigenous children in Canada. In S. McKay, D. Fuchs, & I. Brown (Eds.), *Passion for action in child and family services: Voices from the prairies* (pp. 49–67). Canadian Plains Research Center.

Chandler, S.M., & Giovannucci, M. (2004). Family group conferences: Transforming traditional child welfare policy and practice. *Family Court Review, 42*(2), 216–31. https://doi.org/10.1111/j.174-1617.2004.tb00645.x

Chansonneuve, D. (2005). *Reclaiming connections: Understanding residential school trauma among Aboriginal people.* The Aboriginal Healing Foundation. http://www.ahf.ca/downloads/healing-trauma-web-eng.pdf

Coleman, H., Unrau, Y.A., & Manyfingers, B. (2001). Revamping family preservation services for Native families. *Journal of Ethnic & Cultural Diversity in Social Work, 10*(1), 49–68. https://doi.org/10.1300/j051v10n01_03

Daining, C., & DePanfilis, D. (2007). Resilience of youth in transition from out-of-home care to adulthood. *Children and Youth Services Review, 29*(9), 1158–78. https://doi.org/10.1016/j.childyouth.2007.04.006

DiLorenzo, P., Johnson, R., & Bussey, M. (2001). The role of spirituality in the recovery process. *Child Welfare, 80*(2), 257–73.

di Tomasso, L., & de Finney, S. (2015). A discussion paper on Indigenous custom adoption part 2: Honouring our caretaking traditions. *First Peoples Child & Family Review, 10*(1), 19–38. http://journals.sfu.ca/fpcfr/index.php/FPCFR/article/view/248/230

Ermine, W. (1995). Aboriginal epistemology. In M. Battiste & J. Barman (Eds.), *First Nations education in Canada: The circle unfolds* (pp. 101–12). University of British Columbia Press.

Ferris, P., Simard, E., Simard, G., & Ramdatt, J. (2005). *Weechi-it-te-win Family Services: Utilizing a decentralized model in the provision of bi-cultural services.* https://fncaringsociety.com/sites/default/files/2.WFSPromisingPractices.pdf

Fleming, J., & Ledogar, R.J. (2008). Resilience and Indigenous spirituality: A literature review. *Pimatisiwin, 6*(2), 47–64. http://www.pimatisiwin.com/uploads/404389036.pdf

Graveline, F.J. (1998). *Circle works: Transforming Eurocentric consciousness.* Fernwood.

Green, B.L. (2010). Culture is treatment: Considering pedagogy in the care of Aboriginal people. *Journal of Psychosocial Nursing & Mental Health Services, 48*(7), 27–34. https://doi.org/10.3928/02793695-20100504-04. Medline: 20506971

Green, J., & Thomas, R. (2009). Children in the centre: Indigenous perspectives on anti-oppressive child welfare practice. In S. Strega & J. Carriere (Eds.), *Walking this path together: Anti-racist and anti-oppressive child welfare practice* (pp. 29–44). Fernwood.

Greenwood, M., & de Leeuw, S. (2006). Fostering indigeneity: The role of Aboriginal mothers and Aboriginal early child care in responses to colonial foster-care interventions. In D.M. Lavell-Harvard & J.C. Lavell (Eds.), *Until our hearts are on the ground: Aboriginal mothering, oppression, resistance and rebirth* (pp. 173–83). Demeter Press.

– (2007). Teachings from the land: Indigenous people, our health, our land, and our children. *The Canadian Journal of Native Education, 30*(1), 48–53.

48   Joey Wark, Heather Boynton, and Jo-Ann Vis

Haig-Brown, C. (1988). *Resistance and renewal: Surviving the Indian residential school*. Arsenal Pulp Press.

Harris, B., Russell, M., & Gockel, A. (2007). The impact of poverty on First Nations mothers attending a parenting program. *First Peoples Child & Family Review, 3*(3), 21–30. https://doi.org/10.7202/1069394ar

Hart, M.A. (2002). *Seeking Mino-Pimatisiwin: An Aboriginal approach to helping*. Fernwood.

– (2009). Anti-colonial Indigenous social work: Reflections on an Aboriginal approach. In R. Sinclair, M.A. Hart, & G. Bruyere (Eds.), *Wicihitowin: Aboriginal social work in Canada* (pp. 25–41). Fernwood Publishing.

Hodge, D.R., Limb, G.E., & Cross, T.L. (2009). Moving from colonization toward balance and harmony: A Native American perspective on wellness. *Social Work, 54*(3), 211–19. https://doi.org/10.1093/sw/54.3.211. Medline: 19530568

Isaak, C.A., & Marchessault, G. (2008). Meaning of health: The perspectives of Aboriginal adults and youth in a northern Manitoba First Nations community. *Canadian Journal of Diabetes, 32*(2), 114–22. https://doi.org/10.1016/s1499-2671(08)22008-3

Jackson, L.J., White, C.R., O'Brien, K., DiLorenzo, P., Cathcart, E., Wolf, M., Bruskas, D., Pecora, P.J., Nix-Early, V., & Cabrera, J. (2010). Exploring spirituality among youth in foster care: Findings from the Casey Field Office Mental Health Study. *Child & Family Social Work, 15*(1), 107–17. https://doi.org/10.1111/j.1365-2206.2009.00649.x. Medline: 25057258

Kiliç, C. (2010). Posttraumatic growth in Turkish populations. In T. Weiss & R. Berger (Eds.), *Posttraumatic growth and culturally competent practice: Lessons learned from around the globe* (pp. 49–64). John Wiley & Sons.

LaFrance, J., & Bastien, B. (2007). Here be dragons! Reconciling Indigenous and Western knowledge to improve Aboriginal child welfare. *First Peoples Child & Family Review, 3*(1), 105–26. https://doi.org/10.7202/1069530ar

Lavallée, L.F. (2010). Blurring the boundaries: Social work's role in Indigenous spirituality. *Canadian Social Work Review, 27*(1), 143–6.

Lietz, C.A., & Hodge, D.R. (2011). Spirituality and child welfare reunification: A narrative analysis of successful outcomes. *Child & Family Social Work, 16*(4), 380–90. https://doi.org/10.1111/j.1365-2206.2010.00752.x

Lietz, C.A., & Strength, M. (2011). Stories of successful reunification: A narrative study of family resilience in child welfare. *Families in Society, 92*(2), 203–10. https://doi.org/10.1606/1044-3894.4102

Limb, G.E., & Hodge, D.R. (2010). Helping child welfare workers improve cultural competence by utilizing spiritual genograms with Native American families and children. *Children and Youth Service Review, 32*(2), 239–45. https://doi.org/10.1016/j.childyouth.2009.08.021

Longboat, D. (1987). First Nations control over education: The path to our survival as nations. In J. Barman, Y. Hébert, & D. McCaskill (Eds.), *Indian education in Canada Volume 2: The challenge* (pp. 22–42). University of British Columbia Press.

Manahan, C., & Ball, J. (2007). Aboriginal fathers support groups: Bridging the gap between displacement and family balance. *First Peoples Child & Family Review*, 3(4), 42–49. https://doi.org/10.7202/1069373ar

Maratita, J. (2017). *Intergenerational Historical Trauma and Posttraumatic Growth in an Indigenous Pacific Island Community* (Publication No. 10638236) [Doctoral dissertation, Walden University]. ProQuest Dissertations and Theses Database.

McCormick, R.M. (1994). *The facilitation of healing for the First Nations people of British Columbia* [Doctoral dissertation, The University of British Columbia]. UBC Theses and Dissertations. https://doi.org/10.14288/1.0053949

– (2009). Aboriginal approaches to counselling. In L.J. Kirmayer & G.G. Valaskakis (Eds.), *Healing traditions: The mental health of Aboriginal peoples in Canada* (pp. 337–54). University of British Columbia Press.

Meyerson, D.A., Grant, K.E., Carter, J.S., & Kilmer, R.P. (2011). Posttraumatic growth among children and adolescents: A systematic review. *Clinical Psychology Review*, 31(6), 949–64. https://doi.org/10.1016/j.cpr.2011.06.003. Medline: 21718663

Miller, J.R. (1996). *Shingwauk's vision: A history of Native residential schools.* University of Toronto Press.

Milloy, J.S. (1999). *A national crime: The Canadian government and the residential school system, 1879–1986.* University of Manitoba Press.

Muir, N., & Bohr, Y. (2014). Contemporary practice of traditional Aboriginal child rearing: A review. *First Peoples Child & Family Review*, 9(1), 66–79. http://journals.sfu.ca/fpcfr/index.php/FPCFR/article/view/231/218

Peacock, C., & Morin, D. (2010). Yellowhead Tribal Services Agency Open Custom Adoption Program. In J. Carrière (Ed.), *Aski awasis/Children of the earth: First Peoples speaking on adoption* (pp. 57–82). Fernwood.

Pintarics, J., & Sveinunggaard, K. (2005). Meenoostahtan minisiwin: First Nations family justice "pathways to peace." *First Peoples Child & Family Review*, 2(1), 67–88. https://doi.org/10.7202/1069539ar

Rawana, E., & Brownlee, K. (2009). Making the possible probable: A strength-based assessment and intervention framework for clinical work with parents, children, and adolescents. *Families in Society: The Journal of Contemporary Social Services*, 90(3), 255–60. https://doi.org/10.1606/1044-3894.3900

Richardson, C., & Nelson, B. (2007). A change of residence: Government schools and foster homes as sites of forced Aboriginal assimilation–A paper designed to provoke thought and systemic change. *First Peoples Child & Family Review*, 3(2), 75–83. http://journals.sfu.ca/fpcfr/index.php/FPCFR/article/view/44/80 https://doi.org/10.7202/1069466ar

Robbins, J.A., & Dewar, J. (2011). Traditional Indigenous approaches to healing and the modern welfare of traditional knowledge, spirituality and lands: A critical reflection on practices and policies taken from the Canadian Indigenous example. *International Indigenous Policy Journal*, 2(4). https://doi.org/10.18584/iipj.2011.2.4.2

The Royal Commission on Aboriginal Peoples. (2010). *Highlights from the report of the royal commission on Aboriginal peoples.* Government of Canada: Crown-Indigenous Relations and Northern Affairs Canada. https://www.rcaanc-cirnac.gc.ca/eng/1100100014597/1572547985018

Ryan, J. (1996). Restructuring First Nations' education: Trust, respect, and governance. *Journal of Canadian Studies*, 31(2), 115–32. https://doi.org/10.3138/jcs.31.2.115

Saleebey, D. (2006). *The strengths perspective in social work practice.* Pearson.

Seita, J.R. (2000). In our best interest: Three necessary shifts for child welfare workers and children. *Child Welfare*, 79(1), 77–92.

Shaw, A., Joseph, S., & Linley, P.A. (2005). Religion, spirituality, and posttraumatic growth: A systematic review. *Mental Health, Religion and Culture*, 8(1), 1–11. https://doi.org/10.1080/1367467032000157981

Simard, E. (2009). Culturally restorative child welfare practice: A special emphasis on cultural attachment theory. *First Peoples Child & Family Review*, 4(2), 44–61. https://doi.org/10.7202/1069329ar

Simpson, L. (2006). Birthing and Indigenous resurgence: Decolonizing our pregnancy and birthing ceremonies. In D.M. Lavell-Harvard & J.C. Lavell (Eds.), *Until our hearts are on the ground: Aboriginal mothering, oppression, resistance and rebirth* (pp. 25–33). Demeter Press.

Sterling-Collins, R. (2009). A holistic approach to supporting children with special needs. In R. Sinclair, M.A. Hart, & G. Bruyere (Eds.), *Wicihitowin: Aboriginal social work in Canada* (pp. 65–88). Fernwood Publishing.

Strega, S. (2009). Anti-oppressive approaches to assessment, risk management and file recording. In S. Strega & J. Carriere (Eds.), *Walking this path together: Anti-racist and anti-oppressive child welfare practice* (pp. 142–57). Fernwood.

Strega, S., Fleet, C., Brown, L., Dominelli, L., Callahan, M., & Walmsley, C. (2008). Connecting father absence and mother blame in child welfare policies and practices. *Children and Youth Services Review*, 30(7), 705–16. https://doi.org/10.1016/j.childyouth.2007.11.012

Tedeschi, R.G., & Calhoun, L.G. (1995). *Trauma and transformation: Growing in the aftermath of suffering.* Sage Publications.

– (2004). Posttraumatic growth: Conceptual foundations and empirical evidence. *Psychological Inquiry*, 15(1), 1–18. https://doi.org/10.1207/s15327965pli1501_01

Thompson, G.E., Cameron, R.E., & Fuller-Thomson, E. (2013). Walking the red road: The role of First Nations grandparents in promoting cultural well-being. *The International Journal of Aging and Human Development*, 76(1), 55–78. https://doi.org/10.2190/ag.76.1.c. Medline: 23540159

Timpson, J. (1995). Four decades of literature on Native Canadian child welfare: Changing themes. *Child Welfare: Journal of Policy, Practice, and Program*, 74(3), 525–46.

Trocmé, N., Knoke, D., & Blackstock, C. (2004). Pathways to the overrepresentation of Aboriginal children in Canada's child welfare system. *Social Service Review*, 78(4), 577–600. https://doi.org/10.1086/424545

Van Hook, M. (2008). *Social work practice with families: A resiliency-based approach*. Lyceum.

van Wormer, K. (2003). Restorative justice: A model for social work practice with families. *Families in Society: The Journal of Contemporary Social Services*, 84(3), 441–8. https://doi.org/10.1606/1044-3894.127

Vis, J., & Boynton, H.M. (2008). Spirituality and transcendent meaning making: Possibilities for enhancing posttraumatic growth. *Journal of Religion and Spirituality in Social Work: Social Thought*, 27(1–2), 69–86. https://doi.org/10.1080/15426430802113814

Wade, A. (1995). Resistance knowledges: Therapy with Aboriginal persons who have been subjected to violence. In P.H. Stephenson, S.J. Elliott, L.T. Foster, & J. Harris (Eds.), *A persistent spirit: Towards understanding Aboriginal health in British Columbia* (pp. 167–206). University of Victoria.

Waldram, J.B. (2004). *Revenge of the Windigo: The construction of the mind and mental health of North American Aboriginal peoples*. University of Toronto Press.

Weiss, T., & Berger, R. (Eds.) (2010). *Posttraumatic growth and culturally competent practice: Lessons learned from around the globe*. John Wiley & Sons.

Wilson, K. (2003). Therapeutic landscapes and First Nations peoples: An exploration of culture, health and place. *Health and Place*, 9(2), 83–93. https://doi.org/10.1016/s1353-8292(02)00016-3

3 Spiritual-Trauma-Informed Schools: Supporting Children Exposed to Interpersonal Trauma

HEATHER BOYNTON, JO-ANN VIS,
AND TAYLOR SMITH

Childhood is a time for developmental milestones and new experiences; however, exposure to traumatic events can lead to obstacles and complications in psychological, relational, and academic growth. The spiritual dimension of life can offer children support and strength and can be a pathway to promoting posttraumatic growth through the trauma journey. Social workers, informed with a spiritual lens, can provide support to educators and students in the integration of spirituality within trauma-informed approaches as a means for facilitating posttraumatic growth. Depending on the type of adverse childhood event, the prevalence rates of childhood adversity for school-aged children range from 25–85 per cent (American Psychological Association, 2020; Felitti et al., 1998; Finkelhor et al., 2015). It can be challenging to assess when a child is exposed to a traumatic event due to the complexities of one's development and limited information about the child's psychosocial circumstances. Many schools are adopting trauma-informed approaches. However, the appreciation concerning how spiritual interventions can help build resilience to critical events is lacking (Jerome, 2011; Mata-McMahon et al., 2019). School personnel often support children who have experienced trauma and have an opportunity to intervene to mitigate long-term effects on development and support growth. Spiritual activities include spiritual-mindedness (Jerome, 2011), spiritual strengths-based approaches (Kielty et al., 2017), as well as connections to others, self, environment, or things beyond oneself (Mata-McMahon et al., 2019).

This chapter overviews the types of trauma, the effects that exposure to trauma has on children and their spiritual development, and how spiritual-trauma-informed schools can be implemented as a response. Also, research concerning posttraumatic growth (PTG) and children will be presented as a lens through which spiritual-trauma-informed

(STI) interventions in a school setting can be realized. The aspects of STI approaches that are deemed supportive and helpful for children experiencing adversity are highlighted. In conclusion, suggestions about how social workers can advocate and support the development of STI schools are offered.

Types of Trauma and Its Effects

Within the literature, trauma and traumatic symptoms are often defined within the context of the versions of the *Diagnostic and Statistical Manual* (DSM) regarding criteria for posttraumatic stress disorder (PTSD). The debate over the progression of the DSM classification of PTSD includes how narrowly or broadly to define trauma, symptomatology, and its understanding of prevalence (Brewin et al., 2009; Weathers & Keane, 2007). These areas of tension are amplified when considering the complexity of childhood trauma, duration, and relationships. Children's exposure to trauma has been found to lead to cognitive and emotional disruptions, including dysregulated affect, difficulty concentrating, irritability and hyperarousal (Lubit et al., 2003). Furthermore, "these symptoms might manifest themselves as distractibility, disorganized effect, and disruptive behaviours, all of which occur in ADHD" (Szymanski et al., 2011, p. 54) and can also be symptoms of anxiety.

When looking at the definition of childhood traumatic stress within a school context, where clinical diagnosis is not emphasized, trauma needs to be defined in a general manner so that schools can support a wide range of children experiencing traumatic symptoms (Wolpow et al., 2016). The National Child Traumatic Stress Network (2008) uses a broad definition of traumatic stress applicable to a school setting. It imparts that child traumatic stress occurs when children and adolescents are exposed to traumatic events or traumatic situations, which overwhelms their ability to cope with what they have experienced. This definition allows for educators to be sensitive to the fact that there will be children in their classrooms who have experienced symptoms from a traumatic incident.

Chronic Trauma

While definitions of chronic traumatization are mostly inconsistent in the literature, it can be generally characterized as "repeated exposures to traumatic stressors within the same overall context over time" (Kaysen et al., 2003, p. 248). What separates chronic trauma exposure from an acute traumatic event is the time limitations. While critical trauma occurrences are classified as single-incident events, defining the duration of chronic traumatization is more complicated. This complexity is due to the many variables included in chronic trauma exposure, including the number of recurrences of traumatic stressors and the length of time spent in danger (Kaysen et al., 2003). Regardless, it is noteworthy that chronic traumatization may have significant short and long-term effects.

Interpersonal Trauma

In general, interpersonal trauma involves any of the following traumatic experiences: emotional abuse, emotional neglect, physical abuse, physical neglect, or sexual abuse (Dugal et al., 2016; Mauritz et al., 2013). When individuals experience multiple or prolonged trauma, they can exhibit complex trauma, which has been shown to impact regulatory function and brain development negatively. It is essential to understand the potential effects of trauma across multiple dimensions. As Weathers and Keane (2007) argue, traumatic stress operates on a continuum of severity and that there are numerous dimensions of "complexity, frequency, duration, predictability, and controllability" (p. 108).

In recent years, several authors have identified symptoms exhibited by child and adult survivors of chronic, interpersonal trauma, developed a framework, and argued for a new category of developmental trauma in the DSM (Schmid et al., 2013). It is argued that developmental trauma manifests as difficulties in affect regulation, memory and attention, self-perception, attachment, interpersonal relationships, somatization, and systems of meaning (van der Kolk et al., 2005). Developmental trauma may be a result of various traumatic situations such as child maltreatment, including parental inflicted abuse, neglect, domestic violence, parental substance abuse and mental health struggles.

Ongoing developmental trauma can lead to toxic stress where activation of the stress response is prolonged, and the body is not able to fully recover, which may result in acute effects on healthy brain development. The architecture of the brain is impeded (Franke, 2014). Adverse childhood events and developmental trauma can lead to more significant struggles in the classroom and broader school environment, including cognitive and attentional difficulties, struggles with peers, delinquency, suicidal ideation and self-harm, and can have other long-term health and well-being effects across the lifespan, including early death (Felitti et al., 1998).

Cognitive Impairments

While it is evident that chronic trauma exposure has various adverse effects on children's overall development, cognitive impairments are perhaps the most concrete evidence of suffering. Research has found that "early exposure to stress and trauma [causes] physical effects on neurodevelopment which may lead to changes in the individual's long-term response to stress" (Lubit et al., 2003, p. 128). Considerable brain development occurs in the earliest stages of life. Any interruptions of its construction can cause severe damage to one's functioning, both in the present moment and long term (Bremner, 2006). The establishment and interruption of neural connections depend directly on the child's experiences, and "only those connections and pathways frequently activated are retained" (Hawley, 2000, p. 1). This suggests that a child who is frequently exposed to any sort of abuse would be in a near-constant state of responding to a stressful trigger.

Additionally, these complications grow to be even more involved with the occurrence of multiple trauma, or chronic trauma exposure (Forkey, 2018), significantly influencing cognitive ability. Cognitive factors that support school performance are also impacted by early trauma. Abused and neglected pre-schoolers were found to show lower flexibility and creativity in problem-solving (Egeland et al., 1983). Similarly, older children with a history of abuse and violence exposure were negatively impacted in regards to attention, abstract reasoning, and executive functioning skills (Beers & De Bellis, 2002).

Such challenges with school performance have led many children with a history of trauma to experience impaired school functioning. Children with a history of abuse frequently score lower on academic testing and have a higher academic failure (Eckenrode et al., 1993). Children with histories of trauma have a higher incidence of disciplinary referrals and suspensions (Shonk & Cicchetti, 2001). Across studies, children who have experienced trauma have higher dropout rates and failures than the general population (Boden et al., 2007). These research findings are highly concerning and demonstrate a need to provide trauma supports within the school system.

Academic Functioning

As noted, chronic trauma exposure leads to significant negative impacts on a child's brain development. This has direct implications for students as "studies have consistently found that trauma exposure puts children and adolescents at risk for decreased academic achievement"

(Overstreet & Mathews, 2011, p. 740). Academic success can be hampered by learning difficulties, emotional regulation, and attention deficiencies as they ultimately disrupt a child's educational performance. A child who has been exposed to chronic trauma will often experience a near constant fight-or-flight state resulting in disrupted learning and memory brain functions (Morton & Berardi, 2018). Therefore, a child becomes "unable to engage in academic tasks [as] the central nervous system is in a constant state of high [stress hormone] production" (Morton & Berardi, 2018, p. 488). While the brain's response to stress is constantly overactive, "survival becomes the dominant priority for students [instead of] academic and social learning" (Morton & Berardi, 2018, p. 489). Consequently, when children are continuously in a defensive mode and primarily concerned with protecting themselves at all times, their time spent learning and engaging in the classroom declines, putting not only their academic achievement at risk but their overall well-being.

Mental Health

Children's responses to trauma exposure can take many forms, including various mental health concerns (Lubit et al., 2003; Overstreet & Mathews, 2011; Record-Lemon & Buchanan, 2017). Typically, children will receive a diagnosis such as anxiety, depression, attention deficit hyperactivity disorder (ADHD), oppositional defiant disorder, conduct disorder, or PTSD due to exposure to one or more critical incidents (D'Andrea et al., 2012). There is an abundance of symptoms that can manifest in children after chronic trauma exposure, even without a formal diagnosis. These include fear, anger, digestive problems, nightmares, emotional regulation, social isolation, helplessness, and so on (Walkley & Cox, 2013). When it comes to exposure to violence, the impact on children is profound and long-standing; however, the process of assessing and diagnosing the effect of chronic trauma exposure in children is too complicated (Lubit et al., 2003). Research states that "the crucial issue in assessing the effects of trauma and deciding if a child needs treatment is not whether a child fulfills the criteria for ... a diagnosis, [but rather on] the degree of compromise in social and academic functioning" (Lubit et al., 2003, p. 129–30). While a child may exhibit symptoms of mental illness after chronic trauma exposure, it is not enough to provide a diagnosis. Additionally, young children cannot articulate the complex emotions and responses they experience after chronic trauma exposure (Lubit et al., 2003), especially if the trauma occurred prior to language acquisition and development during the preverbal stage, making it even more challenging to determine when they are struggling.

Inadequate Care

While the variety of professionals involved in ensuring a child's over-arching well-being is always appreciated and significant, it is perhaps not enough to meet the needs of those children who have been exposed to chronic and developmental trauma. Children struggle at times to articulate the complexities associated with a traumatic event, as well as the ability to identify an event as traumatic. As such, it is often left to parents, caregivers, and professionals to pinpoint the need for support; however, important information may be missed (Hawkins & Radcliffe, 2006). For example, parents may not report accurate levels of stress in their child simply because of a lack of knowledge regarding their child's symptoms, effects, and processes. Lubit et al. (2003) stated that the

> ability of children to shift from painful affective states to be able to play leads parents to assume incorrectly that the child has recovered. Studies indicate that counselors and teachers identify fewer than 50% of adolescents with significant, treatable emotional problems. Pediatricians do even more poorly, probably due to their more limited time for interaction, and identify only 25% of those with diagnosable mental disorders. (p. 130)

This lack of awareness points to the absence of knowledge that most parents and caregivers have surrounding children's responses to traumatic events. Additionally, because parents may have contributed to the interpersonal trauma experienced by the child, they are unlikely to report such an event or even be able to define an event as traumatic. Finally, an overall lack of awareness of trauma-informed practice may cause children to fall between the cracks when they are not asked the appropriate questions (Hawkins & Radcliffe, 2006).

These issues suggest a need for a more holistic approach to care, and the collaboration of stakeholders, pointing to trauma-informed schools as a solution and supporting traumatized youth. While most trauma literature focuses on risk factors, there needs to be a richer understanding of how strengths and resiliency factors buffer the risk factors in trauma (Faust & Katchen, 2004). A focus on resilience and strengths-based approaches is especially important in a school setting where educators can help children foster resiliency, mastery and competency skills and potentially facilitate PTG.

Potential for Using a PTG Lens in Establishing Spiritual-Trauma-Informed Schools

Schools aim to provide an education that nurtures the whole child; however, in secular schools in particular, the spiritual aspect seems to be missing. Spirituality is an important dimension for individuals who experience trauma, and needs to be part of trauma informed approaches. Research has found that children can and do experience PTG, particularly when spiritual support is offered (Jerome, 2011; Kilmer et al., 2014; Laceulle et al., 2015; Mata-McMahon, 2019; Yaskowich, 2002). Therefore, it is argued that an STI approach in school settings may foster resilience and support PTG. The domains of PTG outlined by Calhoun and Tedeschi (2006) include having a greater sense of one's strengths and renewed self-perception. Equally important are positive changes in relationships and greater connectedness, changes to one's life philosophy and outlook, having a greater appreciation of and recognition of new possibilities or new interests in life, as well as compassion and spiritual growth. These domains can be fostered through trauma-sensitive school-based initiatives. However, it is vital to understand how PTG may occur in children to consider approaches.

Laceulle et al. (2015) conveyed that rumination and attempts to find meaning in trauma may trigger posttraumatic stress reactions as well as posttraumatic growth. They also identified that children with more peer connectedness and more robust religious engagement demonstrate greater PTG, particularly in spiritual change, appreciation of life, and relating to others. Spiritual themes also promote connectedness within relationships among self, others, and one's environment, creating an opportunity for healthy child development. Effectively building resilience that can be accessed during times of psychological difficulty (Mata-McMahon et al., 2019). Kilmer et al. (2014) imparted that PTG may evolve through the struggle after trauma and the resultant meaning-making and rumination processes, along with coping and adaptation processes. They also highlight the importance and role of caring adults in supporting these processes in children. Yaskowich (2002) found that PTG in youth with cancer was positively correlated with social support especially from teachers and, consequently, surmised that teacher support and social skills training might play a significant role for these children in terms of adjustment and growth. Kielty et al. (2017) suggest that assisting students to develop internal and external strengths to motivate and engage are spiritual contemplative practices that promote reflection of meaning and purpose.

While the school setting is often a place where the adverse effects of trauma are revealed, there is also the potential for the school to contribute to a child's healing and coping. Maynard et al. (2019) argue that there is not enough research on outcomes of trauma-informed approaches in schools. Yet we contend that many aspects of this approach can be helpful such as creating safety and trustworthiness, using strengths-based approaches, providing connections and engaging in collaboration as well as assisting kids in making choices and having control over their decisions (Kielty et al., 2017). Psychological literature has established the developmental importance of the environment to a child's well-being and the mutual interaction between a child and their ecology (Zielinski & Bradshaw, 2006). As Tishelman and colleagues (2010) suggest, "ecological factors can either buffer a child from the full effects of adversity or conversely exacerbate a child's difficulties" (p. 280). Equally, both Benson et al. (2008) and Mata-McMahon et al. (2019) convey that spiritual development is interlinked with developmental growth regardless of one's religious exposure. Therefore, while traditional psychological strategies can assist with behaviour change, encouraging spiritual-mindedness provides hope, encourages relationship connection and seeks to find meaning in traumatic situations (Jerome, 2011).

Educators need to understand that a child's social context can have an impact on the severity and resolution of symptoms. Schools have the potential to be a natural protective fit for children who have experienced trauma as they can be places which are validating and restorative as well as places of refuge which foster connectedness and meaning making. In addition, schools can include a welcoming environment where educators are familiar with trauma's impact on relationships, learning, and behaviour (Cole et al., 2005). In this way, the school community becomes an invaluable connection and relationship resource to help support a child who has experienced trauma.

As noted, a child's experience and response to trauma will vary depending on their age, gender, social health and relationships (Crosby, 2015). Additionally, children's limited vocabulary, articulation and social status influence how they might define and verbalize their experiences to a trusted adult (Lubit et al., 2003). Overstreet and Mathews (2011) support this perspective noting that "national prevalence rates do not generalize equally to all youth; ethnic minority youth living in impoverished urban environments are particularly at risk for exposure to violent trauma" (p. 739). Also important to note is that access to spiritual and religious resources vary depending on a child's developmental level (Benson et al., 2008). Thus, by implementing STI schools, resources can be accessed at the micro, mezzo, and macro level to cater to the needs of the diversity of spirituality for individuals and communities. Advocating for STI schools has the potential to include a wide range of religious and spiritual supports that students and families can seek out following times of adversity (Jerome, 2011). Schools have been presented as valuable environments to provide support to children who have been exposed to chronic traumatic events (Kataoka et al., 2018). Creating an STI school environment offers expanded solutions for the child, family, and community.

Characteristics of Spiritual-Trauma-Informed Schools

Research surrounding the impetus for trauma-informed schools empha-sizes the "importance of participation and collaboration among clinical, teaching, administrative staff, parents, and students" (Record-Lemon & Buchanan, 2017, p. 300). Collaboration is a crucial characteristic and a defining quality of trauma-informed schools. Other experts suggest that when prominence is placed on the collective responsibilities between educators and mental health professionals, support and care can be realized among all stakeholders (Morton & Berardi, 2018). This partner-ship points to the necessity of collaboration and cooperation between a variety of participants. It involves the presence of streamlined educa-tion, communication and alliance involving students, caregivers, edu-cators and administration, leading to a more "holistic understanding of a [child's] functioning" (Yohannan & Carlson, 2018, p. 448). According to Menschner & Maul (2016), a trauma-informed approach assesses a child's overall progress in various domains with support to ensure suc-cessful assessment, intervention and evaluation. In holistic education, however, the spiritual component is typically missing; yet, it is a critical aspect of life for children and, from a social justice lens, a human right.

The creation of STI schools implies a paradigm shift. Ultimately, schools become "models of care and support provision that consider the prevalence of childhood trauma and its subsequent impacts on devel-opment, learning, and well-being" (Record-Lemon & Buchanan, 2017, p. 288). This approach becomes a standard lens through which behaviour and academic evaluation are viewed (Morton & Berardi, 2018). How-ever, an STI model guides how to respond to the spiritual developmen-tal needs of children integrated within psychological, behavioural, or academic aspects. As such, schools that promote spiritual-mindedness challenge students to feel hopeful, optimistic and rely on support from others to find meaning following a tragic event (Jerome, 2011). This phi-losophy reinforces the notion that the building blocks of STI schools include an overall shift in the way curriculum is implemented, while also modifying the school community's culture (Kielty et al., 2017).

Suggested STI Practices to Foster PTG

The Significance of the Relationship

An STI school is one that emphasizes the importance of relationship connection for and among children. Educators, counsellors and admin-istrators in school settings have opportunities throughout the day to engage in positive connections and interactions with children that nurture their soul (Mata-McMahon et al., 2019). Along with safety, they can offer consistency and transparency in their relationships with children. Caring adults can model effective emotion regulation, interpersonal skills, promote relationship repairs, and demonstrate kindness, empathy, compassion, and love. They can acknowledge children and validate them as valuable and significant individuals and foster new interests. It is often through a relationship connection where one begins to value diversity, develop a sense of self and begin to understand what one values (Mata-McMahon et al., 2019). These relationship factors can lead to positive changes and increased connectedness which promote PTG, resilience, and help children move forward.

The Significance of the Environment

School-based environments offer children structure, routine, rules, and boundaries which promote safety so that children know what to expect. They can foster a sense of connection and community for children and establish inclusiveness and respect for diversity. School environments can also provide children with a range of positive experiences that contribute to their growth, development, self-esteem, and sense of mastery. A safe environment that respects the child and provides a refuge from toxic stress, harm and abuse may help to alleviate long-term detrimental effects. Schools often instil positive values, morals, and beliefs that can contribute to a child's developing spiritual foundation (Boynton, 2016). Attention to the environment with a spiritual lens also includes having spaces that are calm, pleasing and stimulating enough to promote inspiration (Mata-McMahon et al., 2019). These types of environments can offer a spiritual oasis for children where they can engage in meaningful reflection without threat or interruption. The STI school environment can be inclusive and restorative depending on its relationships, how its problems are solved, and how disruptive or challenging behaviours are dealt with. If problems are solved through collaborative and restorative justice approaches children can learn the skills for deeper empathy, compassion, meaning making, and connectedness. An STI school could also provide and ensure safe spiritual spaces for engaging in spiritual practices and activities throughout the day.

The Significance of Spiritual Education

Adults and social workers in schools have an excellent opportunity to not only educate children on various mental health topics but also to promote opportunities for spiritual reflection and growth. Psycho-spiritual educational topics, for instance, can open the door for children to reflect on their experiences, strengths, and supports available, as well as how to experience spirituality in broad terms. Art, music, yoga, mindfulness exercises, discussion of religion and connecting to something beyond oneself can be influential in youth development and drawn upon during crises (Benson et al., 2008). Activities that bring joy, passion, and creativity, which are also aspects of spirituality, can assist children in spiritual exploration and develop a sense of mastery within their own spiritual practices, and strengths. Through education and discussion, children's feelings and experiences concerning spirituality or religion can be validated when shared with others. Children can learn not only about the effects of trauma but how spiritual practices can be used as a resource to manage and grow from that experience. A variety of behavioural and spiritual skills can be discovered, practised, and modelled. Emotion regulation, communication strategies, interpersonal skills, relaxation, prayer, self-awareness, compassion, empathy, and advocacy are just some of the myriad of options for teaching and learning. These experiences could foster a new outlook and new possibilities for children contributing to a renewed philosophy of life, facilitating PTG.

The Significance of Strengths-Based Approaches

Dennis Saleebey (2008) introduced the strengths-based concept as a challenge to social workers (and other allied professionals) to forgo assessment through a problem saturated lens. The strengths philosophy suggests that all individuals have internal and external assets, resources and capacities that can be drawn upon to motivate and create change. The importance of believing that one possesses these strengths is paramount. That is, Saleebey (2008) notes that, at times, one has to believe in the other before the individual can believe in oneself. Kielty et al. (2017) add to the strengths perspective with the petition to increase spiritual strengths in children, as this can serve as a shielding factor for critical incident recovery and high-risk behaviour.

Strengths-based approaches are easily implemented in school settings and can have powerful positive effects. Strengths-building strategies, character development, and collaborative problem solving can foster children's development and potentially support the PTG processes mentioned above. Challenging children to aspire to find meaning and purpose in one's life, based on the talents and assets, can influence positive action and goal setting. Collaborative problem solving, which includes the child's voice in the problem-solving outcome, develops competency and self-mastery in the child. This approach changes power dynamics, accesses student strengths, and resources are engaged and supported. A collaborative problem-solving approach within a trauma-informed paradigm changes the lens from "'What is wrong with you?' to considering 'What happened to you?'" (Sweeney et al., 2018, p. 323). Contemplative practices (Kielty et al., 2017) allow children to reflect on how one was able to access one's inner resources to cope through a traumatic event. Externally, strengths can be identified when children reflect on people, places and things in their environment which can be of assistance and support. These strengths-based approaches can build trust, foster hope, and facilitate meaningful connections and PTG.

Implications for School Social Workers

STI schools require significant collaborative support at the micro or classroom level, mezzo or school and community level, and macro or policy and ministry levels. Social workers are well equipped to take a leadership role in partnership with educational institutions seeking to engage students from a trauma-informed perspective. A social worker's understanding of child spiritual development, traumatic effects, person-in-environment and systems models, existential and humanistic theory, and strengths-based treatments offer the holistic perspective required for practical trauma assessment, intervention, and evaluation. Additionally, a social worker can play a large role in helping the school administration develop STI policies. Social workers can collaborate with educators to develop curriculum and lesson plans that incorporate self-regulation and coping skills. Social workers can also advocate for public policy or ministry directives that support mental health funding and the availability of spiritually informed services in schools.

Supporting school communities with trauma-informed practices must include education, support and policy development for educators and school personnel. Equally, providing education, advocacy, support, and coping strategies for students and their caregivers creates a coordinated approach that generates positive outcomes for children (Walkley & Cox, 2013). Educators can utilize the resources of social workers for situations which require assessment or more specific therapy for a child. In these instances, social workers can assist by suggesting evidence-based research approaches that are effective and supportive of PTG. Also, "school social workers can engage in mezzo level interventions by collaborating with professionals within and across systems; ... a key feature of best practice" (Crosby, 2015, p. 228). Strategically situated, social workers can act to bridge the gaps within the school system while promoting and modelling trauma-informed practices. Skills can be used to streamline the process of sharing information with stakeholders and advocating to ensure that youth "receive unified coordination of educational and other services" (Crosby, 2015, p. 228). By applying a PTG lens to trauma-informed school interventions, social workers can model the importance of assessing for strength and resilience in children in order to help them grow from their trauma experiences.

Conclusion

It is evident throughout the literature that children exposed to chronic interpersonal and developmental trauma experience a wide range of effects. Yet, they are not always so easily defined and identified. Still, the results of the trauma will manifest in a multitude of forms, making it even more difficult for parents, caregivers, and professionals to pinpoint the issue, as well as how to resolve it best. Therefore, a broad approach is required to address trauma in school settings.

Implementing STI schools is not only a holistic response to trauma exposure but it offers children opportunities for support and care within a system where they spend a vast amount of their time. Assessment, support, and growth can be provided within a safe space, creating healthy systemic connections among all stakeholders. The domains of PTG can be fostered through the power of secure relationships, a safe environment, psychoeducation, and the inclusion of spiritual strengths-based strategies. Through the involvement of the school community, individual, emotional, and spiritual needs can be met while also promoting the importance of relationships, connectedness, collaboration, exploration, and growth.

REFERENCES

American Psychological Association. (2020). *Children and Trauma*. https://www.apa.org/pi/families/resources/children-trauma-update
Beers, S.R., & De Bellis, M.D. (2002). Neuropsychological function in children with maltreatment-related posttraumatic stress disorder. *American Journal of Psychiatry, 159*(3), 483–6. https://doi.org/10.1176/appi.ajp.159.3.483. Medline: 11870018
Benson, P.L., & Roehlkepartain, E.C. (2008). Spiritual development: A missing priority in youth development. *New Directions for Youth Development, 2008*(118), 13–28. https://doi.org/10.1002/yd.253. Medline: 18642315
Boden, J.M., Horwood, L.J., & Fergusson, D.M. (2007). Exposure to childhood sexual and physical abuse and subsequent educational achievement

outcomes. *Child Abuse & Neglect*, *31*(10), 1101–14. https://doi.org/10.1016
/j.chiabu.2007.03.022. Medline: 17996302

Boynton, H.M. (2016). *Navigating in seclusion: The complicated terrain of
children's spirituality in trauma, grief, and loss* [Unpublished doctoral
dissertation]. Department of Social Work, University of Calgary. https://
doi.org/10.11575/PRISM/27063

Bremner, J.D. (2006). Traumatic stress: Effects on the brain. *Dialogues in Clinical
Neuroscience*, *8*(4), 445–61. https://doi.org/10.31887/dcns.2006.8.4/jbremner

Brewin, C.R., Lanius, R.A., Novac, A., Schnyder, U., & Galea, S. (2009).
Reformulating PTSD for DSM-V: Life after criterion a. *Journal of Traumatic
Stress*, *22*(5), 366–73. https://doi.org/10.1002/jts.20443. Medline: 19743480

Calhoun, L.G., & Tedeschi, R.G. (2006). The foundations of posttraumatic
growth: An expanded framework. In L.G. Calhoun & R.G. Tedeschi (Eds.),
Handbook of posttraumatic growth: Research and practice (pp. 3–23). Lawrence
Erlbaum Associates.

Cole, S.F., O'Brien, J.G., Gadd, G.M., Ristuccia, J., Wallace, D.L., & Gregory, M.
(2005). *Helping traumatized children learn: Supportive school environments for
children traumatized by family violence*. Massachusetts Advocates for Children
Trauma and Learning Policy Initiative. http://traumasensitiveschools.org
/tlpipublications/download-a-free-copy-of-helping-traumatized-children
-learn/

Crosby, S.D. (2015). An ecological perspective on emerging trauma-informed
teaching practices. *Children & Schools*, *37*(4), 223–30. https://doi.org
/10.1093/cs/cdv027

D'Andrea, W., Ford, J., Stolbach, B., Spinazzola, J., & van der Kolk, B.A.
(2012). Understanding interpersonal trauma in children: Why we need
a developmentally appropriate trauma diagnosis. *American Journal of
Orthopsychiatry*, *82*(2), 187–200. https://doi.org/10.1111/j.1939
-0025.2012.01154.x. Medline: 22506521

Dugal, C., Bigras, N., Godbout, N., & Bélanger, C. (2016). Childhood interpersonal
trauma and its repercussions in adulthood: An analysis of psychological and
interpersonal sequelae. *A Multidimensional Approach to Posttraumatic Stress
Disorder – From Theory to Practice*, 71–107. https://doi.org/10.5772/64476

Eckenrode, J., Laird, M., & Doris, J. (1993). School performance and
disciplinary problems among abused and neglected children. *Developmental
Psychology*, *29*(1), 53–62. https://doi.org/10.1037/0012-1649.29.1.53

Egeland, B., Sroufe, L.A., & Erickson, M. (1983). The developmental
consequence of different patterns of maltreatment. *Child Abuse & Neglect*,
7(4), 459–69. https://doi.org/10.1016/0145-2134(83)90053-4

Faust, J., & Katchen, L.B. (2004). Treatment of children with complicated
posttraumatic stress reactions. *Psychotherapy: Theory, Research, Practice and
Training*, *41*(4), 426–37. https://doi.org/10.1037/0033-3204.41.4.426

Felitti, V.J., Anda, R.F., Nordenberg, D., Williamson, D.F., Spitz, A.M., Edwards, V., Koss, M.P., & Marks, J.S. (1998). Relationship of childhood abuse and household dysfunction to many of the leading causes of death in adults: The Adverse Childhood Experiences (ACE) Study. *American Journal of Preventive Medicine, 14*(4), 245–58. https://doi.org/10.1016/s0749 -3797(98)00017-8

Finkelhor, D., Turner, H.A., Shattuck, A., & Hamby, S.L. (2015). Prevalence of childhood exposure to violence, crime, and abuse: Results from the national survey of children's exposure to violence. *JAMA Pediatrics, 169*(8), 746–54. https://doi.org/10.1001/jamapediatrics.2015.0676. Medline: 26121291

Forkey, H. (2018). Children exposed to abuse and neglect: The effects of trauma on the body and brain. *Journal of the Academy of Matrimonial Lawyers, 30*, 307–24.

Franke, H.A. (2014). Toxic stress: Effects, prevention and treatment. *Children, 1*(3), 390–402. https://doi.org/10.3390/children1030390. Medline: 27417486

Hawkins, S.S., & Radcliffe, J. (2006). Current measures of PTSD for children and adolescents. *Journal of Pediatric Psychology, 31*(4), 420–30. https://doi .org/10.1093/jpepsy/jsj039. Medline: 15947119

Hawley, T. (2000). *Starting smart: How early experiences affect brain development.* Ounce of Prevention Fund. https://www.theounce.org/wp-content /uploads/2017/03/StartingSmart.pdf

Jerome, A. (2011). Comforting children and families who grieve: Incorporating spiritual support. *School Psychology International, 32*(2), 194–209. https://doi .org/10.1177/0143034311400829

Kataoka, S.H., Vona, P., Acuna, A., Jaycox, L., Escudero, P., Rojas, C., Ramirez, E., Langley, A., & Stein, B.D. (2018). Applying a trauma informed school systems approach: Examples from school community-academic partnerships. *Ethnicity & Disease, 28*(2), 417–26. https://doi.org/10.18865 /ed.28.s2.417. Medline: 30202195

Kaysen, D., Resick, P.A., & Wise, D. (2003). Living in danger: The impact of chronic traumatization and the traumatic context on posttraumatic stress disorder. *Trauma, Violence, & Abuse, 4*(3), 247–64. https://doi.org/10.1177 /1524838003004003004. Medline: 14697125

Kielty, M.L., Staton, A.R., & Gilligan, T.D. (2017). Cultivating spiritual strength in children and adolescents through contemplative practices in K–12 school settings. *Journal of Child and Adolescent Counseling, 3*(3), 164–74. https://doi .org/10.1080/23727810.2017.1341796

Kilmer, R.P., Gil-Rivas, V., Griese, B., Hardy, S.J., Hafstad, G.S., & Alisic, E. (2014). Posttraumatic growth in children and youth: Clinical implications of an emerging research literature. *American Journal of Orthopsychiatry 84*(5), 506–18. https://doi.org/10.1037/ort0000016. Medline: 25110973

Laceulle, O.M., Kleber, R.J., & Alisic, E. (2015). Children's experience of posttraumatic growth: Distinguishing general from domain-specific correlates. *PLoS One, 10*(12), e0145736. https://doi.org/10.1371/journal.pone.0145736. Medline: 26714193

Lubit, R., Rovine, D., DeFrancisci, L., & Eth, S. (2003). Impact of trauma on children. *Journal of Psychiatric Practice, 9*(2), 128–38. https://doi.org/10.1097/00131746-200303000-00004. Medline: 15985923

Mata-McMahon, J., Haslip, M., & Schein, D. (2019). Early childhood educators' perceptions of nurturing spirituality in secular settings. *Early Child Development and Care, 189*(14), 2233–51. https://doi.org/10.1080/03004430.2018.1445734

Mauritz, M.W., Goossens, P.J., Draijer, N., & Van Achterberg, T. (2013). Prevalence of interpersonal trauma exposure and trauma-related disorders in severe mental illness. *European Journal of Psychotraumatology, 4*(1), 1–15. https://doi.org/10.3402/ejpt.v4i0.19985. Medline: 23577228

Maynard, B.R., Farina, A., Dell, N.A., & Kelly, M.S. (2019). Effects of trauma-informed approaches in schools: A systematic review. *Campbell Systematic Reviews, 15*(1–2). https://doi.org/10.1002/cl2.1018

Menschner, C., & Maul, A. (2016). *Key ingredients for successful trauma-informed care implementation.* Center for Health Care Strategies: National Center for Trauma-Informed Care. https://www.samhsa.gov/sites/default/files/programs_campaigns/childrens_mental_health/atc-whitepaper-040616.pdf

Morton, B.M., & Berardi, A.A. (2018). Trauma-informed school programming: Applications for mental health professionals and educator partnerships. *Journal of Child and Adolescent Trauma, 11*, 487–93. https://doi.org/10.1007/s40653-017-0160-1. Medline: 32318170

The National Child Traumatic Stress Network. (2008). *Child trauma toolkit for educators.* http://rems.ed.gov/docs/NCTSN_ChildTraumaToolkitForEducators.pdf

Overstreet, S., & Mathews, T. (2011). Challenges associated with exposure to chronic trauma: Using a public health framework to foster resilient outcomes among youth. *Psychology in the Schools, 48*(7), 738–54. https://doi.org/10.1002/pits.20584

Record-Lemon, R.M., & Buchanan, M.J. (2017). Trauma-informed practices in schools: A narrative literature review. *Canadian Journal of Counselling and Psychotherapy, 51*(4), 286–305.

Saleebey, D. (2008). Commentary on the strengths perspective and potential applications in school counseling. *Professional School Counseling, 12*(2). https://doi.org/10.1177/2156759x0801200216

Schmid, M., Petermann, F., & Fegert, J.M. (2013). Developmental trauma disorder: Pros and cons of including formal criteria in the psychiatric diagnostic systems. *BMC Psychiatry, 13*(3), 1–12. https://doi.org/10.1186/1471-244x-13-3. Medline: 23286319

Shonk, S.M., & Cicchetti, D. (2001). Maltreatment, competency deficits, and risk for academic and behavioral maladjustment. *Developmental Psychology*, *37*(1), 3–17. https://doi.org/10.1037/0012-1649.37.1.3

Sweeney, A., Filson, B., Kennedy, A., Collinson, L., & Gillard, S. (2018). A paradigm shift: Relationships in trauma-informed mental health services. *BJPsych Advances*, *24*(5), 319–33. https://doi.org/10.1192/bja.2018.29. Medline: 30174829

Szymanski, K., Sapanski, L., & Conway, F. (2011). Trauma and ADHD—association or diagnostic confusion? A clinical perspective. *Journal of Infant, Child and Adolescent Psychotherapy*, *10*(1), 51–9. https://doi.org/10.1080/15289168.2011.575704

Tishelman, A.C., Haney, P., O'Brien, J.G., & Blaustein, M.E. (2010). A framework for school-based psychological evaluations: Utilizing a 'trauma lens.' *Journal of Child & Adolescent Trauma*, *3*, 279–302. https://doi.org/10.1080/19361521.2010.523062

van der Kolk, B.A., Roth, S., Pelcovitz, D., Sunday, S., & Spinazzola, J. (2005). Disorders of extreme stress: The empirical foundation of a complex adaptation to trauma. *Journal of Traumatic Stress*, *18*(5), 389–99. https://doi.org/10.1002/jts.20047. Medline: 16281237

Walkley, M., & Cox, T.L. (2013). Building trauma-informed schools and communities. *Children & Schools*, *35*(2), 123–6. https://doi.org/10.1093/cs/cdt007

Weathers, F.W., & Keane, T.M. (2007). The criterion a problem revisited: Controversies and challenges in defining and measuring psychological trauma. *Journal of Traumatic Stress*, *20*(2), 107–21. https://doi.org/10.1002/jts.20210. Medline: 17427913

Wolpow, R., Johnson, M.M., Hertel, R., & Kincaid S.O. (2016). *The heart of learning and teaching: Compassion, resiliency, and academic success.* Washington State Office of Superintendent of Public Instruction (OSPI) Compassionate Schools. https://www.k12.wa.us/sites/default/files/public/compassionateschools/pubdocs/theheartoflearningandteaching.pdf

Yaskowich, K.M. (2002). *Posttraumatic growth in children and adolescents with cancer* [Unpublished doctoral thesis]. Department of Psychology, University of Calgary. https://doi.org/10.11575/PRISM/20242

Yohannan, J., & Carlson, J.S. (2018). A systematic review of school-based interventions and their outcomes for youth exposed to traumatic events. *Psychology in the Schools*, *56*(3), 447–64. https://doi.org/10.1002/pits.22202

Zielinski, D.S., & Bradshaw, C.P. (2006). Ecological influences on the sequelae of child maltreatment: A review of the literature. *Child Maltreatment*, *11*(1), 49–62. https://doi.org/10.1177/1077559505283591. Medline: 16382091

4 Body-Mind Oriented Trauma Therapy with Childhood Sexual Abuse Survivors: Benefits and Challenges

JOANNE SMIT AND JO-ANN VIS

Authors in trauma research and trauma therapies purport that trauma treatments over the last three decades may be misguided when approached from the mindset that trauma is about a historical narrative that occurred in the past (Briere & Scott, 2015; Ogden & Minton, 2000; van der Kolk, 2014). Researchers suggest that trauma is more about the present, and how it is being lived out in the body. Trauma, different from stress, has neurophysiology well established in neuroscience, rooted in unresolved flight, fight, freeze, and feigned death responses that involve the nervous system and arousal centres of the brain (Courtois & Ford, 2009; Levine, 2010; Ogden & Minton, 2000; van der Kolk, 2014). Trauma changes memory encoding that influences beliefs systems, thoughts, body sensations, intuitive feelings, spiritual connection, and symptoms that define dissociation, with cues that bring a victim back to the moment of an old state of collapse or helplessness (Levine, 2010; Ogden & Minton, 2000; van der Kolk, 2014). When a nervous system does not reset after an overwhelming experience, unresolved physiological distress leads to an array of behavioural, physical, and emotional symptoms (Levine, 2010, Ogden & Minton, 2000; van der Kolk, 2014). Talk therapy limits trauma resolution as the emergence of the slightest implicit memory can trigger dysregulation, and without a concerted effort to work with physiology, re-traumatization can occur (Ogden & Minton, 2000; van der Kolk, 2014).

Adult survivors of childhood sexual abuse report that they continue to struggle with complex sequelae by re-experiencing, avoidance/emotional constriction, hyper-arousal, and that the features associated with these symptom clusters are identified with the complex PTSD profile, as defined in the DSM V (American Psychiatric Association, 2000; Briere & Scott, 2015; Cloitre et al., 2011). Pat Ogden states that working with the body may be the missing link in present-day treatment, and suggests that this can integrate well with psychotherapies (Ogden & Minton, 2000). She argues that we need both "top-down approaches" and "bottom-up approaches" working together since the body is driving the brain in the organism (Ogden & Minton, 2000). Bessel van der Kolk (2014) suggests that talk therapy may be a distraction to the work that is necessary to unlock habitual traumatic patterns, as talking activates in a different part of the brain. Experts in the field suggest that the key to resolving trauma includes body-mind therapies that rely on using body awareness, along with a connectedness to emotional, spiritual, and cognitive experiences, as entry points into exploring a survivor's experience (Nowakowski-Sims & Kumar, 2020; Ogden & Minton, 2000; van der Kolk, 2014). Integrating the body's experience into the healing process is key in rescuing the body from the past and bringing it back to a place of "rest and digest." Research indicates that the practice of sensing the body and inquiry on this level can establish a more profound sense of safety and empowerment within (Cornell & Olio, 1991; Price, 2006), and facilitating dialogue between mind and body serves to support clients in becoming self-focused, gaining control over the internal processes, and re-patterning the nervous system (Levine, 2010; Ogden & Minton, 2000). Recovery needs to ensure that treatment focuses on bringing the body into talk therapies and working with body-mind approaches to facilitate and enrich life.

Social workers can support and aid this process of healing, whether they provide direct clinical intervention, participate through case management, or work from an interprofessional systems approach. Trauma-informed social workers have many options to offer as new research becomes available, and this work bodes well in social work practice with ethical values such as doing no harm and working collaboratively with others (Tan, 2009).

This chapter argues for more inclusion of spiritual body-mind approaches with adult female survivors of childhood sexual abuse, as a result of reviewing historical and present-day research, and it discusses how social workers can assist with this process. Theoretical formulations, well established in the trauma literature over the last three decades, and current research demonstrate the effectiveness of body-mind work and will form the basis to expand beyond traditional psychotherapies and bring the body in with intention for this population. An outline of implications for treatment will then offer social workers, both entry-level and experienced, an understanding of the benefits and challenges that continue to be faced in their work today.

Theoretical Foundations: Body-Mind Therapies

The basis for applying body-mind remedies in trauma work stems from the biological, psychological, spiritual, and behavioural sequelae of childhood traumatization that, when taken into adult life, affect the capacity and ability to live life fully and responsively (Boynton & Vis, 2011; Briere & Scott, 2015; Racco & Vis, 2015; van der Kolk, 2014).

Unresolved and ongoing childhood sexual abuse experienced through developmental stages into adulthood create trauma outcomes that are often complex, resulting in a pervasive pattern that may have included trauma during the preverbal period of life, further complicating their impacts (Alpert et al., 1998; Courtois & Ford, 2009; Finkelhor & Browne, 1985). Maltreatment of a child can also include neglect and abuse, in addition to sexual abuse (Courtois, 2008; Finkelhor & Browne, 1985; van der Kolk et al., 1991). Within caregiving relationships, this leads to pervasive adverse effects in later development and impairment in many domains of functioning (Briere & Scott, 2015; Courtois, 2008; van der Kolk et al., 1991).

Adult survivors of childhood sexual abuse can be found to exhibit some to all of the 11 symptom domains in the DSM V (Cloitre et al., 2011). They may struggle with re-experiencing, avoidance/emotional constriction, hyper-arousal, and those features associated with these symptom clusters identified in the complex PTSD profile, as defined in the DSM V (American Psychiatric Association, 2000; Cloitre et al., 2011). Included are affect dysregulation (highly reactive, or inhibited or explosive anger), behavioural dysregulation (self-harm, aggression to others, risk-taking), relational difficulties (conflictual or chaotic relationships or preoccupation with or avoidance of interactions), attentional disturbances (difficulty following directions or completing tasks), state-like dissociation (de-realization or de-personalization), and troubles in systems of meaning and beliefs (feeling damaged, ineffective or ashamed, loss of purpose within its relatedness to life, and chronic pain (parts of the body are numb or paralysed) (Cloitre et al., 2011). Explicitly found in this population are experiences of traumatic sexualization, experiences of betrayal, powerlessness, spiritual distress, and stigmatization (Alpert et al., 1998; Finkelhor & Browne, 1985; Gall et al., 2007). Emerging themes of hypervigilance along with difficulty with inward focusing, have been found as survivors struggle, often manifesting as hyper-alertness to danger (Wilson, 2010; Wilson et al., 2012). Two defence mechanisms used tend to be denial and dissociation in the face of childhood sexual abuse (Cornell & Olio, 1991). When dissociation is used as a primary defence, the individual is less able to experience capacity for spontaneous emotion and experiences a damaged sense of identity, spirituality and, often, a loss of their history (Cornell & Olio, 1991; Gall et al., 2007). Denial becomes a mechanism through which one can maintain emotional balance (Cornell & Olio, 1991).

Trauma research suggests that trauma struggles are about the present and how they are experienced in the body through negative physical sensation and motor patterns that, in turn, have a reciprocal negative interaction with other systems, such as cognition and emotion (Briere & Scott, 2015; Ogden & Minton, 2000; Ogden et al., 2006).

Trauma responses are identified by a sense of the lack of safety that continues to be activated well after the event is over (Briere & Scott, 2015; Herman, 1992; van der Kolk, 1994, 2014). When traumatization is not processed and the victim is unable to complete the flee or fight response, the trauma response remains fragmented (Courtois & Ford; 2009; Levine, 2010). The entire picture of what happened during the trauma event is not consciously stored in the brain. Rather, people remember images, sights, sounds, and physical sensations without much context (Briere & Scott, 2015; van der Kolk, 1994, 2014).

The theory of embodiment assumes cognition/belief and emotional processes are rooted in human organisms' motor and sense experience, directly affecting the mind (Khoury et al., 2017; Nowakowski-Sims & Kumar, 2020). Sensory systems bring about cognizance of presence, while motor systems are causal of action, and interoception under-lies sentience, emotion, thought, and motivation (Nowakowski-Sims & Kumar, 2020). Top-down processes initiated in the cerebral cortex and bottom-up processes initiated by various somatic senses work with neural processing via ascending pathways from the brainstem to cerebral cortex and are considered to be involved with self-regulation (Nowakowski-Sims & Kumar, 2020).

Ogden posits that traumatic events remain as unconscious proce-dural memories, are "wired" as sensorimotor responses, and become traits through conditioning (Ogden & Minton, 2000; Ogden et al., 2006). These memories are primarily the cause for de-regulation of one's phys-iological response (Ogden & Minton, 2000; Ogden et al., 2006). Physical responses tied to emotion and mood can occur in response to actual cues and nonspecific reminders and are difficult to change (Briere & Scott, 2015; Ogden & Minton, 2000; van der Kolk, 1994, 2014). As exter-nal and internal cues are experienced and neurologically laid down, a repetitive cycle of interaction between sensorimotor, cognition, and emotional processing affect each other and influence behaviour (Ogden & Minton, 2000; Ogden et al., 2006; van der Kolk, 1989, 1994, 2014). For example, a survivor may begin to feel sexually aroused by her partner, and even a pleasurable feeling may trigger a flashback experience of images of childhood sexual abuse, feelings of shame, corresponding with thoughts of "I am a bad person," and she may retreat, or submit to these experiences, creating what is known as re-enactment. Unconscious procedural memory can also lead to a failure to understand the appropriate context, as this process confuses the survivor, leaving her sometimes hyper- or hypo-aroused, resulting in an exaggerated response to present-day situations impacting self, relationships, and adult responsibility (Ogden & Minton, 2000; van der Kolk, 1989). Using the example above, as the survivor is triggered by the sexual experience, she may retreat or submit to these experiences and thus be left feeling exhausted, shut down, and continue to experience herself as a failure.

Implications for Treatment: Effective Body-Mind Therapeutic Interventions

The survivor of complex trauma needs to feel that the traumatic experience is over. This outcome occurs when the body can sense safety and somatic reactivity diminishes (Courtois, 2008; Ogden & Minton, 2000; van der Kolk, 2014). Equally significant is the need to approach trauma intervention in a progressive succession building on the therapeutic relationship and independent stability as the base for ongoing work (Courtois, 2008; Herman, 1992; Ogden & Minton, 2000). Courtois (2008) discusses the need for a three-stage intervention with the opening stage being the most significant. Within this stage, efforts are concentrated on the development of a robust therapeutic alliance, affect regulation, psychoeducation, and skill-building (Cloitre et al., 2011). With success in the first stage, individuals can move to the work of the processing through traumatic material to increase daily functioning (Cloitre et al., 2011). The final stage emphasizes the restructuring of one's life incorporating new narratives beyond that of a sexual abuse victim (Courtois, 2008).

Many trauma-informed therapists theorize that body-mind therapies integrate cognitive, affective, somatic, and spiritual responses to trauma and are effective first-stage interventions (Briere & Scott, 2015; Racco & Vis, 2015; van der Kolk, 2014). Actual recovery must target the deactivation of both hypo- and hyper-arousal responses and bring arousal to a level that is tolerable to ensure no harm, and minimize re-traumatization (Ford et al., 2005; Ogden & Minton, 2000; van der Kolk, 2014). Somatic resources (such as grounding and orienting) are found to increase capacity to manage hyper- and hypo-arousal reactions and to counteract tendencies to dissociate (Briere & Scott, 2015; Ogden et al., 2006; van der Kolk, 2014). Working within a therapeutic "window of tolerance" introduced by Siegel (1999) teaches clients to moderate traumatic material, builds capacity to know *when* and *how* to manage trauma reactivity at will, and regains mastery over one's awareness and subsequent reactions.

Treatment strategies need to ensure an awareness of the cycle of denial and dissociation by both the therapist and the client, and mapping emotional reactivity, cognition, sensation, and related behaviour (Cornell & Olio, 1991; Wilson, 2010; van der Kolk, 1989). These treatment strategies promote pattern awareness since procedural memory is considered unconscious (Ogden & Minton, 2000). Through this work, one can support capacity building to recognize and eventually avoid traumatic re-enactments both in and out of the treatment room (Cornell & Olio, 1991; Ogden & Minton, 2000). Once able to stay in the present moment, individuals are more able to work through traumatic activation effectively. Skills, in turn, help to experience empowerment and promote self-responsibility for self-care (Wilson, 2010): "This is my body, and not anyone else's. You took it, and now I am getting back" (from a Survivor quoted in Wilson, 2010, p. 118).

According to the literature reviewed, top interventions include psychoeducation, emotional regulation, anxiety and stress management, body awareness practices, and narrative and cognitive restructuring (Cloitre et al., 2011; White & Epston, 1990). However, a stage-based treatment approach that incorporates stability and skills development within the initial stage is considered vital for effective trauma treatment (Cloitre et al., 2011; Courtois, 2004, 2008; Ford et al., 2005). The first stage assists individuals to build capacity to stay within a "window of tolerance," and increases a sense of safety, aiming to decrease self-harm, impulsivity and suicidality (Courtois, 2004, 2008; Ford et al., 2005). Initial-stage interventions can occur in an individual or group context; however, case management support through consistent contact also provides direction at the beginning of treatment.

First-Stage Interventions

As discussed, individuals managing complex trauma often balance compound multi-systemic challenges, with limited access to internal and external resources. Attempting to process traumatic experiences before one has built up these resources often results in adverse outcomes. Trauma treatment begins in the initial stage, and can often be enough to offer individuals new opportunities and life benefit outcomes. Likewise, social workers who have limited clinical experience with sexual abuse survivors may avoid providing service, under the pretence that "treatment" only includes work at the second and final stages. This interpretation generates doubts about one's ability to assist if they deem themselves unqualified to address clinical issues at the second and third stages. But, the literature endorses involvement at the initial stage of complex trauma work, affirming the importance of intervention before delving into the trauma experience. Extensive work such as building the needed therapeutic alliance, promoting stabilization and skill development are fundamental goals to be set and evaluated. The following sections discuss these essential initial stage intervention options, utilizing the skill set of trained social workers.

Psychoeducation

Psychoeducation teaches the theory of traumatic stress, its impacts on health and body, the importance of decent nutrition and sleep to recover, differences between emotions, and thoughts and their distortions. Also, topics such as time management, goal setting, assertiveness training, meditation, breath work, mindful body scanning, and guided imagery can help individuals to cope with stressful emotions, thoughts, and body responses (Wilson, 2010; Wilson et al., 2012). Knowledge about the impact of trauma on one's health and spiritual well-being can become a powerful tool for complex trauma survivors. By incorporating information about what one can expect throughout the treatment process, one can anticipate and prepare for ongoing symptom management, assisting in relapse prevention.

Directed Mindfulness

Skills developed in the first stage of treatment may be harmonized with other forms of intervention. Body-mind work attunes a person to one's reactions and emotions and allows one to learn the skills to moderate those reactions (Ogden & Minton, 2000; Price, 2004; Wilson, 2010). Directed mindfulness to observe internal experiences along with deep breathing and stillness practices with non-judgment are used to regulate emotion and cognition within Western Buddhist tradition. These practices are viewed as the primary change agent in the reduction of suffering (Khoury et al., 2017). Central in all mindfulness practices is an integration of bottom-up and top-down processes. While maintaining lucid awareness of external and internal cues, one can regulate one's emotions while reviewing belief experiences, allowing for renewed perspectives (Khoury, et al., 2017). This approach goes beyond the tendency to use mindfulness practice as a behavioural application. Instead, true mindfulness application requires a spiritual approach, seeking out a client's spiritual lived experience and incorporating Buddhist or Christian thoughts as appropriate to expand one's sense of meaning and purpose (Trammel, 2017).

Decreased stress, decreased blood pressure and cortisol levels, combined with an increased mindful awareness of bodily reactions to stress may support improvement to health (Wilson, 2010). Decreasing hypervigilance and hyper-arousal may allow clients to become comfortable in public spaces, providing general enjoyment of physical movement and activity as part of one's daily life. Mindfulness skills developed in individual or group counselling can be transferable to other aspects of an individual's life and may support the building of interpersonal relationships, establishing effective boundaries, and managing relationships with one's family of origin.

Developing the skills to self-regulate and self-soothe may decrease the tolerance for relationships that are not supportive of healthy behaviours. Increased emotional intelligence and the ability to realistically assess danger may allow individuals to relax their guard, own their autonomy, and possibly lead them to better relationship experiences (Brotto et al., 2012). The benefits of incorporating the body into psychotherapy and grounding into the present may allow the survivor time to grieve the betrayals experienced and fully process them in body, mind, and spirit. Increased autonomy and belief in self can, potentially, allow the survivor to circumvent the effects of the stigma placed by other people.

Most body-mind practices bring focused attention to posture with sensation in parts of the body, and then accompany self-care and change strategies to support stabilization (Langmuir et al., 2011; Price, 2006; Wilson et al., 2012). The understanding of physical body movement and organization can support a positive sense of self when working with posture or movement (Ogden & Minton, 2000; Wilson et al., 2012). For example, grounding in the legs by standing up with focused attention to the change the experience, or alignment through the spine by sitting up straight from a collapsed posture, or gesturing stop or welcome with hands to get the feel of body boundaries are simple techniques that build capacity (Ogden & Minton, 2000). Some suggest adding a brief and soft touch to heighten the experience, with the intent to be educational. In this process, one discovers a tolerance of distressful inner experiences which has shown to help with re-owning the body when coupled with self-care practices (Cornell & Olio, 1991). The use of massage with self-care practices, such as directed mindfulness, practised relaxation with tension, and breath work, was also found to support body awareness, reduce pressure, support management of triggers, and create relaxation (Price, 2006). These body-based practices contributed to decreased scores of PTSD and a trend towards lessened dissociation and women reported an increased felt sense of security, which serves to support psychotherapy and recovery (Price, 2006).

The benefits of body-mind therapies in a staged model of intervention with adult sexual abuse survivors could result in shorter courses of treatment while offering new skills that clients can access whenever needed (Price, 2004, 2006; van der Kolk, 2014; Wilson, 2010). Research by Brotto et al. (2012) found that in only two sessions of mindfulness, individuals reported more benefit than 24 weeks of medication. Although these initial conclusions involved a small sample size, the potential for complementary skill development in the initial stages of recovery is promising.

Social workers, generally, are not experts in massage therapy, yoga, other movement therapies, or spiritual practices, and thus, interprofessional teams seem to be a natural progression. An interprofessional approach to post-trauma interventions offers opportunity for allied professionals to work together within mandates of existing organizations and differing cultural, spiritual practices, providing clients with a holistic approach to stabilization and self-care (Nicols, 2015; Price, 2006).

Groupwork

Group therapy formats provide an opportunity to develop and practice skills such as bodily awareness, increased toleration of distress, and soothing capacities. Learning from others, engaging in mutual support, while challenging one another creates an environment ripe with interpersonal opportunity. Good group interaction experiences can lead to an improvement in developing and experiencing interpersonal relationships (Langmuir et al., 2011). Individuals in groups can practice these skills while finding comfort in sharing their trauma narratives and learning they are not alone. Also, the mobilization of natural social support is vital in the treatment of PTSD (Briere & Scott, 2015; van der Kolk, 1989). Through discussions of body experience, felt sensation, and the behavioural impulse to thoughts and feelings supports increased capacity in a real context. Group offers participants the chance to share ones' past and present accurately, transforming their story of survival to an account of what is possible (Langmuir et al., 2011). Another added benefit of group work is the opportunity to enhance interpersonal communication skills and expand one's external support network. Research supports the possibility that a person with complex PTSD, who is often feeling hypervigilant, overwhelmed, or defeated, and has few social supports, can develop relations with others in the group while increasing capacity for independent living (Wilson, 2010; van der Kolk, 2014). Through this group experience, individuals can benefit from collective capacity building, challenging themselves and others, eventually transferring this interaction to other life situations.

How Social Workers Can Assist

It is imperative that all social workers set out as part of their ethical practice to be trauma-informed (Breckenridge & James, 2010). Social workers should strive to be knowledgeable about various trauma-informed assessments and process-orientated models. Understanding the connections between individual and system approaches can be used to coach survivors and assist them in making educated choices about ongoing treatment options (Breckenridge & James, 2010).

Psychosocial-education in and of itself is considered safe practice with complex survivors and can shift a survivor from feeling defeated to curious. Psychosocial-education is a fundamental skill employed by social workers to empower individuals to understand one's current experience to determine what resources are necessary to meet the demand. Introducing an awareness of the biological responses to stress, the mindfulness skills to recognize the internal process, and new skills to initiate healthier behaviours, are potentially new abilities for the complex trauma survivor.

As social workers attend to rigorous evaluation of their work, ensuring understanding of the Buddhist and Christian historical roots of mindfulness will lead to minimizing risks of misappropriating it's true original and spiritual components. Expanding the purpose of mindfulness beyond a behavioural exercise allows for spiritual reflection beyond the conceptual level. This critical evaluation is essential to offer a holistic and diverse approach for complex sexual abuse survivors (Trammel, 2018, 2017).

Working as part of an interprofessional team is another critical social work skill developed through years of education and training. As with any new skill or practice, relapse is often possible or expected, and therefore progression through therapy to independence, and self-supporting, needs to go slowly (Langmuir et al., 2011; van der Kolk, 2014). Using a case management approach provides a logical connection between a client and social work professional who can support and offer reflective evaluation of progress made throughout the initial stage. Through a case management model, social workers can apply their generalist skills aptly, creating the therapeutic alliance, encouraging skill capacity, and strengthening internal and external resources. Social workers can support a team approach by helping to develop a common language within a case management model or team strategy, through the sharing of one's knowledge and systemic understanding.

Social workers already familiar with the importance of using the skills of attunement and compassionate inquiry can assist survivors to experience a greater experience of themselves in connection with original movement. For social workers who require support in this area, one can seek to work with professional teams that include spiritual knowledge keepers, or seek further training in this area with the aim to offer a more diverse healing experience (Nowakowski-Sims & Kumar, 2020; Trammel, 2018).

Social workers are well trained to create and maintain therapeutic relationships. Communication skills and therapy knowledge are vital transferable skills that will be called upon within the initial stage of trauma treatment for complex trauma survivors. Assessment questions focusing on strengths and abilities are equally crucial to those narratives of struggle and difficulty. As a result of the impact of complex traumatic stress on survivors, the social worker must work to create an environment of safety and respect (Cornell & Olio, 1991; Langmuir et al., 2011). This environmental context is one where social workers strive to focus on strengths and possibilities, while educating, stabilizing, and promoting skill development.

In summary, as outlined in the research, key to resolving traumatic maladaptive responses, include body-mind therapies. Body-mind modalities support establishing renewed safety, allow for corrective re-patterning of the nervous system resulting in decreased somatic reactivity, and effective re-ordering of the inner experience. Through three-stage interventions, both entry-level and experienced trauma-informed social workers can, led by ethics, assist effectively through direct clinical work (both in group and individual practice), both with interprofessional teams and through case management. Social workers are arguably well positioned to assist and facilitate this invaluable work for those members of society in need.

REFERENCES

Alpert, J.L., Brown, L.S., & Courtois, C.A. (1998). Symptomatic clients and memories of childhood abuse: What the trauma and child sexual abuse literature tells us. *Psychology, Public Policy, and Law, 4*(4), 941–95. https://doi.org/10.1037/1076-8971.4.4.941

American Psychiatric Association. (2000). *Diagnostic and statistical manual of mental disorders* (4th ed.).

Boynton, H.M., & Vis, J. (2011). Meaning making, spirituality, and creative expressive therapies: Pathways to processing grief with children. *Counselling and Spirituality, 30*(2). 137–59.

Breckenridge, J., & James, K. (2010). Educating social work students in multifaceted interventions for trauma. *Social Work Education, 29*(3), 259–75. https://doi.org/10.1080/02615470902912250

Briere, J. & Scott, C. (2015). *Principles of trauma therapy: A guide to symptoms, evaluation, and treatment* (2nd ed.). Sage Publications.

Brotto, L.A., Seal, B.N., & Rellini, A. (2012). Pilot study of a brief cognitive behavioral versus mindfulness-based intervention for women with sexual distress and a history of childhood sexual abuse. *Journal of Sex & Marital Therapy, 38*(1), 1–27 https://doi.org/10.1080/0092623x.2011.569636. Medline: 22268979

Cloitre, M., Courtois, C.A., Charuvastra, A., Carapezza, R., Stolbach, B.C., & Green, B.L. (2011). Treatment of complex PTSD: Results of the ISTSS expert clinician survey on best practices. *Journal of Traumatic Stress, 24*(6), 615–27. https://doi.org/10.1002/jts.20697. Medline: 22147449

Cornell, W. & Olio, K. (1991). Integrating affect in treatment with adult survivors of physical and sexual abuse. *American Journal of Orthopsychiatry, 61*(1), 59–69. https://doi.org/10.1037/h0079232. Medline: 2006678

Courtois, C.A. (2004). Complex trauma, complex reactions: Assessment and treatment. *Psychotherapy: Theory, Research, Practice, Training, 41*(4), 412–25. https://doi.org/10.1037/0033-3204.41.4.412

– (2008). Complex trauma, complex reactions: Assessment and treatment. *Psychological Trauma: Theory, Research, Practice and Policy, S*(1), 86–100. https://doi.org/10.1037/1942-9681.s.1.86

Courtois, C., & Ford, J. (Eds.). (2009). *Treating complex traumatic stress disorders: Scientific foundations and therapeutic models.* The Guilford Press.

Finkelhor, D., & Browne, A. (1985). The traumatic impact of child sexual abuse: A conceptualization. *American Journal of Orthopsychiatry, 55*(4), 530–41. https://doi.org/10.1111/j.1939-0025.1985.tb02703.x. Medline: 4073225

Ford, J.D., Courtois, C.A., Steele, K., van der Hart, O., & Nijenhuis, E.R.S. (2005). Treatment of complex posttraumatic self–dysregulation. *Journal of Traumatic Stress, 18*(5), 437–47. https://doi.org/10.1002/jts.20051. Medline: 16281241

Gall, T.L., Basque, V., Damasceno-Scott, M., & Vardy, G. (2007). Spirituality and the current adjustment of adult survivors of childhood sexual abuse. *Journal for the Scientific Study of Religion*, 46(1), 101–17. https://doi.org /10.1111/j.1468-5906.2007.00343.x

Herman, J.T. (1992). *Trauma and recovery: The aftermath of violence from domestic abuse to political terror*. Basic Books.

Khoury, B., Knäuper, B., Pagnini, F., Trent, N., Chiesa, A., & Carrière, K. (2017). Embodied mindfulness. *Mindfulness*, 8(5), 1160–71. https://doi.org/10.1007 /s12671-017-0700-7

Langmuir, J.I., Kirsh, S.G., & Classen, C.C. (2011). A pilot study of body-oriented group psychotherapy: Adapting sensorimotor psychotherapy for the group treatment of trauma. *Psychological Trauma: Theory, Research, Practice, and Policy*, 4(2), 214–20. https://doi.org/10.1037/a0025588

Levine, P.A. (2010). *In an unspoken voice: How the body releases trauma and restores goodness*. North Atlantic Books.

Nicols, L. (2015). The use of mind-body practices in counseling: A grounded theory study. *Journal of Mental Health Counseling*, 37(1), 28–46. https:// doi.org/10.17744/mehc.37.1.v432446211272p4r

Nowakowski-Sims, E., & Kumar, J. (2020). Soul work in social work. *Journal of Religion & Spirituality in Social Work*, 39(2), 1–16. https://doi.org/10.1080 /15426432.2019.1706694

Ogden, P., & Minton, K. (2000). Sensorimotor psychotherapy: One method for processing traumatic memory. *Traumatology*, 6(3), 149–73. https:// doi.org/10.1177/153476560000600302

Ogden, P., Pain, C., & Fisher, J. (2006). A sensorimotor approach to the treatment of trauma and dissociation. *Psychiatric Clinics of North America*, 29(1), 263–79. https://doi.org/10.1016/j.psc.2005.10.012. Medline: 16530597

Price, C. (2004). Characteristics of women seeking body-oriented therapy as an adjunct to psychotherapy during recovery from childhood sexual abuse. *Journal of Bodywork and Movement Therapies*, 8(1), 35–42. https:// doi.org/10.1016/s1360-8592(03)00077-9

– (2006). Body-oriented therapy in sexual abuse recovery: A pilot–test comparison. *Journal of Bodywork and Movement Therapies*, 10(1), 58–64. https://doi.org/10.1016/j.jbmt.2005.03.001

Racco, A., & Vis, J. (2015). Evidence based trauma treatment for children and youth. *Child & Adolescent Social Work Journal*, 32, 121–9. https:// doi.org/10.1007/s10560-014-0347-3

Siegel, D.J. (1999). *The developing mind: toward a neurobiology of interpersonal experience*. Guilford Press.

Tan, N.T. (2009). Disaster management and social recovery: Strengths and community perspective. *Journal of Global Social Work Practice*, 2(1), 217–33. http://www.globalsocialwork.org/vol2no1_Tan.html

Trammel, R.C. (2017). Tracing the roots of mindfulness: Transcendence in Buddhism and Christianity. *Journal of Religion & Spirituality in Social Work, 36*(3), 367–83. https://doi.org/10.1080/15426432.2017.1295822

– (2018). A phenomenological study of Christian practitioners who use mindfulness. *Journal of Spirituality in Mental Health, 20*(3), 199–224. https://doi.org/10.1080/19349637.2017.1408445

van der Kolk, B.A. (1989). The compulsion to repeat the trauma: Re-enactment, re-victimization, and masochism. *Psychiatric Clinics of North America, 12*(2), 389–411. https://doi.org/10.1016/s0193-953x(18)30439-8

– (1994). The body keeps the score: Memory and the evolving psychobiology of posttraumatic stress. *Harvard Review of Psychiatry, 1*(5), 253–65. https://doi.org/10.3109/10673229409017088. Medline: 9384857

– (2014). *The body keeps the score: Brain, mind, and body in the healing of trauma.* Penguin Books.

van der Kolk, B.A., Perry, J.C., & Herman, J.L. (1991). Childhood origins of self-destructive behaviour. *The American Journal of Psychiatry, 148*(12), 1665–71. https://doi.org/10.1176/ajp.148.12.1665. Medline: 1957928

White, M., & Epston, D. (1990). *Narrative means to therapeutic ends.* Norton.

Wilson, D.R. (2010). Stress management for adult survivors of childhood sexual abuse: A holistic inquiry. *Western Journal of Nursing Research, 32*(1), 103–27. https://doi.org/10.1177/0193945909343703. Medline: 19955101

Wilson, D.R., Vidal, B., Wilson, W.A., & Salyer, S.L. (2012). Overcoming sequelae of childhood sexual abuse with stress management. *Journal of Psychiatric and Mental Health Nursing, 19*(7), 587–93. https://doi.org/10.1111/j.1365-2850.2011.01813.x. Medline: 22070354

5 Exploring Meaning and Purpose: Underpinnings to Posttraumatic Growth for Front Line Professionals

JO-ANN VIS

Introduction

Individuals who choose professions in first response, health care, child protection, mental health, and other human services, often report a sense of fulfilment; choosing these careers with inspiration to make a difference and offer support to those in need (Avraham et al., 2014; Conrad & Kellar-Guenther, 2006; Rosso et al., 2010). However, despite positive affirmation and reinforcement that their efforts contribute to others' health and well-being, the scope of their accountabilities also invariably exposes them to psychological injury. Current research suggests that continuous exposure to work-related critical workplace incidents could create overwhelming emotional responses that can lead to various psychological stress concerns (Geisler et al., 2019; Randall & Buys, 2013). Equally, critical incident exposure can erode one's sense of meaningful work, creating internal cynicism, diminishing one's professional self-concept (Geisler et al., 2019). Yet, in contrast, other research presents information about the positive implications of meaning-making concerning one's job as a way to promote posttraumatic growth (Conrad & Kellar-Guenther, 2006; Geisler et al., 2019; Regehr et al., 2004).

Finding meaning and experiencing meaningfulness in one's work has been argued as one of the key areas from which individuals can draw relevance in one's life (Martela & Pessi, 2018; Rosso et al., 2010). Engaging in meaningful work creates a sense of purpose. It can aid in overall positive well-being, alongside more expected experiences that offer life fulfilment, such as religious practices and the formation of significant relationships (Martela & Riekki, 2018; Rosso et al., 2010). Social workers often work at the micro, mezzo, and macro levels to offer support to individuals, families, communities, and organizations who have been exposed to work-place critical incidents. Attention to spirituality is an important component in assessment, intervention, and evaluation of workplace wellness.

This chapter will highlight the spiritual and psychological stressors concerning critical incident exposure for front line workers. Specifically, discussion will focus on the impact of critical incidents on the professional's meaning and purpose in the workplace, offering discourse concerning the importance of including spirituality in assessment and intervention as a means to promote posttraumatic growth.

Spiritually Challenging Occupations

There is a well-established appreciation that first responders (firefighters, police, paramedics, soldiers, etc.) may be at increased risk for the development of psychological injury as a result of exposure to critical and traumatic incidents in the workplace (Adams et al., 2013; Alexander & Klein, 2001; Shakespeare-Finch, 2011). Additionally, research has shown that other occupations such as health care providers, child welfare workers, mental health professionals and crisis response workers equally experience critical and traumatic events that involve human suffering (Conrad & Kellar-Guenther, 2006; Huggard et al., 2017; Kessell et al., 2009; Regehr et al., 2002, 2004). Consequently, any front line helping professional bearing witness to human suffering can experience psychological and spiritual challenges regardless of designation. Therefore, the term front line professional is used to capture the variety of helping professionals (paramedics, firefighters, police officers, EMTs, rescue workers, military personnel, nurses and other medical staff, 911 dispatchers, child welfare and mental health crises workers) who assist other individuals in times of crisis.

Upon reviewing the literature concerning the psychological impact in the workplace, the terms critical or traumatic incidents are interchangeable. Posttraumatic stress disorder (PTSD) is the most commonly researched term linked to long-term psychological injury (Halpern et al., 2009). As noted in the *Diagnostic and Statistical Manual of Mental Disorders* (DSM-5; American Psychiatric Association, 2013), an event is traumatic when one encounters "Exposure to actual or threatened death, serious injury, or sexual violence in one (or more) of the following ways: (1) Directly experiencing the traumatic event(s); (2) witnessing, in person, the event(s) as it occurred to others; (3) learning that the traumatic event(s) occurred to a close family member or close friend … (4) experiencing repeated or extreme exposure to aversive details of the traumatic event(s) (e.g., first responders collecting human remains; police officers repeatedly exposed to details of child abuse)." Alternatively, a critical incident provides more of a broader definition, addressing emotional involvement rather than the event's details. In this definition, a critical incident is an event that involves threat, loss of life or tragedy, out of the range of one's typical experience. It can vary in response on a continuum to include various levels of stress to the degree to which one cannot cope. Specifically, for front line workers, a critical incident refers to situations in which front line professionals will experience unusually strong emotional reactions that can hamper one's ability to function either during or following the event (Halpern et al., 2009; Mitchell, 1983).

It is important to note that while these two definitions tend to focus on the implication of life-threatening events, front line employees experience other types of *critical* or *traumatic* incidents that cause psychological distress. Verbal and emotional abuse on the job, exposure to chronic social deprivation, and bearing witness to human atrocities are examples of the other critical incidents that can produce harm (Regehr et al., 2004). As a result, the definition offered by Briere and Scott (2015) will be used for this chapter to define an event as traumatic or critical "if it is extremely upsetting, at least temporarily overwhelms the individual's internal resources, and produces lasting psychological symptoms" (p. 10). Equally important are the pre-existing chronic factors related to a sense of lack of control over one's work demands, ultimately adding to the susceptibility to psychological harm (Regehr et al., 2004). While these chronic factors are not critical, they can create stressors leaving one vulnerable to the effects of critical incident exposure. Consequently, front line employees experience higher and more frequent rates of burnout and contact with critical incidents than the general public. This reality not only increases the potential for deterioration of one's mental health capacity, but one's spiritual health and connection to a sense of meaningful work.

The majority of research concerning trauma exposure for front line workers focuses on the psychological (related emotional and behavioural aspects), with little attention given to an employee's spiritual health's phenomenological impact. Attending to the employee's spiritual connection or meaning to one's work following a traumatic incident is equally important and interconnected to promoting posttraumatic growth, longevity, and health in one's career.

Psychological and Spiritual Consequences of Occupational Exposure to Critical Incidents

Those who work on the front lines mostly present as a vulnerable group due to exposure to critical incident stress through employment. Over the past decades, there have been various terms used to capture the emotional effects of exposure to critical incidents that evoke strong emotive responses in professional helpers. PTSD, secondary traumatic stress (STS), compassion fatigue (CF), vicarious trauma (VT), and occupational stress injury (OSI) are the most commonly used to capture the emotional, physical, psychological, and phenomenological effects felt by front line professionals.

Research indicates many similarities between PTSD and STS in terms of symptomatology. Many who experience repeated critical incidents struggle with maintaining a positive attitude towards their job, family, and lifestyle as they deal with their profession's traumatic nature (Avraham et al., 2014). The most frequent trauma-related disorder reported within emergency medical personnel is PTSD (Cacciatore et al., 2011; Choi, 2011). Specifically, PTSD can be an outcome for front line workers when duties expose employees to repeated direct or indirect exposure to critical and traumatic events (American Psychiatric Association, 2013). The American Psychiatric Association (2013) has endorsed the view that being an ongoing witness through the course of one's employment, even when not being familiar with the victim or being directly at risk, may serve as a traumatic event.

STS refers to a cluster of psychological symptoms that mimic PTSD that one experiences when providing support to others who experienced or have a trauma history (Figley, 1995). Symptoms of STS include intrusion, which involves re-experiencing the traumatic event through nightmares or visions; avoidance, which includes numbness by avoiding thoughts, feelings, activities or certain situations; and arousal, which comprises sleep disturbances, outbursts of anger, difficulties concentrating and hypervigilance (Choi, 2011).

CF presents as a natural consequence for the front line professional who, in a caregiving capacity, bears witness to the suffering of others. In efforts to be empathetic in one's professional role, front line workers are at risk of direct or indirect trauma exposure, pain and suffering of others as a consequence of effectively fulfilling one's position (Figley, 1995). Like STS, CF can cause feelings of anger, exhaustion, depression, and frustration but differ as compassion fatigue occurs cumulatively over time (Anderson, 2000). Often discussed in unification with CF is VT, which encompasses the constructivist self-development theory, the process of cognitive change resulting from sustained empathic engagement with trauma survivors (McCann & Pearlman, 1990). VT alters the helper's sense of self, world view, views of safety, trust, and control. The changes that VT has on front line professionals are pervasive, cumulative, and permanent. McCann and Pearlman (1990) add that a traumatic event could include any experience that would potentially disrupt an individual's frame of reference and understanding of her/his world as they view it.

OSI is another common term found in the literature used to capture a range of experiences following the traumatic event that identifies concerns that can emerge from the trauma event itself and what transpires after. Randall and Buys (2013) note that OSI occurs when the work stressors exceed one's resources, separating the stressors found in work demands from strain, which address the negative stress experience. Interestingly, these authors also suggest that jobs that offer little control or flexibility inevitably cause the most tension, reinforcing OSI's certainty for front line workers. In simplistic terms, the above terminology concerning workplace trauma suggests that participating in or witnessing a critical event invariably produces psychological distress and can, at times, produce emotional disability.

The concern with nearly all of this literature is the assumption that adverse psychological outcomes are created primarily by exposure to the critical event alone. To some extent, this assumption may be related to the overwhelming focus on workers with a diagnosis of PTSD (Cacciatore et al. 2011; Halpern et al., 2009). Nevertheless, there has been very little research to support whether it is, in fact, the traumatic nature of the event itself that precipitates psychological symptoms, or whether there are other factors which may influence the psychological impact after the event. Many different factors emerge following a traumatic event.

For example, the effect of posttraumatic investigations, management and supervisory responses to what happened, report completion, and guilt, are just some of the possible factors which could contribute positively or negatively to an employee's ability to continue to manage at work. Regehr et al. (2002) studied the effects of post-mortem inquiries for emergency personnel following a traumatic incident, to find that these inquiries can be more stressful than involvement in the traumatic event. The workers experienced stress and trauma as a result of having their actions questioned, and the length of time taken to conduct a review was the most significant predictor of posttraumatic stress scores in the study. Also, Regehr et al. 's (2004) research on the impact on child welfare workers of inquiries into the deaths of children for whom they had a responsibility also found that workers experienced negative consequences associated with inquiries. The authors concluded that the combined individual, organizational, and trauma event factors led to posttraumatic stress symptoms. This suggests that interventions at various levels have the potential to address these post-event experiences with probability to challenge and reinforce one's sense of purpose, meaning and, ultimately, one's spiritual fulfilment.

While most research and literature focuses on the negative psychological, physiological and behavioural consequences of occupational critical incident exposure, other authors offer essential information regarding growth for individuals both in the general population and those providing front line service. One key concept of posttraumatic growth suggests ties to the purpose of positive meaning-making. Yet the connection between posttraumatic growth and meaningfulness of work has been scarce in the literature.

According to Clark (2006), spirituality is an essential component of one's world view and how one makes meaning of her or his experiences. Appreciation of spirituality and meaning-making is imperative when working in front line positions. These jobs require individuals to confront one's purpose and connections to others daily, suggesting that spirituality is another factor worthy of consideration for promoting growth and well-being.

Importance of Spirituality for Front Line Workers

How each employee conceptualizes the critical incident and one's ability to access services and supports could be protective factors against the development of PTSD (Adams et al., 2013; Halpern et al., 2009; Shakespeare-Finch, 2011). With this awareness has come increased attention to front line professionals as a vulnerable group and a corresponding interest in identifying risk or protective factors that may help mitigate psychological vulnerability (Huggard et al., 2017; Regehr et al., 2004; Shakespeare-Finch, 2011).

Meaning-making exploration following a traumatic event appears to play an important role, with a greater sense of self-worth and sentiments of more significant goodwill globally, contributing to lower PTSD symptoms prospectively (Park & Ai, 2006). Martela and Riekki (2018) define meaningfulness of work as "the subjective experience of how significant and intrinsically valuable people find their work to be" (p. 2). Finding meaning and purpose in one's life often includes a connection to spirituality or religion (Park & Ai, 2006). One's work or vocation has emerged as a realm where one finds meaning and purpose, especially when one experiences a positive correlation between one's belief that she/he can make a difference in the world alongside evidence that reinforces this hope (Rosso et al. 2010; Wrzesniewski et al., 1997). Although conversation among co-workers directly linked to spirituality may be rare, many employees find themselves reflecting on their work in spiritual terms (Rosso et al., 2010). Especially significant are those employees who believe that their religious or spiritual beliefs inform their work choices and conduct, with a sense of being *called* to a particular profession because of innate talents and abilities (Wrzesniewski et al., 2003).

Interestingly, the idea of a *calling* from a secular view is remarkably similar, including work that one would perceive as moral, social and offers personal significance (Wrzesniewski et al., 1997). Regardless of the religious or secular context, callings are unique beliefs tied to one's work that reflects one's abilities, which is reinforced when one experiences success in one's career.

Despite the lack of scholarly discourse regarding the meaningfulness of work, the tension between critical incident exposure and preserving a healthy spiritual outlook of one's work in the front lines is timely and essential. Authenticity, a sense of self-connectedness and social responsibility are terms used to describe experiences of meaning and purpose through one's work, linking a personal or spiritual connection to an intention or innate obligation to enter a profession that requires and reflects one's abilities or gifts. These discernments reinforce a sense of congruence with one's job and personal values, leading to an overall understanding of meaningfulness (Conrad & Kellar-Guenther, 2006; Martela & Riekki, 2018; Rosso et al., 2010). Exploration of meaning for those struggling with occupational stress is an underpinning factor in posttraumatic growth and stabilization.

Upon reviewing the literature concerning meaningfulness in one's life and work, themes addressing issues of purpose, value, ability, resilience, calling, and relationship with self and others continue to emerge. While various authors suggest different categories, Martela and Riekki (2018) provide a helpful compilation that addresses these themes in four "pathways" that capture the multiple components of meaningfulness in a concise and useful way. The four pathways include *autonomy*, providing a sense of connectedness between what one does with what one values; *competence*, which contains the feeling of confidence that one can perform tasks in a skilled manner; *relatedness*, which describes a sense of connection and relationship within one's relational system; and *beneficence*, a feeling that one's work is of benefit or help to others (Martela & Riekki, 2018).

Similarly, Rosso et al. (2010) offer two related but separate components to describe the meaning of work. One part involves the type of importance that an employee might make of one's work, with the second being the significance or meaningfulness that one might attach to it. Employees in front line positions hold personal importance to a sense of meaningfulness in their work. If employees believe that they make a difference for the people they serve, that one has talents and skills that make one suited for the work that one does and that employees strive to help those in need, meaningfulness is maintained (Conrad & Kellar-Guenther, 2006; Martela & Riekki, 2018; Rosso et al., 2010). Based on this thesis, the four pathways are used to highlight the implication of meaningful work, particularly for front line employees exposed to critical incidents in efforts to promote posttraumatic growth.

Autonomy

Employees who work in emotionally high-risk positions typically describe their work as meaningful, believing that they contribute to society in a way that offers protection or care to members of the community (Conrad & Kellar-Guenther, 2006; Halpern et al., 2009). Often employees in these positions discuss their draw to work as more of a desire to care for others or make a difference versus to collect a pay check or other perceived job benefits (Geisler et al., 2019). Therefore, reinforcing a belief held individually and usually supported externally, the work in these front line positions has meaning; van Dorssen-Boog et al. (2020) expands on the discussion of autonomy within the self-leadership theory. The authors conclude that even in highly controlled environments, such as those in health care, individuals can experience autonomous motivation, positively impacting an employee's enthusiasm and health. Self-leadership naturally rewards strategies such as seeking out pleasurable activities at work or focusing on positive aspects of one's job can influence one's motivation and meaning, leading to positive health outcomes. Ultimately, building an individual's sense of self-leadership through reflection concerning positive experiences and gains from one's work creates an opportunity for autonomy, despite high-risk professions where limiting policies and procedures are many.

Competence

Examples of competence include situations where front line employees can perform their duties to bring about positive change while amid a critical incident. When cases end in death or pain or employees are abused and discredited in the process, one begins to doubt her/his ability (see Halpern et al. 2009, for example). According to Rosso et al. (2010), a person's self-concept and evaluation of competence is fragile and can change in response to various experiences and work contexts. This would be particularly true for front line employees. Avraham and colleagues' (2014) research supports this suggestion based on their finding that employees in the front lines can have fluctuating empowering or disempowering experiences following a critical incident, which influences one's sense of competence.

Despite efforts and adherence to protocol, adverse outcomes can occur even when one performs one's job duties effectively. Such is the reality of work in the front lines. Research demonstrates that employees often face additional external factors that reinforce doubt and ability. Assessment of one's meaning about work is typically an individual exercise. However, one's organization, peers, and community are also influential in this meaning-making process. Management, societal bias and negative media can create additional stressors, casting self-doubts regarding outcomes (Avraham et al., 2014; Regehr et al., 2004). As a result, confidence must be re-storied to promote posttraumatic growth, while using this growth to mitigate other psychological stressors.

Relatedness

Strong collegial bonds have the potential to reinforce the sense of positive meaning regarding one's work, particularly following critical incident exposure. However, weak and negative interactions among colleagues can influence one's purpose to work differently. Working among peers who share the same perceptions concerning the importance of one's work, and the belief that providing service to others offers a sense of purpose contributes to a peer environment that continually provides cues that reinforce front line service as meaningful work. Wrzesniewski et al. (2003) suggest that peer relationships can build upon one's sense of purpose when witnessing others demonstrating care when interacting in service to others. When an employee hears a peer describe their work as a privilege or calling. The authors describe this as interpersonal sense-making, which can have a positive or negative outcome. When a peer culture is healthy, interpersonal relatedness is consistent and supportive. A robust reinforcement of meaning-making concerning one's work can act as an antidote to psychological stress following a critical incident. Equally, cynicism can also become the relatedness breeding ground for pessimism and discontent in an adverse peer environment, leaving one without support and direction when needed.

Beneficence

Many employees experience fulfilment due to caring for others or a sense of giving back to society. This is often one reason for seeking these careers, describing rewards beyond that of a financial nature. These employees believe that they have talents, skills and abilities suited to work and that feedback from peers, clients and managers reinforces this belief. These examples lead to the perception that these positions provide one with the opportunity to help others and make the world in which we live a better place. When this gets reinforced by individuals, management, media, and society at large, a continued sense of beneficence can be experienced internally (Rosso et al., 2010). However, when employees start to become cynical and instil beliefs that they work in a thankless job, they will never make a difference; or, they are no longer capable of performing the job effectively in which beneficence is lost.

Meaning-Making Is Part of Posttraumatic Growth

Posttraumatic growth has gained traction in the past decades challenging common perceptions that all individuals exposed to trauma will be left to struggle with negative consequences. Researchers focused on posttraumatic growth have found that some individuals can show growth and strength following traumatic incidents while others struggle. In examining ambulance paramedics in Australia, Shakespeare-Finch et al. (2003) found that growth occurred for many paramedics following a traumatic event. In this research, the positive change rate was far more frequent than negative posttraumatic changes scored on the Posttraumatic Growth Inventory. A sense of meaningfulness or a reinforced belief that one's work is valuable and worth doing appears to have a direct positive growth experience for the person doing the work (Martela & Pessi, 2018).

Calhoun and Tedeschi (1999) describe posttraumatic growth as a positive change experience that emerges from struggling with a traumatic event. The authors clarify that progress does not negate the struggle and loss associated with trauma, but a traumatic experience can lead to meaning-making and growth. This alternative provides hope and opportunity to see a positive outcome while one attempts to move forward and cope. Overall the authors determined that individuals report development in "three major domains: change in relationships with others, change in the sense of self, and change in philosophy of life" (p. 11). When one considers the experience of front line workers exposed to traumatic events daily, as part of one's duties, autonomy, competence, relatedness, and beneficence emerge as themes that are effortlessly related to the three major domains linked posttraumatic growth.

Associated with the concept of posttraumatic growth, but specific to the importance of resilience is vicarious resilience (VR). VR is described in the literature by Hernández et al. (2007) as a new concept for consideration that suggests those who work with trauma survivors can experience a positive effect as a result of witnessing the resilience of those they assist. Building on the concept of VT, the authors propose that helpers can be vicariously impacted positively through observing a survivor's strength. They discuss a list of elements that contribute to a sense of empowerment, including bearing witness to client stories, observing healing, and incorporating spirituality. Similar to posttraumatic growth, VR offers another opportunity for processing meaning-making that emphasizes resilience. Understanding that one can become more resilient due to seeing the resilience in those who have experienced a horrific event suggests growth and strength. VR is another essential concept to consider when assisting front line workers to become reacquainted with one's sense of purpose and competence, as reinforcing factors for professional growth and stability.

**Implications for Social Work: Assessment,
Intervention, and Evaluation**

Social workers are one of the key providers of community mental health services (Bell, 1995). Social work services often range to include individual, couple, family, group, and organizational development. Therefore, it is probable that social workers frequently offer support and intervention to front line employees, particularly at the micro and mezzo levels of engagement. Social workers use system concepts to understand the importance of an individual's environment, of which work plays a significant part. When employees struggle with the psychological effects of unresolved critical exposure to the degree that it permeates one's professional and home life, it is central to incorporate the conversation concerning phenomenological and spiritual challenges as part of a holistic approach. Clark (2006) offers a practice model that creates space for understanding that allows for spiritual and culturally sensitive social work. Focusing on meaning within one's lived experience provides the opportunity to interpret one's place in the world. Therefore, questions concerning meaning and purpose regarding one's work are essential complements to the more commonly assessed categories of psychological and physiological changes in efforts to promote posttraumatic growth.

Cadell et al. (2003) argue that it is essential that all helping professionals understand the importance of posttraumatic growth so that they can facilitate it, noting that spirituality plays a role in its formation. According to Martela and Riekki (2018), the focus on meaningful work and clarifying one's calling has increased in counselling psychology. As part of the bio-psycho-social assessment, spirituality is an equally important component given front line workers' exposure to traumatic incidents. As trauma-informed counsellors, social workers can help explore meaning and purpose as part of the recovery process.

Assessment

The importance of a social work assessment for front line workers concerning their exposure to traumatic events is part of a trauma-informed practice. Regardless of the presenting issues, questions concerning one's work and the impact of trauma exposure on meaning exploration are paramount. Attention to shifts or cynicism regarding autonomy, competence, relatedness, and beneficence are essential considerations. Assessment questions in these areas link to the three major domains concerning posttraumatic growth. By carefully posing open-ended reflection questions, clients can become aware of how ongoing exposure has challenged or reinforced their sense of purpose and calling.

Intervention

Closely connected to the assessment exploration is a social workers' opportunity to explore the client's strengths regarding her/his autonomy, competence, relatedness, and beneficence. Inventions should provide for reflection concerning what called the individual to this particular type of work. Questions that encourage discussion about positive experiences, personal and professional gains can promote self-leadership competence, offering a sense of autonomy. Exploring one's prior and existing skill sets can allow employees to remember what she/he brings to one's job. Questions that reflect how these skills are noted and appreciated by one's peers can reinforce one's perspective of competence and relatedness when this has been doubted. Discussions concerning an employee's particular skills and how did she/he believe that she/he was making a difference for the people they served offers an opportunity for reflection and reinforcement of beneficence. Education, support, and phenomenological exploration are vital intervention strategies that can equip the front line employee with a deeper understanding of how one's meaning and purpose are compromised and what may be necessary for rebuilding this sense of purpose.

Education intervention at a group level could also offer substantial benefit when organizations approach social workers to address morale or cynicism issues, particularly following a series of calls that involved critical incident exposure of various kinds. While typical education and support sessions include attention to physiological, psychological, and behavioural symptoms, including spiritual symptoms, it provides a holistic approach that addresses pessimism and spiritual decay. Introduction to spirituality in the workplace presents an often-neglected perspective that is vital to promote posttraumatic growth for the individual and one's peer community.

Evaluation

Identified growth in the areas of autonomy, competence, relatedness, and beneficence are central considerations for evaluation. When an employee can recount one's reason for pursuing front line work, identify strengths and abilities that reinforce a sense of competence, and believe that one is making a difference in the work that one does, posttraumatic growth is evident. Employee peers who can recount encouragement and reinforcement experiences demonstrate significant workplace relatedness, establishing a posttraumatic work culture.

Conclusion

Social workers will inevitably offer services to individuals who experience traumatic events through front line service delivery. Appreciating the importance of spirituality in the context of meaning-making of one's vocation is vital for opening up a dialogue that explores the impact of critical incident exposure beyond psychological and behavioural implications. Attending to psychological stressors and injuries must include spiritual assessment and interventions as underpinning concepts for posttraumatic growth.

REFERENCES

Adams, B.D., Davis, S.A., Brown, A., Filardo, E., & Thomson, M.H. (2013). *Posttraumatic stress disorder (PTSD) in emergency responders scoping study: Literature review.* Human Systems Incorporated. http://www.emscc.ca /docs/postings/PTSD/PublishedBibliography.pdf

Alexander, D.A., & Klein, S. (2001). Ambulance personnel and critical incidents: Impact of accident and emergency work on mental health and emotional well-being. *The British Journal of Psychiatry, 178*(1), 76–81. https://doi.org/10.1192/bjp.178.1.76. Medline: 11136215

American Psychiatric Association. (2013). *Diagnostic and statistical manual of mental disorders* (5th ed.).

Anderson, D.G. (2000). Coping strategies and burnout among veteran child protection workers. *Child Abuse & Neglect, 24*(6), 839–48. https://doi.org/10.1016/s0145-2134(00)00143-5

Avraham, N., Goldblatt, H., & Yafe, E. (2014). Paramedics' experiences and coping strategies when encountering critical incidents. *Qualitative Health Research, Vol. 24*(2), 194–208. https://doi.org/10.1177/1049732313519867. Medline: 24495988

Bell, J.L. (1995). Traumatic event debriefing: Service delivery designs and the role of social work. *Social Work, 40*(1), 36–43. https://doi.org/10.1093/sw/40.1.36

Briere, J. & Scott, C. (2015). *Principles of trauma therapy: A guide to symptoms, evaluation, and treatment* (2nd ed.). Sage Publications.

Cacciatore, J., Carlson, B., Michaelis, E., Klimek, B., & Steffan, S. (2011). Crisis intervention by social workers in fire departments: An innovative role for social workers. *Social Work, 56*(1), 81–8. https://doi.org/10.1093/sw/56.1.81. Medline: 21314074

Cadell, S., Regehr, C., & Hemsworth, D. (2003). Factors contributing to posttraumatic growth: A proposed structural equation model. *American Journal of Orthopsychiatry, 73*(3), 279–87. https://doi.org/10.1037/0002-9432.73.3.279. Medline: 12921208

Calhoun, L.G., & Tedeschi, R.G. (1999). *Facilitating posttraumatic growth: A clinician's guide* (I.B. Weiner, Ed.). Lawrence Erlbaum Associates.

Choi, G.Y. (2011). Organizational impacts on the secondary traumatic stress of social workers assisting family violence or sexual assault survivors. *Administration in Social Work, 35*(3), 225–42. https://doi.org/10.1080/03643107.2011.575333

Clark, J.L. (2006). Listening for meaning: A research-based model for attending to spirituality, culture and worldview in social work practice. *Critical Social Work, 7*(1), 1–25. https://ojs.uwindsor.ca/index.php/csw/article/download/5771/4710 https://doi.org/10.22329/csw.v7i1.5771

Conrad, D., & Kellar-Guenther, Y. (2006). Compassion fatigue, burnout, and compassion satisfaction among Colorado child protection workers. *Child Abuse & Neglect, 30*(10), 1071–80. https://doi.org/10.1016/j.chiabu.2006.03.009. Medline: 17014908

Figley, C. (1995). Compassion fatigue: Towards a new understanding of the cost of caring. In B.H. Stamm (Ed.), *Secondary traumatic stress: Self-care issues for clinicians, researchers, and educators* (pp. 3–28). The Sidran Press.

Geisler, M., Berthelsen, H., & Hakanen, J.J. (2019). No job demand is an island – Interaction effects between emotional demands and other types of job demands. *Frontiers in Psychology, 10.* https://doi.org/10.3389/fpsyg.2019.00873. Medline: 31057472

Halpern, J., Gurevich, M., Schwartz, B., & Brazeau, P. (2009). What makes an incident critical for ambulance workers? Emotional outcomes and implications for intervention. *Work & Stress, 23*(2), 173–89. https://doi.org/10.1080/02678370903057317

Hernández, P., Gangsei, D., & Engstrom, D. (2007). Vicarious resilience: A new concept in work with those who survive trauma. *Family Process, 46*(2), 229–41. https://doi.org/10.1111/j.1545-5300.2007.00206.x. Medline: 17593887

Huggard, P., Law, J., & Newcombe, D. (2017). A systematic review exploring the presence of vicarious trauma, compassion fatigue, and secondary traumatic stress in alcohol and other drug clinicians. *Australasian Journal of Disaster and Trauma Studies, 21*(2), 65–72.

Kessell, E.R., Alvidrez, J., McConnell, W.A. & Shumway, M. (2009). Effect of racial and ethnic composition of neighborhoods in San Francisco on rates of mental health-related 911 calls. *Psychiatric Services, 60*(10), 1376–8. https://doi.org/10.1176/ps.2009.60.10.1376. Medline: 19797379

Martela, F. & Pessi, A.B. (2018). Significant work is about self-realization and broader purpose: Defining the key dimensions of meaningful work. *Frontiers in Psychology, 9.* https://doi.org/10.3389/fpsyg.2018.00363. Medline: 29632502

Martela, F., & Riekki, T.J.J. (2018). Autonomy, competence, relatedness and beneficence: A four multicultural comparison of the four pathways to meaningful work. *Frontiers in Psychology, 9*, 1–14. https://doi.org/10.3389/fpsyg.2018.01157. Medline: 30042710

McCann, I.L., & Pearlman, L.A. (1990). Vicarious traumatization: A framework for understanding the psychological effects of working with victims. *Journal of Traumatic Stress, 3*, 131–49. https://doi.org/10.1007/bf00975140

Mitchell, J.T. (1983). When disaster strikes: The critical incident stress debriefing process. *Journal of Emergency Medical Services, 8*(1), 36–9.

Park, C.L., & Ai, A.L. (2006). Meaning making and growth: New directions for research on survivors of trauma. *Journal of Loss and Trauma, 11*(5), 389–407. https://doi.org/10.1080/15325020600685295

Randall, C., & Buys, N. (2013). Managing occupational stress injury in police services: A literature review. *International Public Health Journal, 5*(4), 413–25.

Regehr, C., Goldberg, G., & Hughes, J. (2002). Exposure to human tragedy, empathy, and trauma in ambulance paramedics. *American Journal of Orthopsychiatry, 72*(4), 505–13. https://doi.org/10.1037/0002-9432.72.4.505. Medline:15792036

Regehr, C., Hemsworth, D., Leslie, B., Howe, P., & Chau, S. (2004). Predictors of posttraumatic distress in child welfare workers: A linear structural equation model. *Children and Youth Services Review, 26*(4), 331–46. https://doi.org/10.1016/j.childyouth.2004.02.003

Rosso, B.D., Dekas, K.H., & Wrzensniewski, A. (2010). On the meaning of work: A theoretical integration and review. *Research in Organizational Behavior, 30*, 91–127. https://doi.org/10.1016/j.riob.2010.09.001

Shakespeare-Finch, J. (2011). Primary and secondary trauma in emergency personnel. *Traumatology: An International Journal, 17*(4), 1–2. https://doi.org/10.1177/1534765611431834

Shakespeare-Finch, J.E., Smith, S.G., Gow, K.M., Embelton, G., & Baird, L. (2003). The prevalence of posttraumatic growth in emergency ambulance personnel. *Traumatology, 9*(1), 58–71. https://doi.org/10.1528/trau.9.1.58.21634

van Dorssen-Boog, P., de Jong, J., Veld, M., & Van Vuuren, T. (2020). Self-leadership among healthcare workers: A mediator for the effects of job autonomy on work engagement and health. *Frontiers in Psychology*, 11. https://doi.org/10.3389/fpsyg.2020.01420. Medline: 32765341

Wrzesniewski, A., Dutton, J.E., & Debebe, G. (2003). Interpersonal sensemaking and the meaning of work. *Research in Organizational Behavior, 25*, 93–135. https://doi.org/10.1016/s0191-3085(03)25003-6

Wrzesniewski, A., McCauley, C., Rozin, P., & Schwartz, B. (1997). Jobs, careers, and callings: People's relations to their work. *Journal of Research in Personality, 31*(1), 21–33. https://doi.org/10.1006/jrpe.1997.2162

6 Grief and Loss: A Shifting Landscape

SUSAN CADELL

Introduction

There is a popular song that says "Love is all around us." I agree. And I add that grief is all around us. Love and grief are inextricably linked. "Grief is the price we pay for love and we must all be prepared to pay it" (Parkes, 2015, p. 3). Growth can also be part of what is around us while spirituality can be an important facet of the process.

I learned nothing about grief in my own social work studies. Now I spend a great deal of time thinking about grief. I think about it personally and professionally. I think about it when caring for aging parents. I think about it when friends and family die. I think about it professionally when I work with those who are grieving or do research on the subject. When I teach about death, dying and grief, I often hear from students that they are learning about it for the first time.

The focus of this chapter is on expanding the knowledge base of social workers about grief and how that can, but does not necessarily, include growth, trauma, and spirituality. I begin with the premise that everyone dies and that each human will experience the death of someone (or of many people) that they care for or about. Some may say that we live in a death-denying culture; I agree with Macdonald (2020) that we live in a grief-denying society. Social workers and social work education are located in that society. Little or no education on grief is provided to social workers in training (Stein et al., 2019; Thieleman & Cacciatore, 2019). At the same time, growth can occur in grief and in other difficult circumstances. Spirituality can be an important part of the process of growth. I continue this chapter with examples of growth in caregiving and grief gathered from years of research and conclude with discussing how the landscape of grief is shifting.

First some definitions will provide context. Grief occurs as the result of loss; this can happen after any kind of loss, not just death. There are those that differentiate between bereavement and grief. There are languages in which there is only one word while in English we have more than one. I use them interchangeably because I believe that most people outside the specialized field of thanatology, the study of death, dying and bereavement, do not make that differentiation. Posttraumatic growth, or simply growth, can occur in the face of stressful circumstances. Despite the name, it does not need to be after a trauma. Tedeschi and Calhoun (2004, p. 4) define it as "a change in people that goes beyond an ability to resist and not be damaged by highly stressful circumstances; it involves a movement beyond pre-trauma levels of adaptation … It has a quality of transformation, or a qualitative change in functioning." It is not the difficult event that encourages growth; it is the struggle after the event that can lead to such growth (Tedeschi & Calhoun, 1995). Spirituality has many definitions. The one that inspires me is Hardy's (1982, p. 154), who describes it as "that attitude, that frame of mind which breaks the human person out of the isolating self. As it does that, it directs him or her to another in relationship to whom one's growth takes root and sustenance."

Grief Theory

There are a lot of myths and misconceptions about grief. One of the pioneers in the field, Elisabeth Kübler-Ross (1970), proposed five aspects of experience that dying people underwent. Somehow this idea transformed into the five stages of grief that apply not to those who are dying but to those who are left behind when someone dies: the bereaved. Simplistic and outdated notions based on this model are described in fiction and perpetuated by popular culture as well as by health professionals (Breen, 2011; Breen et al., 2013, 2014). This idea also persists in social work textbooks and beyond (Corr, 2018, 2019). Our understanding of grief has shifted dramatically over the past several decades.

Theorists in this field now work from far more complex and sophisticated models. For instance, Rubin's (1999) two-track model of bereavement considers one track of function and the other of relationship to the deceased. Both tracks have positive and negative aspects. Stroebe et al.'s (2005) oscillation model offers an illustration of how grievers may oscillate or vary wildly from restoration orientation to loss orientation in their coping. Both these theories acknowledge the complexity of the experience of grief.

The theory of continuing bonds (Klass et al., 2014; Klass & Steffen, 2017) revolutionized the scholarly view of grief in two ways. It moved away from the pathological view that sees grief work as needing to focus on severing ties with the person who died to one that recognizes that healthy grieving involves the establishment of a new kind of relationship with the deceased person. It also firmly challenged the notion of stages of grief. Michael White had been advocating for a similar approach years before in inviting clients in therapy to greet and speak to the person who died (Furlong, 2008; White, 1988).

Klass (2014, p. 11) wrote: "Continuing bonds ... are the relationship that individuals, communities, and cultures maintain with those who have died." Klass (2014) has done extensive work with bereaved parents and has written about rituals for these parents: "The parents are all too aware ... that their experiences of their children's continuing presence lack social acceptance. Rituals play an important role in affirming that the parents' bonds with the dead children are a social reality, not just an internal reality" (p. 13). Klass (2014) contests the notion that grief is solely an individual psychological experience as it is often defined to be (Granek, 2010). Klass (2014) defines grief as intersubjective experience that includes the social. This includes the seeking of connection to others as consolation to the experience of grief. The seeking of connection is part of the definition of spirituality (Hardy, 1982). Both Rubin (1999) and Stroebe et al. (2005) acknowledge the ongoing relationship in their respective models.

A recent addition to our understanding of grief is the public health model of bereavement support. The model arises out of the palliative care context in Australia. The authors proposed "that all bereaved people should have access to information about bereavement and relevant local supports" (Breen et al., 2017, p. 275). They hypothesized that for the majority of people (about 60 per cent), their friends, families, and communities would be sufficient support when grieving. A smaller proportion of bereaved people, about 30 per cent, could benefit from more formal opportunities for support, while only 10 per cent of bereaved people would be in need of specialist intervention. They then tested their theory with 678 bereaved people by measuring the risk of complicated grief (Aoun et al., 2015). The proportions of risk for complicated grief were strikingly similar to the hypothesis: 58.4 per cent at low risk, 35.2 per cent at moderate, and 6.4 per cent at high risk of complicated grief. It is important to note that 100 per cent of people would benefit from an increased capacity in their friends, families, and communities to support them when they are grieving.

Our understanding of grief has changed and expanded over time. Kübler-Ross (1970) did a great service by allowing us as a society to be more open to talking about death and dying. However, the ongoing legacy of five stages oversimplifies the experience of grief. It remains one of the myths that needs challenging. The death positive movement, championed by YouTube's "Ask a Mortician" personality, Caitlin Doughty, and including death cafés (deathcafe.com), has allowed some to be even more open.

The public health framework and the compassionate communities' movement contribute to these changes by urging us to consider the care of our most vulnerable to be the duty of communities, not just institutions (Aoun et al., 2018; Kellehear, 1999). Rumbold (2017, p. 76), in reflecting on spirituality in palliative care, says it well: "Fundamentally, public health reminds us that health is created in communities in all aspects of their life together, not something delivered by experts to the community." However, few of these undertakings include grief beyond mentioning the word (Breen et al., 2020). We would benefit as a society by becoming more grief literate, not just death literate.

Posttraumatic Growth

As social workers, many of us have not been prepared to assess strengths and anticipate the possibility of growth, especially in circumstances that include life-limiting illness, caregiving and/or grief. Saleebey's (2006) strengths perspective in social work played a pivotal part in my professional life by undergirding that people have the possibility within them of experiencing positive change.

When I undertook PhD studies, I knew that I wanted to do something related to HIV/AIDS. I came to study positive aspects and posttraumatic growth in bereaved HIV carers. I was very inspired by the work of Susan Folkman. She had worked on an important model of stress and coping (Lazarus & Folkman, 1984) earlier in her career. Folkman headed up a ground-breaking longitudinal study of HIV caregiving and bereavement in San Francisco in which the original questions did not involve any positive aspects. It was the HIV carer participants who suggested that the researchers were missing out; questions were added about positive aspects of their lives (Folkman et al., 1997). As a result, Folkman (1997) reworked the original model of stress and coping to include positive emotions even when there was not a favourable resolution to the stressful event.

I was equally inspired by the work of Richard Tedeschi and Laurence Calhoun, two psychologists who coined the term posttraumatic growth (Tedeschi & Calhoun, 1995; Tedeschi et al., 1998; Calhoun & Tedeschi, 2014). As psychologists, they had done a great deal of work with widows and realized that the theory of the time was not sufficient to explain how these people were changing. The single most important aspect of posttraumatic growth as conceptualized by Tedeschi and Calhoun, in my opinion, is that there is ongoing distress along with growth. While they have changed the models over time, the ongoing positives and negatives are an ongoing feature, one that is shared with Folkman's (1997) revised model as well.

For my PhD, I did a mixed methods study of bereaved HIV carers. In a survey of 174 individuals from all over Canada, I examined factors that allowed for growth in the circumstances. Overall, the bereaved HIV carers did experience growth (Cadell, 2007). The resulting model (Cadell et al., 2003) illustrated that the carers experienced greater growth when they had greater social support, stronger spirituality and increased levels of stress. While the first two findings were expected, the third concerning more stress resulting in greater growth, was unexpected.

The follow-up interviews with 17 people were chosen based on the scores of posttraumatic growth (Cadell & Sullivan, 2006). An effort was made to interview both those with high scores as well as those demonstrating less growth. The most intriguing finding of this mixed methods approach was that those with low scores of growth told many stories of positive aspects of their lives. For instance, one participant had been HIV-positive himself for many years while caring for and grieving many friends (Cadell et al., 2006; Cadell, & Haubrich, 2006). He had renamed the HIV virus into his own personal motto. HIV in French is VIH which for him meant "Vivre Intensément l'Humain" or in English to "Live Humanity Intensely." This man who had been living with HIV for more than 10 years at the time of the interview considered that instead of it being a death sentence, HIV was an opportunity for him to live his life to the fullest. He considered that this interpretation had allowed him to survive and thrive for so long.

In the overall sample of bereaved HIV carers, there were many relationships to the person or people who had died. In studying separately those whose partners had died, we were able to specifically examine how they grieved after the caregiving and the death of the partner (Cadell & Marshall, 2007). In using an inclusion of other into self-model, we demonstrated how seven gay and transgender carers were able to reconstruct themselves, both as individuals and as carers, after the death of the partner. The meaning in the caregiving and the relationship was pivotal to this process. Spirituality, in the sense of connection to others and growth (Hardy, 1982), played an important role for many of the participants. They shared how their struggles moved them to be stronger and to reach out to others in a new way. One of transgender partners commented about her strength: "The process made me stronger. And it has given me an even stronger acceptance for who I am" (Cadell & Marshall, 2007, p. 544). Another participant had changed his own career path in order to manage a scholarship in his partner's name. Another had begun to do presentations in schools. He commented: "I understood that we each have a mission in life ... It has been five years since I have been doing [prevention work] with young people. I know that I am doing good because I save, maybe in a class, 2 lives and that gives me the strength to continue. I could say that it's my breath of life" (p. 544).

Later I led another mixed methods study of caregiving and bereaved parents in the context of paediatric palliative care. We examined factors allowing for growth in that population of parents. The resulting model with 273 caregiving parents in Canada and the United States demonstrates similar results to the HIV carers (Cadell et al., 2014). What is different, however, is that the meaning in caregiving is pivotal to the model (see Figure 6.1). The meaning that the parents make about their experience determines how much growth they experience. This is an important finding in general in terms of posttraumatic growth, but it is particularly exciting for social work. We have a role to play in helping shape how people view their circumstances. Spirituality can be key in meaning-making as well.

In addition, in interviews, parents identified how treacherous their landscapes were in the circumstances (Davies et al., 2012). The sand was shifting below their feet as they were navigating their children's conditions and treatments. This experience of shifting landscapes in caregiving is similar to the grief experience in that aspects change constantly.

Recently in Canada a new legislation allows for death with medical assistance (Health Canada, 2019). This has shifted the landscape of death and dying and may have an impact on grief. Little is known about the grief experience after an assisted death, even in jurisdictions where it has existed for decades (Andriessen et al., 2019). However, with that little evidence exists, there is no indication that grief is adversely affected after an assisted death. Stigma and silence may complicate grief but the assistance itself does not seem to. There is a need for further research in this area.

Figure 6.1. Model of posttraumatic growth

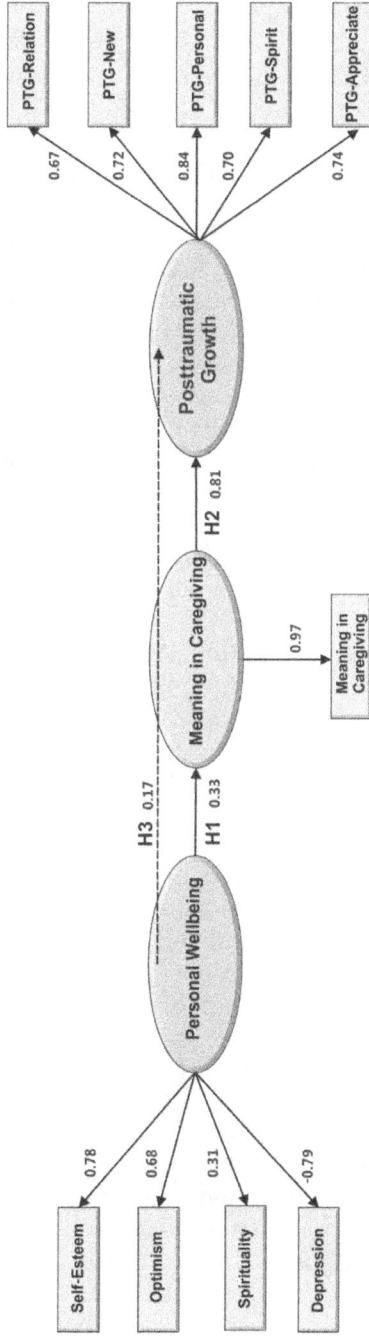

Abbreviations: PTGI NP: Posttraumatic Growth Inventory New Possibilities; PTGI RO: Relating to Others; PTGI PS: Personal Strength; PTGI AL: Appreciation of Life; PTGI SC: Spiritual Change.

Copyright © 2014, Global Alliance for Behavioral Health and Social Justice. Reproduced with permission. Cadell, Hemsworth, Smit Quosai, Steele, Davies, Liben, Straatman, & Siden, 2014, p. 126

Conclusion

Thieleman and Cacciatore (2019) observed: "It is vital that social workers do not react to clients' expressions of grief after the death of a loved
one in an avoidant or dismissive way and instead maintain a steady,
empathic presence for their clients' wellbeing. This is especially important when dealing with traumatic bereavement" (p. 472). I support this
statement with one caveat and would like to expand upon it. While I
began this chapter with the notion that love is all around us and that
grief is the price that we pay for love, I avoid the use of the term "loved
one." As social workers, we should be well aware of the complexities
of human relationships, especially those in a family. We should never
assume that because an individual is caring or has cared for someone
and/or is grieving that person's death, that the person was loved.
Like the presence of ongoing distress in growth, it is important not
to oversimplify love. There are many reasons for providing care and
experiencing grief. The term "loved one" is easily replaced by using
the individual's name or naming the relationship. That way we avoid
assumptions and respect all reasons for caring and grieving that may
not involve love.

In addition, I build on the above statement to say that it is true of
all humans interacting with grieving individuals that we not avoid or
dismiss grief. Everyone can benefit if individuals of all ages, families,
communities, and societies were more grief literate and better able to
support one another. We are making progress in acknowledging that
death is a part of life, but we have a way to go in making sure that we
are comfortable with acknowledging grief and the grievers in our midst.

In this shifting landscape of new awareness of death and dying as
well as new approaches to it, I urge us all as human beings and social
workers to increase our own individual and our collective knowledge
about grief and develop our own and others' grief literacy. One possible avenue for exploring grief, spirituality, growth and meaning is
to inquire about people's tattoos, either planned (Eschler et al., 2018)
or existing (Cadell et al., 2020). Tattoos that honour someone who has
died are an expression of continuing bonds that challenge the stigma of
both grief and tattoos. As social workers, we can discover much about
peoples' narratives by asking about tattoos.

Saleebey's (2006) work shifted my own understanding of social work
by giving me language to articulate the focus on strengths that I thought
was missing. The work in the positive aspect of stress and coping (Folkman, 1997) and posttraumatic growth (Tedeschi & Calhoun, 2004) further expanded my own views and that of many others. Similar to those

paradigms shifts, I particularly want social work to contribute to further shifting the landscape so that our societies are more grief aware and prepared to support one another.

REFERENCES

Andriessen, K., Krysinska, K., Dransart, D.A.C., Dargis, L., & Mishara, B.L. (2019). Grief after euthanasia and physician-assisted suicide: A systematic review. *Crisis*, *41*, 255–72. https://doi.org/10.1027/0227-5910/a000630. Medline: 31657640

Aoun, S.M., Breen, L.J., Howting, D.A., Rumbold, B., McNamara, B., & Hegney, D. (2015). Who needs bereavement support? A population based survey of bereavement risk and support need. *PloS one*, *10*(3), e0121101. https://doi.org/10.1371/journal.pone.0121101. Medline: 25811912

Aoun, S.M., Breen, L.J., White, I., Rumbold, B., & Kellehear, A. (2018). What sources of bereavement support are perceived helpful by bereaved people and why? Empirical evidence for the compassionate communities approach. *Palliative Medicine*, *32*(8), 1378–88. https://doi.org/10.1177/0269216318774995. Medline: 29754514

Breen, L.J. (2011). Professionals' experiences of grief counseling: Implications for bridging the gap between research and practice. *OMEGA: Journal of Death and Dying*, *62*(3), 285–303. https://doi.org/10.2190/om.62.3.e. Medline: 21495536

Breen, L.J., Aoun, S.M., Rumbold, B., McNamara, B., Howting, D.A., & Mancini, V. (2017). Building community capacity in bereavement support: Lessons learnt from bereaved caregivers. *American Journal of Hospice and Palliative Medicine*, *34*(3), 275–81. https://doi.org/10.1177/1049909115615568. Medline: 26566928

Breen, L.J., Fernandez, M., O'Connor, M., & Pember, A.J. (2013). The preparation of graduate health professionals for working with bereaved clients: An Australian perspective. *OMEGA: Journal of Death and Dying*, *66*(4), 313–32. https://doi.org/10.2190/om.66.4.c. Medline: 23785983

Breen, L.J., Kawashima, D., Joy, K., Cadell, S., Roth, D., Chow, A., & Macdonald, M.E. (2020). Grief literacy: A call to action for compassionate communities. *Death Studies*. https://doi.org/10.1080/07481187.2020.1739780

Breen, L.J., O'Connor, M., Hewitt, L.Y., & Lobb, E.A. (2014). The "specter" of cancer: Exploring secondary trauma for health professionals providing cancer support and counseling. *Psychological Services*, *11*(1), 60–7. https://doi.org/10.1037/a0034451. Medline: 24079353

Cadell, S. (2007). The sun always comes out after it rains: Understanding posttraumatic growth in HIV caregivers. *Health & Social Work*, *32*(3), 169–76. https://doi.org/10.1093/hsw/32.3.169. Medline: 17896673

Cadell, S., & Haubrich, D. (2006). Vivre intensément l'humain: Une exploration du deuil après le VIH-sida. *Reflets: Revue ontaroise d'intervention sociale et communautaire, 12*(1), 127–43. https://doi.org/10.7202/013441ar

Cadell, S., Hemsworth, D., Smit Quosai, T., Steele, R., Davies, E., Liben, S., Straatman, L., & Siden, H. (2014). Posttraumatic growth in parents caring for a child with a life-limiting illness: A structural equation model. *American Journal of Orthopsychiatry, 84*(2), 123–33. https://doi.org/10.1037/h0099384. Medline: 24826928

Cadell, S., Janzen, L. & Haubrich, D.J. (2006). Engaging with spirituality: A qualitative study of grief and HIV/AIDS. *Critical Social Work, 7*(1), 27–43. https://doi.org/10.22329/csw.v7i1.5770

Cadell, S., Lambert, M.R., Davidson, D., Greco, C., & Macdonald, M.E. (2020). Memorial tattoos: Advancing continuing bonds theory. *Death Studies*, 1–8. https://doi.org/10.1080/07481187.2020.1716888. Medline: 31994454

Cadell, S., & Marshall, S. (2007). The (re)construction of self after the death of a partner to HIV/AIDS. *Death Studies, 31*(6), 537–48. https://doi.org/10.1080/07481180701356886. Medline: 17726828

Cadell, S., Regehr, C. & Hemsworth, D. (2003). Factors contributing to posttraumatic growth: A proposed structural equation model. *American Journal of Orthopsychiatry, 73*(3), 79–287. https://doi.org/10.1037/0002-9432.73.3.279. Medline: 12921208

Cadell, S., & Sullivan, R. (2006). Posttraumatic growth in bereaved HIV caregivers: Where does it start and when does it end? *Traumatology, 12*(1), 45–59. https://doi.org/10.1177/153476560601200104

Calhoun, L.G., & Tedeschi, R.G. (Eds.). (2014). *Handbook of posttraumatic growth: Research and practice*. Routledge.

Corr, C.A. (2018). Elisabeth Kübler-Ross and the "five stages" model in a sampling of recent American textbooks. *OMEGA: Journal of Death and Dying, 82*(2), 294–322. https://doi.org/10.1177/0030222818809766. Medline: 30439302

– (2019). Elisabeth Kübler-Ross and the "five stages" model in a sampling of recent textbooks published in 10 countries outside the United States. *OMEGA: Journal of Death and Dying.* https://doi.org/10.1177/0030222819840476. Medline: 30975028

Davies, B., Cadell, S., Steele, R., & Liben, S. (2012, 9–12 October). *Shifting sands: Personal growth in parents of children with chronic, complex, life-limiting conditions* [Conference session]. The 19th International Congress on Palliative Care, Montreal, Quebec, Canada.

Eschler, J., Bhattacharya, A., & Pratt, W. (2018). Designing a reclamation of body and health: Cancer survivor tattoos as coping ritual. In *Proceedings of the 2018 CHI conference on human factors in computing systems* (pp. 1–12). Association for Computing Machinery. https://doi.org/10.1145/3173574.3174084

Folkman, S. (1997). Positive psychological states and coping with severe stress. *Social Science & Medicine, 45*(8), 1207–21. https://doi.org/10.1016/s0277 -9536(97)00040-3

Folkman, S., Moskowitz, J.T., Ozer, E.M., & Park, C.L. (1997). Positive meaningful events and coping in the context of HIV/AIDS. In B.H. Gottlieb (Ed.), *Coping with chronic stress* (pp. 293–314). Springer. https://doi.org/10.1007/978-1-4757 -9862-3_11

Furlong, M. (2008). The multiple relationships between the discipline of social work and the contributions of Michael White. *Australian Social Work, 61*(4), 403–20. https://doi.org/10.1080/03124070802428530

Granek, L. (2010). Grief as pathology: The evolution of grief theory in psychology from Freud to the present. *History of Psychology, 13*(1), 46–73. https://doi.org/10.1037/a0016991. Medline: 20499613

Hardy, R.P. (1982). Christian spirituality today: Notes on its meaning. *Spiritual Life, 28*, 151–9.

Health Canada. (2019). *Fourth interim report on medical assistance in dying in Canada*. https://www.canada.ca/content/dam/hc-sc/documents/services /publications/health-system-services/medical-assistance-dying-interim -report-april-2019/medical-assistance-dying-interim-report-april-2019-eng.pdf

Kellehear, A. (1999). *Health promoting palliative care*. Oxford University Press.

Klass, D. (2014). Grief, consolation, and religions: A conceptual framework. *OMEGA: Journal of Death and Dying, 69*(1), 1–18. https://doi.org/10.2190 /om.69.1.a. Medline: 25084706

Klass, D., Silverman, P.R., & Nickman, S.L. (Eds.). (2014). *Continuing bonds: New understandings of grief*. Taylor & Francis.

Klass, D., & Steffen, E.M. (Eds.). (2017). *Continuing bonds in bereavement: New directions for research and practice*. Routledge.

Kübler-Ross, E. (1970). *On death and dying*. Tavistock.

Lazarus, R.S., & Folkman, S. (1984). *Stress, appraisal, and coping*. Springer Publishing Company.

Macdonald, M.E. (2020). The denial of grief: Reflections from a decade of anthropological research on parental bereavement and child death. In M.H. Jacobsen & A. Petersen (Eds.), *Exploring grief: Towards a sociology of sorrow* (pp. 125–49). Routledge.

Parkes, C.M. (2015). *The price of love: The selected works of Colin Murray Parkes*. Routledge.

Rubin, S.S. (1999). The two-track model of bereavement: Overview, retrospect, and prospect. *Death studies, 23*(8), 681–714. https://doi.org/10.1080 /074811899200731. Medline: 10848088

Rumbold, B. (2017). Spirituality in palliative care. In L. Béres (Ed.), *Practising spirituality: Meaning-making in personal and professional contexts* (pp. 165–80). Palgrave MacMillan.

Saleebey, D. (2006). *The strengths perspective in social work practice*. Pearson.

Stein, G.L., Berkman, C., & Pollak, B. (2019). What are social work students being taught about palliative care? *Palliative & Supportive Care, 17*(5), 536–41. https://doi.org/10.1017/s1478951518001049. Medline: 30714548

Stroebe, M., Schut, H., & Stroebe, W. (2005). Attachment in coping with bereavement: A theoretical integration. *Review of General Psychology, 9*(1), 48–66. https://doi.org/10.1037/1089-2680.9.1.48

Tedeschi, R.G., & Calhoun, L.G. (1995). *Trauma and transformation: Growing in the aftermath of suffering*. Sage Publications.

– (2004). Posttraumatic growth: Conceptual foundations and empirical evidence. *Psychological Inquiry, 15*(1), 1–18. https://doi.org/10.1207/s15327965pli1501_01

Tedeschi, R.G., Park, C.L., & Calhoun, L.G. (Eds.). (1998). *Posttraumatic growth: Positive changes in the aftermath of crisis*. Routledge.

Thieleman, K., & Cacciatore, J. (2019). 'Experiencing life for the first time': The effects of a traumatic death course on social work student mindfulness and empathy. *Social Work Education, 38*(4), 470–84. https://doi.org/10.1080/02615479.2018.1548588

White, M. (1988). Saying hullo again: The incorporation of the lost relationship in the resolution of grief. *Dulwich Centre Newsletter, 3*, 29–36.

7 The Soulful Journey: A Spiritual-Based Group for Treatment

SHELLEY POLUCHOWICZ AND HEATHER BOYNTON

Introduction

The integration of spirituality in mental health treatments is becoming more prevalent as it is recognized as a strength, support, and resource, an aspect of resilience, and it can facilitate and contribute to psycho-spiritual transformation and posttraumatic growth (PTG). In many regions in Canada, the mental health system is taxed with an increasingly high demand for service which has resulted in extensive waitlists and ultimately the denial of timely access to vital services for those in need. This has created a trend towards group therapies as an avenue to meet these demands. Group therapy offers an opportunity to build capacity for self-management and self-determination, and the inclusion of spirituality offers individuals a greater focus on connection, meaning and purpose. The psychosocial rehabilitation model principles and the cardinal values of social work include the individual's right to access resources that serve to strengthen their capacity to grow and develop. Spirituality as an avenue for PTG can be easily infused and creatively employed in group therapy.

This chapter will discuss a spirituality-based treatment group, the Soulful Journey, for individuals experiencing severe mental health struggles, complex grief, and trauma, along with participant evaluations of the group. A brief review of the literature regarding the definition of spirituality, the impact of spirituality on recovery and well-being, and group work are highlighted. A program evaluation of the ten-week group was conducted with quantitative and qualitative measures, however this chapter will focus on the qualitative inquiry aspects. Finally, the implications for social work and considerations for practice are discussed.

The Soulful Journey Group was originally developed by a spiritual care associate, an occupational therapist, and a manager (social worker, and one of the authors) in an outpatient mental health program in Northwestern Ontario. The group employed an integrative spiritual approach informed and grounded in existential and transpersonal theories and several widely utilized therapeutic modalities such as integrative therapy, relational self-psychology, solution-focused brief therapy, narrative therapy, acceptance and commitment therapy (ACT), cognitive behavioural therapy (CBT), dialectical behavioural theory (DBT) and family systems therapy. The goal of the Soulful Journey Group was to assist participants in improving the quality of their lives through exploration of meaning, purpose, and connectedness in relationships to self and beyond. Moreover, it provided an avenue for participants to enhance their capacity for discovering their strengths through increased self-talk, and improving the quality of their relationship with themselves, others, and beyond. It assisted with refining emotional regulation, cultivating the ability to reflect and gain insight, strengthening resilience, and fostering self-acceptance and adaptation to daily life challenges. The aspects of PTG outlined by Tedeschi and Calhoun (1996) include appreciation of life, relationships with others, new possibilities in life, personal strength, and spiritual change, and these were embedded throughout the group.

Understanding Spirituality and Recovery

Spirituality is unique and diverse and can be expressed through a variety of approaches. "Spirituality is defined as the experiences and expressions of one's spirit in a unique and dynamic process reflecting faith in god or a supreme being; a connectedness with oneself, others, nature, or God; and an integration of all human dimensions" (Meraviglia, 1999, p. 18). Canda and Furman (2010) purported that "spirituality may be expressed through religious forms or it may be independent of them" (p. 59). Other dimensions of spirituality found in the literature include a unifying life force and integrative energy, a transcendent self, love and belonging, hope, peace, empathy and compassion, gratitude, guidance from a higher power, death concerns and resolution, appreciation of art and beauty, and moral and ethical issues (Galek et al., 2005; McCarroll et al., 2005).

Fisher (2010) developed the Spiritual Health and Life-Orientation Measure (SHALOM) with a person-centred holistic conceptualization and themes of spirituality and religion. Fisher (2010) spoke of spiritual wellness and viewed spirituality within four domains:

> Personal domain: wherein one intra-relates with oneself with regards to meaning, purpose, and values in life. Self-awareness is the driving force or transcendent aspect of the human spirit in its search for identity and self-worth.
>
> Communal domain: as shown in the quality and depth of interpersonal relationships, between self and others, relating to morality, culture, and religion. These are expressed in love, forgiveness, trust, hope and faith in humanity.
>
> Environmental domain: beyond care and nurture for the physical and biological, to a sense of awe and wonder; for some, the notion of unity with the environment.
>
> Transcendent domain: relationship of self with something or some-One beyond the human level (i.e. ultimate concern, cosmic force, transcendent reality, or God). This involves faith towards, adoration and worship of, the source of Mystery of the universe. (p. 107)

Research utilizing these definitions is beginning to demonstrate that inclusion of spirituality in treatment has the potential to significantly influence one's mental health and well-being (Fallot, 2001; Ivtzan et al., 2013; Vis & Boynton, 2008) and facilitate post-traumatic growth.

The psycho-social rehabilitation (PSR) approach to treatment focuses on a client's self-determination with respect to his or her own healing and recovery. Jacobson and Greenley (2001) asserted: "Recovery is not synonymous with cure. Recovery refers to both internal conditions experienced by persons who describe themselves as being in recovery-hope, healing, empowerment, and connection-and external conditions that facilitate recovery-implementation of human rights, a positive cultural healing, and recovery-oriented services" (p. 482).

Although the PSR approach does incorporate diversity, the spiritual domains of an individual's recovery are often not directly addressed. Boynton (2014) argues that the "incorporation of spirituality is seen as a necessary component to treatment" (p. 236). Congruently, one of the core competencies of PSR practice involves integrating physical, psychological, social, cultural and spiritual dimensions in assessing an individual's strengths and needs (PSR/RPS Canada, 2017). Vis and Boynton (2008) asserted that inclusion of spirituality in treatment can promote the reframing of one's thinking, coping ability, and provide a greater awareness of and renewed meaning making and purpose in life. These factors are beneficial in the healing process and contribute to areas of PTG.

Many individuals struggling with mental health, trauma and adversity experience a deepening of and stronger commitment to their spirituality and faith, engage in spiritual coping and spiritual activities, rituals and practices, and experience spiritual growth and development along with improved spiritual well-being and quality of life. Corrigan et al. (2003) found that 90 per cent of 1,783 individuals living with mental illness viewed themselves as either religious or spiritual, lending support to the inclusion of spirituality in treatment. In a cross-cultural study with 728 adults, Peres et al. (2018) found that meaning and peace were the most important aspects of spirituality and religiosity related to better mental health, quality of life, and well-being. Vis and Boynton (2008) espoused that "spirituality is an extension of world view, coping, and meaning making, and is an essential component in healthy posttraumatic processing" (p. 70). They proposed that including spirituality in treatment can lead to spiritual change and PTG where individuals experience renewed or increased personal strengths, appreciation of life and new life priorities, and enhanced intimate relationships.

Spaniol (2002) suggests: "Recovery, as a spiritual path, can be seen as a journey by which people with psychiatric disabilities rebuild and further develop their connectedness to themselves, to others, to their living, learning, and working environments, and to larger meaning and purpose" (p. 322). Research has highlighted connectedness as having a significant importance within the recovery process (Leamy, et al., 2011; Lee, 2014; Slade, 2009; Young, 2015) and moreover belonging and spiritual connection have been identified as important contributors to the development of meaning and purpose in life (Drageset et al., 2017). Tremendous growth can occur when an individual derives meaning in his or her difficult experience and is able to utilize that understanding to restore hope and successfully cope with the challenge with which he or she has been presented.

Steinberg (2010) purported that group work is a best practice for social work and described group work mutual aid as "a process through which people develop collaborative, supportive, and trustworthy relationships, identify and use existing strengths and/or develop new ones, and work together towards individual and or collective psychosocial goals" (p. 54). Social workers aid participants in discovering and employing their inherent strengths, abilities, and capacities towards wellness. In addition to the role social workers may have in facilitating the discovery of personal resiliency, mutual aid groups also possess the inherent capacity, with respect to connections formed among members, to be an instrumental support in the recovery process. Gilbert (2000) purports that "group members form an exponential number of helping relationships in which they can share information, gain mutual support, normalize emotional and behavioural reactions to experiences, participate in problem solving" (p. 77). Mustain and Helminiak (2015) assert that sharing in recovery groups aids participants to feel a sense of connection, normalizes experiences and expands the participants' perceptions through introspection allowing for restructuring to occur. Groups offer clients opportunities to find hope, feel a sense of belonging or connection, obtain support and awareness of commonalities among members, and create opportunities for learning from others as well as the facilitating therapist (Kelly, 2017). Therefore, groups are a method of best practice that enhance support, relationships, strengths, and connectedness, and the inclusion of spirituality would likely further these aspects.

Pargament (2007) suggested that those seeking mental health assistance may view their issues through a spiritual lens despite religious or spiritual issues not being reported as the presenting problem. Vis and Boynton (2008) stated that "spirituality and meaning are not only discovered through private and internal processing, but also through interactive and communal activities" (p. 78). Holistic and client-centred social work group interventions should include spirituality as they offer opportunities for members to "gain a sense of personal, interpersonal, and environmental control over their lives" (Cohen & Graybeal, 2007, p. 44) within a supportive and collaborative nature (Hyde, 2013). Furman et al. (2007) concluded that inclusion of spirituality enhances the client's resources and support base. In addition, Gilbert (2000) asserted that the inclusion of "spiritual content was necessary to work holistically with clients" (p. 78). The incorporation of spirituality must be considered best practice in social work services that are client centred as its immersion has potential to enhance and elicit both internal and external resources that can significantly aid a client in his or her personal recovery.

For the reasons cited above, a spiritually infused group intervention was developed. The implementation of the spiritually based Soulful Journey group was evaluated to determine its efficacy and value of the intervention, as a quality improvement measure, to inform policy development, and for further decision-making. A mixed method approach was employed using both quantitative and qualitative data. Standardized subjective assessments pertaining to spiritual well-being and quality of life were administered and are discussed in another forthcoming publication. Qualitative questions were assessed through a thematic approach. Grinnell et al. (2016) conveyed that the results of evaluation can provide crucial information and transfer of knowledge for the social work profession. Therefore, it is our hope that other social workers can benefit from this evaluation and incorporate spirituality into their treatments and facilitate PTG, and that clients will ultimately benefit from enhanced connectedness, meaning making, and garner a sense of meaning in life events and in their own life purpose.

Methodology

Participants

Six participants experiencing severe mental health challenges related to mood disorders, relational trauma, grief, and loss who were referred to the group were informed of the program evaluation and its purpose of determining program effectiveness and value. All six participants were female and were 55 years and above and provided informed consent to participate.

Overview of the Soulful Journey Group

The Soulful Journey Group was offered for two hours once per week for a total of ten weeks. During the first half of each of the ten sessions, the two facilitators presented psychoeducational, reflective, experiential, spiritual, and relational information exercises, and short videos to the participants. The latter part of each weekly session focused on the here and now and provided participants with the opportunity to reflect upon the three main questions of the sacred whole exercise: (1) What am I present to? (2) What am I struggling with? (3) What am I grateful for? The sacred three questions offered participants the opportunity to identify and process feelings, thoughts, and experiences as well as witness the human condition of each member in the group with an empathic and supportive presence. Finally, closing reflections or inspirational quotes were shared weekly with the group. The facilitators remained cognizant of members and offered a one on one session if support was needed. There was an expectation that participants would be willing to communicate, and appropriately self-disclose during the sessions.

- **Week 1: Introductory Session – Introducing Spirituality.** In the first session, the facilitators reviewed the group framework, principles, topics of focus, objectives, housekeeping items, and confidentiality. Participants introduced themselves and engaged in activities to increase rapport and trust, and to encourage sharing, discussion, openness, compassion, and listening. The construct of spirituality was introduced and explored. Group members participated in self-awareness activities that facilitated the exploration of one's own spirituality by reflecting on spiritual identity, spiritual distresses, and spiritual resources and by reflecting on alternative perspectives and information shared by others.
- **Week 2: Mystery of Life and Connectedness.** The second week focused on the themes of suffering, life challenges, coping, meaning-making, purpose, connection, and values. Videos and exercises facilitated the exploration of the meaning and purpose in life and values of relationships, vocation, personal growth, and health. Connections with the people, places, animals, and the transcendent as significant resources for mitigating mental health and relational challenges were explored and discussed. Group members practised displaying an empathic and supportive presence, demonstrating active listening, and reflecting the emotions and meanings communicated by others. An inspirational reading and closing reflections were shared.
- **Week 3: Pain, Suffering, and My Spiritual Understanding.** Participants explored beliefs of pain and suffering and the impact on thoughts, emotions, health, relationships, and spirituality. Passages from Viktor Frankl's (1946) *Man's Search for Meaning* illustrated the effects of perspective on the suffering experience. Participants explored and processed the impact of their own cognitions, emotions, and appraisals of life challenges on their mental health and well-being.
- **Week 4: Love, Fear, and Home.** The notion and aspects of fear were explored, reflected upon and one's own fears were articulated. Reactions and personal coping strategies were shared and the notion of not being alone in their challenges was facilitated. A guided meditation relating to fear and courage helped with learning to approach fear in a non-judgmental accepting manner. Closing reflections on the spiritual nature of love were read aloud by each group member.
- **Week 5: Trauma, Healing, and Resiliency.** Psychoeducational materials relating to basic human needs, and trauma symptoms, risk factors, common treatment approaches and the concept of

posttraumatic growth were reviewed. A video by Brené Brown aided in understanding the difference between empathy and sympathy. Participants completed a posttraumatic growth inventory and wrote a trauma narrative. The four stages of treatment progression, (1) Deal, (2) Feel, (3) Heal, and (4) Seal, were explained and discussed. A choice regarding the creation of their own path forward, and how spiritual and cultural beliefs help to inform, and shape meaning was considered. Symbolism and its significance and power in relation to daily living was discussed.

– **Week 6: Guilt, Forgiveness, and Reconciliation.** Written material was supplied relating to the emotional states of shame and guilt. The group reviewed how they both can negatively impact one's well-being and create or perpetuate fear and anxiety. In pairs, members enquired about each other's perspectives regarding forgiveness, enabling them to recognize, process, and move towards acceptance of a personal injury or harm done to them. The emotional freedom technique (EFT) was modelled and then practised. Closing reflections pertaining to a holistic perspective regarding reconciliation were read.

– **Week 7: Acceptance and Rejection.** Psychoeducational materials relating to physical and emotional rejection and abandonment and their long-term consequences were reviewed. Self-esteem and self-acceptance were discussed as well as learned beliefs and impacts on self-worth, satisfaction, happiness, and confidence. Positive self-talk, reframing thoughts, and how to love yourself were explored. A self-love meditation and reading of the closing reflections were completed.

– **Week 8: Inner Strength and Control.** Inner strength, self-confidence, embracing and accepting all aspects of self, and healthy boundaries were areas of focus. Establishing boundaries, remaining flexible with respect to challenges, being receptive to learning and requesting assistance from others, and having a loving relationship with self and spirit were discussed. In order to facilitate an understanding of flexible thinking, a comparison between the *"Mighty Oak"* and the *"Swaying Palm"* portrayed the importance of flexibility during challenging or painful experiences. The session also included a poem, inspirational reflections and the sacred three questions.

– **Week 9: Compassion, Empathy, and Appreciation of Beauty.** The role of self-criticism and the destructive influence it can inflict on one's progress in life was discussed. Group members explored their own self-criticisms. The power of self-compassion, mindfulness, connectedness, and self-kindness were reviewed. A writing activity on self-compassion was conducted. Members wrote a letter to themselves from the perspective of a loving, kind, and compassionate imaginary friend. Each person was encouraged to generate a compassionate mantra to focus on during times of self-doubt. The sacred three questions and closing reflections relating to compassion, beauty, and self-love were completed.

- **Week 10: Gratitude, Hope, and Celebration – Closing.** The final week of the Soulful Journey was spent examining gratitude. A written outline regarding the method and advantages of keeping a gratitude journal was reviewed. Members wrote a letter to their future selves that included ways in which they had begun to love and accept themselves emotionally, mentally, physically, socially, and spiritually. This became an expression of gratitude to themselves for progressing through life's challenges. They included their understanding of novel insights learned through participation in the Soulful Journey, and ended with a supportive wish that they had for themselves. A celebration concluded the Soulful Journey Group. The facilitators offered two additional drop-in dates during which this particular group could meet to check in on their progress.

Results

Responses to the qualitative questions relating to participants' experience in the Soulful Journey Group, its beneficial impact in their lives, the interaction with the facilitators, as well as suggestions for group process improvements were analysed. All group members indicated that they would recommend the Soulful Journey Group to others for rationales including self-awareness and learning. Most of the responses were attributed to the themes of self-awareness, self-compassion, belonging-ness, and meaning.

Theme: Self-Awareness

All participants reported an increase in personal knowledge and aware-ness. One participant stated: "I learned a lot about myself and others." Fisher (2013) states that "self-awareness is the driving force or transcen-dent aspect of the human spirit in its search for identity and self worth" (p. 107). This is captured in the personal domain where one intra-relates to self and further develops awareness, meaning, purpose and values. Several participants voiced similar comments such as "I have learned things about myself that I need to address or applaud" and "I am more aware of changes I have to make in my life." The members' statements illustrated how the group process facilitated an increased awareness of identity and a strengthened motivation to change aspects of self that no longer resonated.

Theme: Self-Compassion

Participants described feelings of acceptance towards themselves in a non-judgmental and positive manner upon completion of the ten-week program. Common comments included: "It certainly made me think about myself, with humility and love," "I feel empathy, sadness, happiness, and joy for myself and others which sometimes I was wondering if I was losing all emotion," and "group reminded me not to be too hard on myself. I've come a long way lately." Individuals with a higher degree of self-compassion have been reported to have less depression and anxiety leading to greater life satisfaction (Neff et al., 2007).

Theme: Belonging/Connection

It was apparent that an awareness of connections with others within the group as well as within their personal lives was facilitated. "My sense of connection has changed as I am more open to what other people feel and cope with life." "It encouraged me to stop avoiding difficult conversations with friends and family, when they are needed." "I can reflect on other's experiences and their way to handle them-it helps me find my way." Fisher's (2013) communal domain relates to the "quality and depth of interpersonal relationships between self and others" (p. 107) and it is apparent interpersonal relationships were enhanced. In their systematic review pertaining to personal recovery, Leamy et al. (2011) found that connectedness was identified, with high frequency, with respect to the recovery process.

Theme: Relationship with Transcendent/Meaning

Participants perceived increases in meaning and purpose in life as well as a greater yearning for or sense of spiritual connection. "I'm feeling a deeper sense of meaning in my life. A stronger connection to a higher power and I'm getting a better sense of purpose for my life going forward." "My takeaway is that I want and need to put a spiritual practice in place for myself." As suggested by Vis and Boynton (2008), groups that incorporate spirituality offer an opportunity to reframe thinking, coping, meaning-making and purpose. Allick's (2012) cited meaning in life as an identified inherent beneficial outcome seen when clients included spirituality in their lives.

Theme: Accepted and Supported

Participants described feelings of being supported while participating in the Soulful Journey Group. "All were heard and acknowledged and made to feel important." "The open-minded personality of each member allows for a very peaceful atmosphere. Very inclusive group." "Members of the group were very understanding and helpful and open-minded." "The group was very helpful, non-judgmental." Social support is an important mechanism through which an individual's mental health can improve (Gonçalves et al., 2015). The experience of a compassionate group who provides opportunities for its members to be heard attentively also fosters resiliency and acts as a resource to those participating (Jacobs, 2018).

Interaction with Facilitators

Group members described the facilitators as caring, helpful, accepting, knowledgeable, and encouraging. "They were both very accepting, respectful, and patient. They encouraged each one of us to open up, but respected our privacy- we felt very much at ease." "They were both very caring and helpful. I found it was encouraging when both facilitators shared in a vulnerable way." "Kind, caring, well educated in this field." Gilbert (2000) suggested that the revealing of some personal information, by the group worker was "believed to enhance feelings of connectedness and to facilitate practical solutions" (p. 76).

Discussion

The Soulful Journey provided an opportunity to integrate the spirituality of its group members within a mutual aid process. Gonçalves et al. (2015) stated that interventions that shift one's thinking, enhance acceptance of illness or distress, provide social support, and a deeper understanding of one's connectedness improve mental health, and these factors were articulated by participants in our group. According to Jacobs (2018), opportunities to experience sharing through the presence of another's undivided attention and deep listening in a compassionate community is a significant resource for peers that fosters resilience.

The Soulful Journey participants' subjective responses underscored the importance of feeling supported. They described how feeling understood from a non-judgmental, empathic, and compassionate approach helped in the development of personal awareness, self-acceptance, and ultimately the strengthening of their capacity for growth and resiliency.

Vis and Boynton (2008) contended that the inclusion of spirituality in treatment can promote "positive reconstruction of worldview, coping, and transcendent meaning making" (p. 69). Meaning centred group therapy has been found to be positively correlated with improved quality of life and reduced symptoms of depression and hopelessness (Breitbart et al., 2015). Participants of the Soulful Journey Group reported perceived increases in meaning and purpose in life as well as an increased sense of spiritual connection. Members of the group reported greater personal understanding of themselves and others from an empathic stance. Opportunities for awareness in the commonalities of life challenges existed among participants and encouraged hope and resiliency. The results from this evaluation demonstrate that the Soulful Journey Group offered benefit in enhancing participants' capacity for strengthening resilience and self-exploration of meaning, purpose, interpersonal relations, fostering self-acceptance, providing an avenue to discover strengths through increased self-talk, and improving quality of relationships with self, other, and beyond.

Considerations

Inclusion of spirituality in the treatment process, with its permeation of all areas of one's life, is important in assisting with the goal of optimization of psychosocial well-being for the client, and with improving self-transcendence, meaning-making, connectedness, and a sense of purpose. Furthermore, incorporating spirituality supports a social worker's ethical responsibility to advocate for change in the best interest of the client, dyads, families, groups, organizations, and communities for the benefit of society. A fully holistic approach that includes spirituality provides an added opportunity for the individual to gain insight into their intrinsic potential to adapt in life. It is important, however, to consider competency when developing, implementing, and assessing interventions that incorporate a spiritual dimension. According to Hodge (2011), "spiritual competence is perhaps best understood as a continuous construct" (p. 154). The social worker should strive to become aware of their own beliefs and biases in addition to gaining a thorough understanding of their clients' spiritual world view (Hodge, 2011). A social worker's critical awareness of his or her own spiritual world view is imperative to ensure that treatment is client directed and not influenced by the beliefs of the therapist. The Soulful Journey provided insights into the beneficial impact of incorporating a spiritual component into service delivery.

Conclusion

Groups with a spiritual focus hold potential for the discovery and awareness of intrinsic resources available for participants and can offer more than symptom alleviation and control. This group had an influence on the physical, psychological, social/communal, environmental, personal, and transcendental aspects of the participants' lives within a short time frame. Participants reported changes in self-awareness, self-compassion, belonging, connection, meaning, and purpose through their participation, which are all important aspects of spirituality and healing. It is recommended that social workers and their interprofessional collaborators gain and maintain competence in the nature and provision of spiritually-focused group interventions through education, training, and self-awareness regarding their attitudes, personal spiritual practices, and beliefs. Shifting to approaches that include spiritual beliefs and practices promotes excellence, diversity, and inclusiveness in the care delivered to those in need and can facilitate posttraumatic growth.

REFERENCES

Allick, D.M. (2012). *Attitudes toward religion and spirituality in social work practice* [Master's research paper, University of St. Thomas]. Social Work Master's Clinical Research Papers. https://ir.stthomas.edu/ssw_mstrp/136
Boynton, H.M. (2014). The healthy group: A mind-body-spirit approach for treating anxiety and depression in youth. *Journal of Religion & Spirituality in Social Work: Social Thought, 33*(3–4), 236–53. https://doi.org/10.1080/15426432.2014.930629
Breitbart, W., Rosenfeld, B., Pessin, H., Applebaum, A., Kulikowski, J., & Lichtenthal, W.G. (2015). Meaning-centered group psychotherapy: An effective intervention for improving psychological well-being in patients with advanced cancer. *Journal of Clinical Oncology, 33*(7), 749–54. https://doi.org/10.1200/jco.2014.57.2198. Medline: 25646186
Canda, E.R., & Furman, L.D. (2010). *Spiritual diversity in social work practice: The heart of helping* (2nd ed.). Oxford University Press.
Cohen, M.B., & Graybeal, C.T. (2007). Using solution-oriented techniques in mutual aid groups. *Social Work with Groups, 30*(4), 41–58. https://doi.org/10.1300/j009v30n04_04

Corrigan, P., McCorkle, B., Schell, B., & Kidder, K. (2003). Religion and spirituality in the lives of people with serious mental illness. *Community Mental Health Journal*, *39*(6), 487–99. https://doi.org/10.1023/b:comh .0000003010.44413.37

Drageset, J., Haugan, G., & Tranvåg, O. (2017). Crucial aspects promoting meaning and purpose in life: Perceptions of nursing home residents. *BMC Geriatrics*, *17*(254), 1–9. https://doi.org/10.1186/s12877-017-0650-x. Medline: 29084511

Fallot, R.D. (2001). Spirituality and religion in psychiatric rehabilitation and recovery from mental illness. *International Review of Psychiatry*, *13*(2), 110–16. https://doi.org/10.1080/09540260120037344

Fisher, J. (2010). Development and application of a spiritual well-being questionnaire called SHALOM. *Religions*, *1*(1), 105–21. https:// doi.org/10.3390/rel1010105

– (2013, 26 August). *The SHALOM tool for assessment of patient's spiritual needs* [Presentation] Catholic Health Australia National Conference, Melbourne, Australia. https://cha.org.au/images/2012_Conference/CHA%2013 %20Dr%20John%20Fisher.pdf

Frankl, V. (1946). *Man's search for meaning*. Beacon Press.

Furman, L.D., Zahl, M.A., Benson, P.W., & Canda, E.R. (2007). An international analysis of the role of religion and spirituality in social work practice. *Families in Society: The Journal of Contemporary Social Services*, *88*(2), 241–54. https://doi.org/10.1606/1044-3894.3622

Galek, K., Flannelly, K.J., Vane, A., & Galek, R.M. (2005). Assessing a patient's spiritual needs. *Holistic Nursing Practice*, *19*(2), 62–9. https:// doi.org/10.1097/00004650-200503000-00006. Medline: 15871588

Gilbert, M.C. (2000). Spirituality in social work groups: Practitioners speak out. *Social Work with Groups*, *22*(4), 67–84. https://doi.org/10.1300 /j009v22n04_06

Gonçalves, J.P.B., Lucchetti, G., Menezes, P.R., & Vallada, H. (2015). Religious and spiritual interventions in mental health care: A systematic review and meta-analysis of randomized controlled clinical trials. *Psychological Medicine*, *45*(14), 2937–49. https://doi.org/10.1017/s0033291715001166. Medline: 26200715

Grinnell, R.M., Gabor, P.A., & Unrau, Y.A. (2016). *Program evaluation for social workers: Foundations of evidenced-based programs* (7th ed.). Oxford University Press.

Hodge, D.R. (2011). Using spiritual interventions in practice: Developing some guidelines from evidence-based practice, *Social Work*, *56*(2), 149–58. http://www.jstor.org/stable/23719368

Hyde, B. (2013). Mutual aid group work: Social work leading the way to recovery-focused mental health practice. *Social Work with Groups*, *36*(1), 43–58. https://doi.org/10.1080/01609513.2012.699872

Ivtzan, I., Chan, C.P.L., Gardner, H.E., & Prashar, K. (2013). Linking religion and spirituality with psychological well-being: Examining self-actualisation, meaning in life, and personal growth initiative. *Journal of Religious Health, 52*, 915–29. https://doi.org/10.1007/s10943-011-9540-2. Medline: 21968697

Jacobs, C. (2018). Reflection on the role of the spirit in finding meaning and healing as clinicians. *Journal of Pain and Symptom Management, 55*(1), 151–4. https://doi.org/10.1016/j.jpainsymman.2017.11.011. Medline: 29154892

Jacobson, N., & Greenley, D. (2001). What is recovery? A conceptual model and explication. *Psychiatric Services, 52*(4), 482–5. https://doi.org/10.1176/appi.ps.52.4.482. Medline: 11274493

Kelly, B.L. (2017). Group work in health care settings. In C.D. Garvin, L.M. Gutiérrez, & M.J. Galinsky (Eds.), *Handbook of social work with groups* (2nd ed., pp. 203–19). The Guilford Press.

Leamy, M., Bird, V., Le Boutillier, C., Williams, J., & Slade, M. (2011). Conceptual framework for personal recovery in mental health: Systematic review and narrative synthesis. *The British Journal of Psychiatry, 199*(6), 445–52. https://doi.org/10.1192/bjp.bp.110.083733. Medline: 22130746

Lee, E.S. (2014). The impact of social and spiritual connectedness on the psychological well-being among older Americans. *Journal of Religion, Spirituality, and Aging, 26*(4), 300–19. https://doi.org/10.1080/15528030.2013.879090

McCarroll, P., O'Connor, T.S.J., & Meakes, E. (2005). Assessing plurality in spirituality definitions. In A. Meier, T.S.J. O'Connor, & P.L. VanKatwyk (Eds.), *Spirituality & health: Multidisciplinary explorations* (pp. 43–61). Wilfred University Press.

Meraviglia, M.G. (1999). Critical analysis of spirituality and its empirical indicators: Prayer and meaning in life. *Journal of Holistic Nursing, 17*(1), 18–33. https://doi.org/10.1177/089801019901700103. Medline: 10373840

Mustain, J.R., & Helminiak, D.A. (2015). Understanding spirituality in recovery from addiction: Reintegrating the psyche to release the human spirit. *Addiction Research & Theory, 23*(5), 364–71. https://doi.org/10.3109/16066359.2015.1011623

Neff, K.D., Kirkpatrick, K.L., & Rude, S.S. (2007). Self-compassion and adaptive psychological functioning. *Journal of Research in Personality, 41*(1), 139–54. https://doi.org/10.1016/j.jrp.2006.03.004

Pargament, K.I. (2007). *Spirituality integrated psychotherapy: Understanding and addressing the sacred.* The Guilford Press.

Peres, M.F.P., Kamei, H.H., Tobo, P.R., & Lucchetti, G. (2018). Mechanisms behind religiosity and spirituality's effect on mental health, quality of life and well-being. *Journal of Religion and Health, 57*(5), 1842–55. https://doi.org/10.1007/s10943-017-0400-6. Medline: 28444608

PSR/RPS Canada. (2017). *Competencies of practice for Canadian recovery-oriented psychosocial rehabilitation practitioners* (2nd ed.). PSR/RPS Canada: Partners in Recovery. https://psrrpscanada.ca/files/pdf/PSR-practice -competencies.pdf

Slade, M. (2009). *Personal recovery and mental illness: A guide for mental health professionals.* Cambridge University Press.

Spaniol, L. (2002). Spirituality and connectedness. *Psychiatric Rehabilitation Journal, 25*(4), 321–2. https://doi.org/10.1037/h0095006. Medline: 12013259

Steinberg, D.M. (2010). Mutual aid: A contribution to best-practice social work. *Social Work with Groups, 33*(1), 53–68. https://doi.org/10.1080 /01609510903316389

Tedeschi, R.G., & Calhoun, L.G. (1996). The Posttraumatic Growth Inventory: Measuring the positive legacy of trauma. *Journal of Traumatic Stress, 9*(3), 455–71. https://doi.org/10.1002/jts.2490090305

Vis, J., & Boynton, H.M. (2008). Spirituality and transcendent meaning making: Possibilities for enhancing posttraumatic growth. *Journal of Religion and Spirituality in Social Work: Social Thought, 27*(1–2), 69–86. https://doi.org/10.1080/15426430802113814

Young, D. (2015). Positive effects of spirituality in facilitating recovery for people with severe mental illness. *International Journal of Psychosocial Rehabilitation, 19*(1), 5–12.

8 Offering Social Work Care for Spiritual Needs at the End of Life

KATHY KORTES-MILLER

Social workers encounter dying, death, loss, and grief in all settings of practice. Those who work in end-of-life settings are confronted by both the existential concerns of individuals who are dying alongside more common stressors such as family support, financial needs and care planning (Daaleman et al., 2008). The need for spiritual support and understanding becomes more salient as the people social workers serve approach the end of life. The founder of the hospice movement, Dame Cicely Saunders, was a social worker before becoming a physician and understood well some of the spiritual needs people face at the end of their lives (Brogan, 2006). She recognized that everyone has a spiritual dimension to their lives that is uniquely connected to who they are. This is recognized in her often-quoted statement, "You matter because you're you, and you matter to the end of your life. We will do all we can not only to help you to die peacefully, but also to live until you die." Spirituality in social work is increasingly being viewed with interest, specifically in health care settings.

As our population ages, there will be an increased demand for social work in palliative and end-of-life care. The Canadian Hospice Palliative Care Association (2015) defines palliative care as "An integrated palliative approach to care focuses on meeting a person and families' full range of needs – physical, psychosocial and spiritual – at all stages of frailty or chronic disease, not just at the end of life" (p. 2). Additionally, in this chapter, the term *end of life* will be used to refer broadly to the period after diagnosis of a serious illness or condition that cannot be cured. Palliative Care recognizes that each aspect of the person's care – biological, psychological, social, and spiritual can influence the other. Social work plays a key role in this care as part of an interprofessional team (Duncan-Daston et al., 2016).

Most social workers are aware that their clients have spiritual needs at the end of life but most feel ill equipped to address them (Wesley et al., 2004). This chapter will examine the need for social workers to have a level of spiritual competence in their interactions with people who are dying and emphasize the need for interprofessional collaboration to enhance this form of care. It will offer practical guidance for providing spiritual support as part of the care that social workers are responsible for.

Spiritual Needs at the End of Life

Spirituality is most often recognized as "a sense of life purpose, meaning, and connectedness" (Callahan, 2009, p. 172). Kellehear (2000) extends this idea by stating that spirituality reflects "the human need to transcend, to go beyond the immediacy of suffering and to find meaning in that experience" (p. 153). He describes spiritual needs at the end-of-life as multidimensional and recognizes three major groupings: situational, moral and biographical, and religious. Kellehear (2000) portrays "situational" needs as including concerns about purpose, hope and the meaning of life, connections with others, and social networks. Peace and reconciliation, forgiveness and closure are encompassed in the "moral and biographical" grouping. The third major grouping "religious" includes divine forgiveness and support, religious rites/ sacraments, connection to religious community and clergy, and discussion about a higher being (God) and eternal life (Kellehear, 2000).

In the past, spiritual needs have been neglected at the end of life but more recently the health care community is becoming more open and accepting of spirituality and spiritual well-being as an essential component of the dying process (Kirby et al., 2004; Callahan, 2009). When a person is facing the end of their life or has been diagnosed with a life-limiting illness it is not unusual for them to have fears and uncertainty and lack an understanding of what both the dying process and death mean to them. They may also acknowledge a stronger orientation to their spirituality and need for connection and meaning making than healthy people (Daaleman & VandeCreek, 2000). In addition, they may find themselves having existential questions that do not have easy, straightforward answers such as: Why is this happening to me? Why now? What is the meaning of my life? What is the meaning of my death? Is there life after death (Wiebe, 2014)? The need to acknowledge death as a part of life can be a powerful stimulus for people at the end of their lives as described by Jacobs (2004): "It is because life is finite, that one strives to connect with the infinite. The knowledge that suffering occurs, moves people to seek meaning and comfort. It is because some-times neither life nor death makes sense that one strives to find and to conform to a belief system in which the contradictions of living and dying, joy and terror, order and absurdity are reconciled" (p. 191).

Spiritual concerns that people facing the end-of-life may include matters pertaining to understanding the meaning of life, the changing aspects of hope, desire for forgiveness and reconciliation with others and a need for connection (Puchalski, 2008). Considering the end of life can challenge people existentially, examining death and life bring up some big questions: What was it all for? Is there life after death? What meaning did I find in my life? Whether someone describes themselves as religious or not, contemplating these kinds of questions might help someone to feel connected with something bigger than themselves. This kind of contemplation can serve to deepen connections with others and the act of living. It also can help navigate the act of dying (Kortes-Miller, 2018). However, if someone reviews their life and finds it lacking or the experience negative, spiritual suffering or distress may occur (Stephenson & Berry, 2014). This spiritual pain or distress may manifest in various ways including unrelieved physical pain, increased anxiety, guilt, or despair (Brunjes, 2010). It is well recognized that spirituality is an important dimension of quality of life, and that the end of life provides opportunity for people to reflect on their life and work to find some meaning as they live until they die (Puchalski, 2008). A sense of meaning and connection at the end of life is important for people to end their lives well (Duncan-Daston et al., 2016).

Role of Social Work at the End of Life

Good palliative and end-of-life care prioritizes psychosocial and spiritual care alongside pain and symptom management. According to Wang et al. (2018), social workers generally support people who are dying and their families in three primary areas: they are called upon to address psychosocial and spiritual concerns of dying persons and their families, to help the dying persons engage in the advance care planning process or establish goals of care, and to provide grief counselling for family members and friends. The social work profession offers an important perspective to palliative and end-of-life care from an ecological approach that considers the person in their environment and the influences of family and culture. Social workers are uniquely positioned to work in palliative and end-of-life care because the values that underpin the profession are closely linked with the values of a palliative approach to care (Csikai, 2004). In their role supporting people at the end of life, social workers are tasked with addressing the physical, psychological, social, and practical issues of clients (Bosma et al., 2008). In an effort to articulate the role of social work in palliative and end of life care a Canadian group of social workers developed competencies highlighting the following areas of practice: advocacy, assessment, care delivery, care planning, community capacity building, evaluation, decision-making, education, research, information sharing, interdisciplinary team participation, and self-reflective practice (Bosma et al., 2008). Additionally, a study conducted by Kramer (2013) with one group of social workers revealed that they most frequently attended to: "psychological and emotional responses of family members (94%) and elder (88%), funeral planning (92%), grief issues (92%), caregiver involvement (89%), spiritual issues (76%), and coordination with facilities (65%)" (p. 313).

Frequently, social workers are part of an interprofessional team and bring expertise focussing on systems, family dynamics, diversity, grief and loss, communication, advocacy, and ethics in palliative care (Gwyther et al. 2005). The team is at the heart of a palliative approach to care with professionals from different disciplines including medicine, nursing, physical and occupational therapy, and spiritual care. At the centre of the care team are the patient and family. The interprofessional team has been found to be a useful model in palliative care to facilitate comprehensive and holistic care and relieve hardship on any one health care discipline (Csikai, 2004). These partnerships and approaches to shared care informs care plans and decision-making. The approach utilized by the social worker is informed by input and knowledge from other team members. The social work lens adds an important perspective to understanding of the needs of the patient and family by highlighting the social determinants of health, the person in environment, impact of systems and actively informs care plans. Often social workers are also the link between settings of care and varied health care services.

Spiritual Care for People at the End of Life

Increasingly, social workers are called upon to address spiritual aspects of care for people who are dying and their families and friends (Callahan, 2009; Duncan-Daston et al., 2016). The ability to offer spiritual support has been acknowledged as a competency by the National Association of Social Workers (Csikai, 2004). Overall, there has been an emerging growth of recognition of the importance of spirituality in social work practice (Kvarfordt et al., 2017; Oxhandler & Pargament, 2014) and social workers are encouraged to learn about spirituality and how it can benefit the support and care they provide for their clients, peers and ultimately themselves. The guiding goals of social work, anti-oppression and cultural sensitivity, align well with the complex and wide-ranging qualities of spirituality (Canda, 2002; Holloway & Moss, 2010). Thus, it may be reasoned that social workers are well positioned to offer spiritual support as part of their practice as they already provide a wide range of services and psychosocial support (Francoeur et al., 2016) and, therefore, must be prepared to provide spiritual support to people at the end of their lives and their families (Wesley et al., 2004).

There are a wide variety of situations and reasons that social workers providing care at the end of life may find themselves focusing on spiritual needs. Social workers are well positioned to support and reinforce the values and beliefs that guide the lives of the people they serve. It is not unusual for social workers to be on the receiving end of the fears, hopes and questions that patients and family members have while navigating the end of life (Miller et al., 2019). As Stewart (2014) states: "Entering into the conscious acknowledgement of death, not just as a possibility but as a certainty, in every human being's life, has the potential to enhance the coping of a patient" (p. 63).

The kind of spiritual support that a social worker may participate in facilitating with individuals at the end of life may include life review, meaning making, processing of difficult life events and emotions, and working towards achieving a sense of peace as defined by the individual (Callahan, 2013a). Additionally, they may be called upon by other professionals who see spiritual care as part of the social work role particularly when a specialist spiritual care advisor is not available or when that professional needs support because they lack experience companioning people at the end of life (Reith & Payne, 2009).

While social workers may not describe the focus of their work at end of life as spiritual care, Canda and Furman (2010) describe this type of care as "spiritually sensitive practice" and perceive it as "a way of being and relating throughout the entire helping process" (p. 214). Social workers engaging in this work need to be aware of their own values and beliefs and how these may influence their practice. While social workers receive education about empathy and the importance of being non-judgmental, the ability to be open and accepting of different spiritual values and belief systems is a life-long skill which continually needs to be nurtured and developed (Duncan-Daston et al., 2016). This openness and acceptance is particularly important in the spiritual relational model that Callahan (2013a) outlines.

Callahan (2017) describes relational spirituality as "the experience of relationships that enhance life meaning. The therapeutic relationship can inform a client's worldview and sustain a social worker's capacity to care" (para. 1). This model positions spiritual care with beginning at the onset of the professional therapeutic encounter. It requires the willingness of both the health care provider and the recipient of care (patient) to discuss and address spirituality and engage in an assessment of spiritual concerns and strengths. Consent to address spiritual issues must be sought. Callahan's (2013a) relational model addresses a number of aspects of spiritual care including the importance of presence and listening, recognizing the uniqueness of the individual and the power of touch. Additionally this model extends to supporting the family and friends of the person who is dying through providing education about what to expect when someone is dying (Duncan-Daston et al., 2016).

Spiritual Assessment

The relationship a person has with their sense of spirituality generally evolves and changes over a lifetime so it is important that social workers offer spiritually sensitive care that is both respectful and compassionate for that individual and meets them where they are at. This is particularly relevant when someone is facing the end of their life as this can be a time of instability, vulnerability, and confusion as people adjust to this new stage in life (Nelson-Becker et al., 2006). For some people, the adjustment to the last stages of life may be obvious and easily recognized while others may hold their experiences more internally and keep their emotions hidden making it more challenging for others to identify or appreciate (Miller et al., 2019). Social workers may accompany individuals whose spiritual beliefs are strengthened as they face the end of their lives and others whose beliefs are challenged. For example, an unexpected diagnosis for which there is no cure can threaten a person's identity or how they understand their place in the world. It could also serve to reaffirm their beliefs or strengthen their reliance in their spiritual faith. One of the goals of the social worker is to focus on how the individual understands their illness and what it means to them. In order to do this, it is helpful to consider a spiritual component within the social work assessment and plan.

Throughout the years social workers have suggested different models and assessment strategies for exploring spirituality with clients. Nelson-Becker et al. (2006) proposed eleven domains as a basis for providing a comprehensive understanding of an individual's relationship to their spirituality. Additionally, assessing these different domains can also help a social worker to ascertain if there is a need for counselling or referral to other members of the interprofessional team. The domains articulated by Nelson-Becker et al. (2006) are not a formula for social workers to follow but rather a guide or outline for deeper engagement. They suggest beginning with exploratory questions to set the stage and assess if further questions might be welcome. Examples of exploratory questions are: "Is spirituality, religion, or faith important in your life? And, what kind of language do you prefer?" (p. 336). Additionally, Steinhauser et al. (2006) suggest asking if spiritual/religious needs are being supported and if an individual would describe themselves as being at peace.

The spiritual assessment domains may include (1) spiritual affiliation, (2) spiritual belief, (3) spiritual behaviour, (4) emotional qualities of spirituality, (5) values, (6) spiritual experiences, (7) spiritual history, (8) therapeutic change factors, (9) social support, (10) spiritual well-being, and (11) extrinsic/intrinsic spiritual focus (Nelson-Becker et al., 2006). While Nelson-Becker et al. (2006) offer a detailed framework using these domains and provide sample assessment questions, many social workers may be initially looking for shorter assessment tools which would allow them to ascertain if this more detailed assessment is needed. Two such tools, well utilized at end of life include the FICA and the HOPE models.

Perhaps the most well-known spiritual assessment tool is the FICA, developed by physician Dr. Christine Puchalski in 1996 in collaboration with other physician colleagues, which is based on the key pieces of information that a health care provider would want to know about a person in a clinical setting (Borneman et al., 2010). The FICA tool is based on four domains of spiritual assessment: Faith (belief, or meaning); the Importance of spirituality for an individual and the influence that belief system or values may have on any health care decision-making; the individual's spiritual Community; and interventions used or required to Address spiritual needs (Puchalski & Romer, 2000). The acronym of FICA is used to support clinicians to remember to address the different spiritual domains. It can be used to assist social workers to guide conversation that focuses on religion/spirituality and connection to health and illness in clinical settings.

The second tool also developed by physicians Anandarajah and Hight (2001) with an easy to remember acronym to support clinicians is the HOPE tool. The HOPE concepts are similar to the FICA and include the following: H – sources of hope, strength, comfort, meaning, peace, love and connection; O – the role of organized religion for the patient; P – personal spirituality and practices; E – effects on medical care and end-of-life decisions (Anandarajah & Hight, 2001). These concepts provide opportunity for social workers to explore general spiritual concerns and issues. Specifically, social workers may find this tool helpful if they are looking to incorporate a spiritual assessment into their clinical assessment

An additional tool that social workers might find helpful is the Posttraumatic Growth Inventory (PGI; Engelkemeyer & Marwit, 2008; Tedeschi & Calhoun, 1996). This provides an opportunity for social workers to assess five domains of growth that people face at the end of their lives or who are grieving may be reporting. These domains include: renewed appreciation of life, new possibilities, enhanced personal strength, improved relationships with others, and spiritual change. It is important to note that while death is most often viewed as a normative life event, Tedeschi and Calhoun (2004) speak about a "seismic event" or use the metaphor of an earthquake when referring to posttraumatic growth. Many people describe the death of a loved one as a transformative or ground shifting experience which then aligns with posttraumatic growth which is said to only be possible if the event is so impactful that it forces people to find and embrace new mechanisms of cognitive processing. Tedeschi and Calhoun (1996) described using the PGI as an opportunity to deepen the recognition of how people naturally work to make meaning and develop understanding of their situation and/or trauma. Social workers may find incorporating these domains into their work as particularly relevant as they provide support to individuals with terminal illness who are striving to plan for the end of life.

These tools serve as a starting off point for social workers to engage in spiritually focused goals and interventions with the people they are serving at the end of life. For example, this might include supporting the completion of a spiritually and culturally appropriate care plan that aligns with the health care team and establishing that there is space for appropriate rituals during the dying process and after death. Social workers may also be involved in connecting with clergy and spiritual leaders in the community and advocating to ensure that there is appropriate spiritual care in response to any experience of spiritual distress (Miller et al., 2019).

All three tools, the FICA, HOPE, and PGI, provide a framework for social workers to ask questions about the role of spirituality at the end of life. The choice of words may not be a fit for all social workers so they are encouraged to practice using the tools and use their own language to elicit information from individuals about what is important to them and their spiritual selves. An example of such a question is "what or who is it that gives meaning to your life?" (Best et al., 2020). Social workers need to determine that the assessment process they choose to use to examine spirituality is well conceptualized and relevant for their practice setting and the individuals they serve (Rumbold, 2007).

Challenges with the Social Work Role at the End of Life

Many of the people that social workers encounter are requesting increased attention to the spiritual dimension of their lives, especially at the end of life. Thus, it is important that social workers expand their offering of psychosocial care to include learning about the spiritual beliefs and practices of the people they are caring for, the role those beliefs may play in health care decision-making and how spiritual beliefs can be included in the care to enhance comfort and a sense of peace at the end of life.

In order to achieve this, it is essential that a social worker strives to create a supportive and non-judgmental space in which spiritual concerns and issues can be openly acknowledged and shared. In Western culture, spirituality is often viewed as a personal and, potentially, a private position. Therefore it is not unusual for people to only offer information pertaining to their spiritual needs when they are asked about it explicitly (Nelson-Becker et al., 2006). Social workers need to develop a level of comfort and competence to ask about spirituality and have the knowledge to refer to others when additional help is required.

Additionally, social workers may have concerns working in a spiritual context if they do not have spiritual beliefs themselves or encounter clients and families with different spiritual beliefs than themselves. In this situation, Reith and Payne (2009) recommend concentrating on more universal beliefs such as meaning making and life review as opposed to specifics of a particular faith or religion. Social workers need to remain open and non-judgmental to the beliefs and spiritual expression of those they are supporting at the end of life.

A commitment to ongoing self-awareness and reflection is essential for social workers caring for people and their families at the end of life. They need to possess a strong awareness of their own personal value and belief systems before engaging with the belief systems of others or there is the possibility of unintended harm (Miller et al., 2019). Miller et al. (2019) suggest that social workers ask the following of themselves: "Am I able to distance myself from my personal beliefs and attitudes in order to sufficiently respect and support the spiritual and/or religious beliefs and observances of the populations I serve?" (p. 144). It is important that social workers develop their own self-care and spiritual practices before engaging in this work in order to ensure that they find the work to be sustaining and rewarding as opposed to depleting of self.

Conclusion

There are enduring opportunities for social workers to infuse spirituality into the care they provide for people and their families at the end of life. As integral members of the palliative care team, they share an obligation to improve and develop their ability and comfort level around the provision of competent and compassionate spiritual care. Creativity and commitment are central to this process as social workers engage in the rich work of supporting people in their care to identify and strengthen their spiritual resources in the environment of uncertainty and opportunity end of life offers.

REFERENCES

Anandarajah, G., & Hight, E. (2001). Spirituality and medical practice: Using the HOPE questions as a practical tool for spiritual assessment. *American Family Physician, 63*(1), 81–9. https://doi.org/10.1016/s1443-8461(01)80044-7

Best, M., Leget, C., Goodhead, A., & Paal, P. (2020). An EAPC white paper on multi-disciplinary education for spiritual care in palliative care. *BMC Palliative Care, 19*(9). https://doi.org/10.1186/s12904-019-0508-4. Medline: 31941486

Borneman, T., Ferrell, B., & Puchalski, C.M. (2010). Evaluation of the FICA tool for spiritual assessment. *Journal of pain and symptom management, 40*(2), 163–73. https://doi.org/10.1016/j.jpainsymman.2009.12.019. Medline: 20619602

Bosma, H., Johnston, M., Cadell, S., Wainwright, W., Abernathy, N., Feron, A., Kelley, M.L., & Nelson, F. (2008). *Canadian social work competencies for hospice palliative care: A framework to guide education and practice at the generalist and specialist levels.* Canadian Hospice Palliative Care Association. http://www.chpca.net/interest_groups/social_workers -counselors/social-work_counsellors_competencies.html

Brogan, G. (2006). Inventing the good death. *Registered Nurse J Pat Advocacy, 102,* 10–14.

Brunjes, G.B. (2010). Spiritual pain and suffering. *Asian Pac J Cancer Prev, 11*(Suppl 1), 31–6.

Callahan, A.M. (2009). Spiritually-sensitive care in hospice social work. *Journal of Social Work in End-of-Life & Palliative Care, 5*(3–4), 169–85. https:// doi.org/10.1080/15524250903555098

– (2013a). A relational model for spiritually-sensitive hospice care. *Journal of Social Work in End-of-Life & Palliative Care, 9*(2–3), 158–79. https://doi.org/10 .1080/15524256.2013.794051. Medline: 23777232

– (2013b). [Review of the book *Spiritually integrated psychotherapy: Understanding and addressing the sacred*, by K.I. Pargament]. *Journal of Religion & Spirituality in Social Work: Social Thought*, 32(1), 104–8. https://doi.org/10.1080/15426432.2013.750523

– (2017, February). Relational spirituality. *Social Work Today: Web Exclusive.* https://www.socialworktoday.com/archive/exc_0217.shtml

The Canadian Hospice Palliative Care Association. (2015). *The way forward national framework: A roadmap for an integrated palliative approach to care.* Government of Canada. http://www.hpcintegration.ca/media/60044/TWF-framework-doc-Eng-2015-final-April1.pdf

Canda, E.R. (2002). A world wide view on spirituality and social work: Reflections from the USA experience and suggestions for internationalization. *Currents: New Scholarship for the Human Services, 1*(1), 11.

Canda, E.R., & Furman, L.D. (2010). *Spiritual diversity in social work practice: The heart of helping* (2nd ed.). Oxford University Press.

Csikai, E.L. (2004). Social workers' participation in the resolution of ethical dilemmas in hospice care. *Health & Social Work, 29*(1), 67–76. https://doi.org/10.1093/hsw/29.1.67. Medline: 15024920

Daaleman, T.P., Usher, B.M., Williams, S.W., Rawlings, J., & Hanson, L.C. (2008). An exploratory study of spiritual care at the end of life. *The Annals of Family Medicine, 6*(5), 406–11. https://doi.org/10.1370/afm.883. Medline: 18779544

Daaleman, T.P., & VandeCreek, L. (2000). Placing religion and spirituality in end-of-life care. *Jama, 284*(19), 2514–17. https://doi.org/10.1001/jama.284.19.2514. Medline: 11074785

Duncan-Daston, R., Foster, S., & Bowden, H. (2016). A look into spirituality in social work practice within the hospice setting. *Journal of Religion & Spirituality in Social Work: Social Thought, 35*(3), 157–78. https://doi.org/10.1080/15426432.2015.1102672

Engelkemeyer, S.M., & Marwit, S.J. (2008). Posttraumatic growth in bereaved parents. *Journal of Traumatic Stress, 21*(3), 344–6. https://doi.org/10.1002/jts.20338. Medline: 18553420

Francoeur, R.B., Burke, N., & Wilson, A.M. (2016). The role of social workers in spiritual care to facilitate coping with chronic illness and self-determination in advance care planning. *Social Work in Public Health, 31*(5), 453–66. https://doi.org/10.1080/19371918.2016.1146199. Medline: 27187806

Gwyther, L.P., Altilio, T., Blacker, S., Christ, G., Csikai, E.L., Hooyman, N., Kramer, B., Linton, J.M., Raymer, M., & Howe, J. (2005). Social work competencies in palliative and end-of-life care. *Journal of Social Work in End-of-Life & Palliative Care, 1*(1), 87–120. https://doi.org/10.1300/j457v01n01_06. Medline: 17387058

Holloway, M., & Moss, B. (2010). *Spirituality and social work*. Macmillan International Higher Education.

Jacobs, C. (2004). Spirituality and end-of-life care practice for social workers. In J. Berzoff & P.R. Silverman (Eds.), *Living with dying: A handbook for end-of-life healthcare practitioners* (pp. 187–205). Columbia University Press.

Kellehear, A. (2000). Spirituality and palliative care: A model of needs. *Palliative Medicine, 14*(2), 149–55. https://doi.org/10.1191/026921600 674786394. Medline: 10829149

Kirby, S.E., Coleman, P.G., & Daley, D. (2004). Spirituality and well-being in frail and nonfrail older adults. *The Journals of Gerontology Series B: Psychological Sciences and Social Sciences, 59*(3), P123–9. https://doi.org/10.1093/geronb/59.3.p123. Medline: 15118015

Kortes-Miller, K. (2018). *Talking about death won't kill you: The essential guide to end-of-life conversations*. ECW Press.

Kramer, B.J. (2013). Social workers' roles in addressing the complex end-of-life care needs of elders with advanced chronic disease. *Journal of Social Work in End-of-Life & Palliative Care, 9*(4), 308–30. https://doi.org/10.1080/15524256.2013.846887. Medline: 24295099

Kvarfordt, C.L., Sheridan, M.J., & Taylor, O. (2017). Religion and spirituality in social work curriculum: A survey of Canadian educators. *The British Journal of Social Work, 48*(5), 1469–87. https://doi.org/10.1093/bjsw/bcx069

Miller, D.R., Stewart, M., & Sumser, B. (2019). Spiritual, religious, and existential dimensions of care. In B. Sumser, M.L. Leimena, & T. Altilio (Eds.), *Palliative care: A guide for health social workers*. Oxford University Press.

Nelson-Becker, H., Nakashima, M., & Canda, E.R. (2006). Spiritual assessment in aging: A framework for clinicians. *Journal of Gerontological Social Work, 48*(3–4), 331–47. https://doi.org/10.1300/j083v48n03_04. Medline: 17210536

Oxhandler, H.K., & Pargament, K.I. (2014). Social work practitioners' integration of clients' religion and spirituality in practice: A literature review. *Social Work, 59*(3), 271–9. https://doi.org/10.1093/sw/swu018. Medline: 25076651

Puchalski, C.M. (2008). Spirituality and the care of patients at the end-of-life: An essential component of care. *OMEGA: Journal of death and dying, 56*(1), 33–46. https://doi.org/10.2190/om.56.1.d. Medline: 18051018

Puchalski, C., & Romer, A.L. (2000). Taking a spiritual history allows clinicians to understand patients more fully. *Journal of Palliative Medicine, 3*(1), 129–37. https://doi.org/10.1089/jpm.2000.3.129. Medline: 15859737

Reith, M., & Payne, M. (2009). *Social work in end-of-life and palliative care*. The Policy Press.

Rumbold, B.D. (2007). A review of spiritual assessment in health care practice. *Medical Journal of Australia, 186*(S10), S60–2. https://doi.org/10.5694/j.1326-5377.2007.tb01044.x. Medline: 17516887

Steinhauser, K.E., Voils, C.I., Clipp, E.C., Bosworth, H.B., Christakis, N.A., & Tulsky, J.A. (2006). "Are you at peace?" One item to probe spiritual concerns at the end of life. *Archives of Internal Medicine, 166*(1), 101–5. https://doi.org/10.1001/archinte.166.1.101. Medline: 16401817

Stephenson, P.S., & Berry, D.M. (2014). Spirituality and uncertainty at the end of life. *Oncology Nursing Forum, 41*(1), 33–9. https://doi.org/10.1188/14 .onf.33-39. Medline: 24368237

Stewart, M. (2014). Spiritual assessment: A patient-centered approach to oncology social work practice. *Social Work in Health Care, 53*(1), 59–73. https://doi.org/10.1080/00981389.2013.834033. Medline: 24405239

Tedeschi, R.G., & Calhoun, L.G. (1996). The Posttraumatic Growth Inventory: Measuring the positive legacy of trauma. *Journal of Traumatic Stress, 9*(3), 455–71. https://doi.org/10.1002/jts.2490090305

– (2004). A clinical approach to posttraumatic growth. In P.A. Linley & S. Joseph (Eds.), *Positive psychology in practice* (pp. 405–19). John Wiley & Sons. https://doi.org/10.1002/9780470939338

Wang, C.W., Chan, C.L.W., & Chow, A.Y.M. (2018). Social workers' involvement in advance care planning: A systematic narrative review. *BMC Palliative Care, 17*(5). https://doi.org/10.1186/s12904-017-0218-8. Medline: 28693527

Wesley, C., Tunney, K., & Duncan, E. (2004). Educational needs of hospice social workers: Spiritual assessment and interventions with diverse populations. *American Journal of Hospice and Palliative Medicine®, 21*(1), 40–6. https://doi.org/10.1177/104990910402100110. Medline: 14748522

Wiebe, M. (2014). Social work, religion, and palliative care. *Journal of Religion & Spirituality in Social Work: Social Thought, 33*(3–4), 339–52. https://doi.org/10.1080/15426432.2014.930638

9 Addressing the Effects of Trauma Using Holistic and Creative Mindfulness-Based Practices and Concepts

DIANA COHOLIC

Introduction

In my recent book, *Facilitating Mindfulness: A Guide for Human Service Professionals* (Coholic, 2019), I discussed how mindfulness is a holistic philosophy and practice that encourages us to live our lives present-focused with non-judgment about our feelings, thoughts, and behaviours. Mindfulness supports us to accept our feelings and approach them with curiosity seeking to understand the feeling's trigger and purpose. Mindfulness also inspires us to appreciate the moments of our lives, to be self-compassionate and empathic, and to be self-aware internally and externally so that we can make informed decisions rather than reacting. Social work brings distinct characteristics to the study and practice of mindfulness such as a holistic and strengths-based lens coupled with creative social group work expertise. Importantly, while practising mindfulness can lead to both personal and professional benefits such as improved mood and therapeutic presence, recognizing our interconnectedness, mindfulness encourages us to work for social justice and change for the well-being of all.

The purpose of this chapter is to briefly explore how learning mindfulness-based practices and concepts can help us address the many effects of trauma such as overwhelming feelings, intrusive thoughts, distraction, rumination, and so on. I present some examples of arts-based mindfulness activities that can be used to teach, learn, and practice mindfulness and its concepts. These activities have been tested for over ten years in our arts-based mindfulness program with a variety of marginalized populations (Coholic et al., 2012, 2018, 2019). Importantly, mindfulness is not just meditation practice. Mindfulness-based concepts are also vital to learn and apply.

Kabat-Zinn (1990) identified these as the attitudinal foundation of mindfulness practice and they include non-judgment, patience, beginner's mind, trust, non-striving, acceptance, and letting go. For example, non-judgment has to do with learning to have compassion and understanding for ourselves when challenging memories and feelings arise, and developing understanding of our choices, behaviours, and so on. For instance, many women blame themselves for being sexually assaulted. Susan is a young woman I worked with in my private practice. She blamed herself for being sexually assaulted while she was on vacation because she let herself be persuaded to go for a walk with a man she recently met; he led her to a secluded area where he assaulted her. In my work with her, it was important to process her ideas that the assault happened because of her naivety and poor decision-making, which fostered feelings of shame that persisted. Negatively judging herself and the resultant shame was a huge roadblock that prevented the exploration of the effects and meaning of this traumatic event for which she was not responsible. Learning self-compassion and understanding were crucial components of her recovery and included developing an analysis of how and why women are blamed for the assaults they suffer.

Mindfulness and Trauma

Indeed, both the practice of mindfulness and the understanding and application of some of its concepts such as self-compassion and acceptance can help address the effects of trauma, which can overwhelm a person's ability to cope and regulate arousal (Kelly & Garland, 2016). Researchers have studied the effects of some mindfulness-based interventions (MBIs) especially for posttraumatic stress disorder (PTSD) symptoms although the research in this area is not yet extensive. This being said, in a review of this work, Hopwood and Schutte (2017) found that MBIs were effective in lessening symptoms of PTSD. Stephenson et al. (2017) extended previous research by exploring certain facets of mindfulness and clusters of PTSD symptoms. They found that greater non-reactivity and acting with awareness was best correlated with lower PTSD symptoms. Thus, they concluded that being able to act with awareness may help decrease PTSD symptoms because people can be more aware of the present moment and not become lost in the past or worry about the future.

Ortiz and Sibinga (2017) examined trauma caused by adverse childhood experiences such as neglect and abuse, low socioeconomic status, and prolonged stress, and stated that learning mindfulness can enhance self-regulation and resilience in daily life in the face of these types of stressors and trauma. Thus, improving resilience (successful coping with stress) is important for mitigating the consequences of adverse childhood experiences, and practising mindfulness can help youth reduce symptoms of depression, anxiety, and PTSD, and improve coping with stress and functioning in school. In another study, Pillay and Eagle (2019) argued that training in mindfulness practices may be especially useful in contexts of high and ongoing violence exposure, and in underserviced areas. For example, learning to be mindful entails learning to focus on one's breath, bodily sensations, sensory perceptions, cognitions, and emotions while having an attitude that is curious, accepting, and non-judgmental. People who practice mindfulness are aware and accepting of what they are experiencing, which promotes emotion regulation, flexibility in thinking, feelings of self-compassion, and empathy for others.

In summary, there is support for the two best-known MBIs, mindfulness-based stress reduction (MBSR; Kabat-Zinn, 1990), and mindfulness-based cognitive therapy (MBCT; Segal et al., 2002), for veterans with PTSD and related symptoms, and for women who have experienced childhood abuse or intimate partner violence (Frewen et al., 2015). Also, it has been reported that MBIs have lower attrition rates compared to other evidence-based treatments (Boyd et al., 2018). In general, therapeutic benefits of MBIs for PTSD symptoms include improving attention and ability to be present (not ruminating or anxious); changing cognitions so that one is less judgmental and more self-compassionate and empathic; and lessening psycho-physiological arousal, and emotional numbing (Frewen et al., 2015).

Finally, consistent with our own research exploring an arts-based mindfulness group intervention with marginalized youth (Coholic, 2019; Coholic & Eys, 2016), Horesh and Gordon (2018) stated that while MBIs with traumatized adolescents have not been widely studied, they may be particularly advantageous because there is a focus on moving one's body (for example, through yoga movements and walking meditations), which is effective for youth mental health and enables youth to cope with challenging emotions and thoughts in a non-verbal indirect manner. Second, learning self-compassion and nonjudgment have been shown to be helpful for adolescents, and third, there are many benefits of group work for youth including support and social inclusion. Finally, MBIs do not require sharing of deeply personal issues, which can appeal to youth (and others).

Addressing the Symptoms of Trauma with Mindfulness

Awareness of Thoughts and Feelings

In general, many people who have experienced trauma have difficulty attending to and regulating their feelings and thoughts. Learning how to be more mindful can improve the ability to pay attention and focus. Thus, we can develop self-awareness of our thought patterns thereby understanding negative thoughts as passing events rather than valid reflections of reality. Just because we think something does not mean the thought is accurate. Learning mindfulness can also promote more flexible thinking and responses as opposed to becoming stuck in rumination or anxiety. In fact, the power of mindfulness is this ability to make choices about our feelings rather than acting out. As Kelly and Garland (2016) stated, rather than change a thought itself, MBIs teach people to change their relationship with their thoughts.

In the arts-based mindfulness group program we have developed, we introduce the concept of mindfulness using an activity we call the "Thought Jar." In the Thought Jar activity, feelings and thoughts are represented by an assortment of beads, which are dropped one by one into a jar half filled with water. Once there are enough beads (thoughts and feelings) in the jar, the jar is shaken, which makes it difficult to identify the individual beads. This is akin to when we feel distracted/anxious/overwhelmed and our thoughts and feelings are swirling around in our minds too quickly. Once we stop shaking the jar, all the thoughts and feelings will settle to the bottom, which symbolizes a more mindful mind when we feel focused and calm, and we can identify our thoughts and feelings. Therefore, a mindful person does not have fewer thoughts and feelings, but they can look internally and identify what these are (Coholic, 2019). Internal self-awareness and mindfulness help us to be in control of our responses and the choices we make about our experiences.

Kelly and Garland (2016) used a trauma informed MBSR to facilitate awareness and exposure of conditioned trauma responses without reacting or avoiding these experiences. They used mindful breathing and body scanning methods to help people control their activation so they could process their feelings and memories without repressing or dissociating from these experiences. They also taught participants to develop self-compassion and insight into their coping mechanisms to reduce feelings of shame. Mindful breathing is one way to meditate and practice focusing our attention on the breath (there are many ways to meditate). A simple mindful breathing exercise entails sitting comfortably with your feet flat on the floor and with your hands resting on your thighs or in your lap. In a relaxed way, you should breathe deeply through your nose and exhale through your mouth trying to breathe slowly. Practice paying attention to your breath as it goes in and out of your body. This can be done with your eyes closed or open but focused on one point (your eyes should not be scanning the environment). Sometimes when we are learning and/or practising mindful breathing, our minds will wander a lot. Just notice the thought, try not to judge it or yourself, and bring your focus back to your breath and breathing. In mindful breathing, we can practice this ability to notice our feelings and thoughts, understanding that we do not have to engage with them. With practice, we can be more aware of emerging feelings and thoughts so that we can make decisions about these processes. If it appeals to you or someone you are working with, there are many apps and even watches that can help you remember to practice mindful breathing, for example, a two-minute breathing activity where your breathing is synced with an expanding and contracting circle.

This ability to regulate feelings is important not just in mindfulness-based practice but in regular trauma treatment. It is challenging or impossible to process an event or memory if feelings are not contained and manageable. Kelly and Garland (2016) found that for women who had experienced interpersonal violence/trauma, participating in a trauma-informed model of MBSR significantly decreased symptoms of PTSD, depression, and anxious attachment. They speculated that learning mindfulness helped participants reduce reactivity to thoughts and emotions thereby increasing distress tolerance. Participants were taught how to be more self-aware of their reactions such as dissociation and to use mindfulness-based practices such as breathing to help them cope with automatic responses such as a fight, flight, or freeze response. Learning present moment awareness coupled with less emotional reactivity may have also helped them feel more secure in relationships, which is important for survivors of trauma who can have challenges with forming healthy attachments.

Non-judgment and Acceptance

People can respond better to intrusive memories if they are not ruminating or feeling anxious, fearful or angry about a thought (Pillay & Eagle, 2019). Pillay and Eagle (2019) explained that in practising mindfulness, a person is encouraged to be aware of and accept their internal and external worlds. So whatever rises can be tolerated and addressed, which is important because avoidance is recognized as a primary trauma symptom cluster that exacerbates and maintains unhealthy outcomes. Practising mindfulness can create a relationship with a person's thoughts, feelings and body sensations in which they non-judgmentally observe these things without becoming too attached or too detached from them thereby achieving a balance between being overwhelmed or too removed from their experiences (Pillay & Eagle, 2019). As noted earlier, negative self-judgment and the need to develop self-compassion is of paramount importance in working with many people who have suffered trauma. When someone tells themselves that they should not feel something, it creates a roadblock and the feeling remains repressed or suppressed, creating further problems (van der Kolk, 2014). Self-compassion includes the ideas that self-kindness helps people to tolerate and understand their challenges without judging their pain and suffering (Neff, 2003).

An arts-based mindfulness activity that promotes discussion about acceptance, non-judgment, and control, and that has been well received by our group participants, is called "Bad Day Better." A piece of paper is folded in half and then opened again. On the left side of the page, a participant paints a bad day. Once this picture is completed, the paper is folded and pressed down, which creates a mirror image on the right side of the page. Next, the right side is painted to turn it into a good day. When this picture is completed, the paper is folded again and pressed together which creates a large picture of a good day. After the bad day has been made better, discussion can be had about the painting and how we have the ability to make our bad days better depending on what we focus on, how grateful we feel, and our actions (Coholic, 2019). Many people focus on people and things they cannot control, and it can be helpful to shift that focus to things we can control such as the choices we make and how we express ourselves, which can help us to feel more in control of our lives. This process is especially relevant for survivors of trauma as intrusive memories and triggered feelings can make someone feel out of control. However, it is important to also normalize that having a bad day is a normal part of life and that the point of being mindful is not to avoid difficult feelings but to learn how to feel and express these in healthy and helpful ways, moment by moment, as they arise.

Another example of a simple activity used to promote self-compassion that we use in every arts-based mindfulness group is called "Warm Fuzzies." This activity nurtures positive feelings between group members and can help develop self-compassion, empathy, and self-esteem. Each group member decorates a small white envelope with their name on it. We hang these envelopes on a string with wooden clothespins symbolizing the group members' connection. In every group session, the group members are encouraged to write a warm fuzzy (a compliment, praise, something positive) about each group member and about themselves, and then place these messages in the envelopes (Coholic, 2019). This past academic year, one of my Master of Social Work students studied our group program with women who had left abusive intimate relationships and who were staying at the local transition house (McMahon, 2019). In her thesis, she quotes one of the participants who discussed this activity in a post-group interview:

> I found it challenging to have this envelope … I've never been told I was loved. I was never told that I did anything right. I was an abused child, and coming into this program, the other women all told me what I was by the little notes I have in my envelope … it lifted me so much. To know myself, to know who I am. The love that poured towards me, so positive and strong, because when you're not loved, and you're told you're nothing from a young child; when you're told how good you are or what you are; when you see what others see in you – they can't all be liars, you know? This activity was beautiful. (McMahon, 2019, p.116)

This woman's experience illustrates how a simple activity coupled with group support can shift negative thoughts about oneself promoting more self-compassion and an understanding of setting the context for recovery and growth from trauma.

Posttraumatic Growth

Posttraumatic growth (PTG) is a process of positive transformation and growth following a traumatic experience (Tedeschi & Calhoun, 1996). As Kilmer (2006) explained, the growth surpasses an original state, and thus, is different from resilience. PTG alterations usually occur in five domains: seeing new possibilities, relating to others, identifying personal strengths, appreciation of life, and spiritual change. Regarding the connections between PTG and mindfulness, there appears to be potential for mindfulness-based practices to have an effect on PTG as mindfulness can help improve empathy, self-awareness, and appreciation of strengths (as discussed earlier), which are convergent with the domains of improvement in PTG.

Hanley et al. (2015) found that people who practised contemplative practices reported higher levels of trait mindfulness and PTG, and that trait mindfulness may be an important protective factor for dealing with trauma. Much of the research exploring PTG and mindfulness-based interventions involved people with medical trauma/cancer. In a systematic review examining this research, Shiyko et al. (2017) found a small positive effect of mindfulness-based training on PTG. Similarly, Lianchao and Tingting (2020) concluded that mindfulness had a positive association with PTG and that it helped cancer patients search for meaning and make sense of traumatic events. Shiyko et al. (2017) concluded that the results of their meta-analysis supported the use of mindfulness for promoting PTG and indicated a need for research in this area beyond traumatic health experiences. Finally, In some of our earlier research with children who experienced trauma, we speculated that some of the positive benefits reported by the children and/or their guardians as a result of having participated in our arts-based mindfulness group, may have been indicative of PTG: children identified their strengths as survivors, they developed self-understanding, and were better able to relate to others (Coholic et al., 2009). However, PTG has also not been extensively studied with children and youth.

Concluding Thoughts: Creativity and Caution

The use of arts-based approaches in facilitating mindfulness has not been widely studied. However, in our own work we have argued that using a creative approach is highly engaging for participants. It promotes an accessible and effective way to learn and practice mindfulness that promotes success, and participants can learn important skills and capacities through an enjoyable experience; that is, healing from trauma does not have to be wholly pain-filled (Coholic, 2017). In fact, art has been used extensively in working with trauma often with the purpose of helping people express their thoughts and feelings (Carey, 2006). Indeed, when social workers use arts-based methods in their practices, it is often to both promote self-expression and the understanding of others' experiences especially for people from cultures where art is associated with communicating stories or where people do not feel comfortable talking about or sharing their experiences (Sinding et al., 2014). A commonality exists between creating art and practising mindfulness in that "the practice of being in the present moment in an accepting and non-judgmental manner" is true for each process (Kalmanowitz & Ho, 2016, p. 59). By combining making art with mindfulness, participants could be helped to both contain and regulate their feelings and express their emotions and stories. Creating art externalizes thoughts and feelings, and thus, these can be seen in a different way potentially leading to change (Kalmanowitz & Ho, 2016).

Learning and practising mindfulness is not going to appeal to everyone and it is not a panacea for all our challenges. Importantly, there may be people who need to learn grounding and containment techniques first before they will be comfortable focusing on their breathing or meditating. In a review of MBIs for the treatment of PTSD, adverse effects of engaging in the MBI were not often mentioned but did sometimes occur; one study noted that one participant's symptoms worsened (Hopwood & Schutte, 2017). Burrows (2018) stated that we need to better understand the potential drawbacks of introducing mindfulness as some people may feel worse as a result of mindfulness-based meditations. In her studies, she found that for students who were dealing with emotionally charged issues, meditation could bring about feelings of disconnection, feeling emotionally overwhelmed, and heightened self-criticism. Context is important to consider as much of her research has to do with teaching mindfulness to students in classrooms and schools. Thus, within a helping relationship, for some people dealing with the effects of trauma, it may be best to implement training in mindfulness in combination with other best practice interventions (Pillay & Eagle, 2019). Within classrooms, we need to be careful if encouraging students to meditate and/or engage in a mindful breathing exercise. We can choose simple mindful breathing activities that might be less likely to trigger challenging feelings, and we can caution students that if they are currently dealing with traumatic material that they may not want to engage in a meditative exercise.

In conclusion, for those who are ready and willing to learn mindfulness-based practices and concepts, Horesh and Gordon (2018) explained that mindfulness can teach people how to be less fearful and reactive towards their memories; understand that their symptoms are not who they are; avoid one's thoughts less; and become more self-aware of triggers. Pillay and Eagle (2019) pointed out that learning mindfulness can build resilience and be a preventative approach to having to deal with ongoing trauma. Additionally, as a group intervention, it can be cost-effective and incorporated into existing practices. It is a holistic form of intervention that could even be delivered by non-professionals. Moreover, it is an approach where there is minimal risk of harm as the methods are non-intrusive and practised in a way that personally resonates for participants; it does not engage directly with traumatic material. And the benefits of learning mindfulness endure when it becomes a trait or disposition and a way of life.

REFERENCES

Boyd, J.E., Lanius, R.A., & McKinnon, M.C. (2018). Mindfulness-based treatments for posttraumatic stress disorder: A review of the treatment literature and neurobiological evidence. *Journal of Psychiatry and Neuroscience, 43*(1), 7–25. https://doi.org/10.1503/jpn.170021. Medline: 29252162

Burrows, L. (2018). *Safeguarding mindfulness in schools and higher education: A holistic and inclusive approach.* Routledge.

Carey, L. (Ed.) (2006). *Expressive and creative arts methods for trauma survivors.* Jessica Kingsley Publishers.

Coholic, D. (2017). Holistic arts-based social work. In B.R. Crisp (Ed.), *The Routledge handbook of religion, spirituality, and social work* (pp. 320–8). Routledge.

– (2019). *Facilitating mindfulness: A guide for human service professionals.* Northrose Educational Resources.

Coholic, D., & Eys, M. (2016). Benefits of an arts-based mindfulness group intervention for vulnerable children. *Child & Adolescent Social Work Journal, 33*, 1–13. https://doi.org/10.1007/s10560-015-0431-3

Coholic, D., Eys, M., & Lougheed, S. (2012). Investigating the effectiveness of an arts-based and mindfulness-based group program for the improvement of resilience in children in need. *Journal of Child and Family Studies, 21*, 833–44. https://doi.org/10.1007/s10826-011-9544-2

Coholic, D., Eys, M., McAlister, H., Sugeng, S., & Smith, D. (2018). A mixed method pilot study exploring the benefits of an arts-based mindfulness group intervention with adults experiencing anxiety and depression. *Social Work in Mental Health, 16*(5), 556–72. https://doi.org/10.1080/15332985 .2018.1449774

Coholic, D., Lougheed, S., & Cadell, S. (2009). Exploring the helpfulness of arts-based methods with children living in foster care. *Traumatology, 15*(3), 64–71. https://doi.org/10.1177/1534765609341590

Coholic, D., Schinke, R., Oghene, O., Dano, K., Jago, M., McAlister, H., & Grynspan, P. (2019). Arts-based interventions for youth with mental health challenges. *Journal of Social Work, 20*(3), 269–86. https://doi.org/10.1177 /1468017319828864

Frewen, P., Rogers, N., Flodrowski, L., & Lanius, R. (2015). Mindfulness and metta-based trauma therapy (MMTT): Initial development and proof-of-concept of an internet resource. *Mindfulness, 6*, 1322–34. https:// doi.org/10.1007/s12671-015-0402-y. Medline: 26609330

Hanley, A.W., Peterson, G.W., Canto, A.I., & Garland, E.L. (2015). The relationship between mindfulness and posttraumatic growth with respect to contemplative practice engagement. *Mindfulness, 6*, 654–62. https://doi.org/10.1007/s12671-014-0302-6

Hopwood, T.L., & Schutte, N.S. (2017). A meta-analytic investigation of the impact of mindfulness-based interventions on post traumatic stress. *Clinical Psychology Review*, 57, 12–20. https://doi.org/10.1016/j.cpr.2017.08.002. Medline: 28806536

Horesh, D., & Gordon, I. (2018). Mindfulness-based therapy for traumatized adolescents: An underutilized, understudied intervention. *Journal of Loss and Trauma*, 23(8), 627–38. https://doi.org/10.1080/15325024.2018.1438047

Kabat-Zinn, J. (1990). *Full catastrophe living: Using the wisdom of your body and mind to face stress, pain and illness.* Delta.

Kalmanowitz, D., & Ho, R.T.H. (2016). Out of our mind. Art therapy and mindfulness with refugees, political violence and trauma. *The Arts in Psychotherapy*, 49, 57–65. https://doi.org/10.1016/j.aip.2016.05.012

Kelly, A., & Garland, E.L. (2016). Trauma-informed mindfulness-based stress reduction for female survivors of interpersonal violence: Results from a stage I RCT. *Journal of Clinical Psychology*, 72(4), 311–28. https://doi.org/10.1002/jclp.22273. Medline: 27002222

Kilmer, R.P. (2006). Resilience and posttraumatic growth in children. In L.G. Calhoun & R.G. Tedeschi (Eds.), *Handbook of posttraumatic growth: Research and practice* (pp. 264–88). Psychology Press.

Lianchao, A., & Tingting, M. (2020). Mindfulness, rumination and posttraumatic growth in a Chinese cancer sample. *Psychology, Health & Medicine*, 25(1), 34–44. https://doi.org/10.1080/13548506.2019.1612079. Medline: 31038362

McMahon, S. (2019). *Beyond shelter: The power of women stepping into connection* [Unpublished master's thesis]. The Department of Social Work, Laurentian University. https://zone.biblio.laurentian.ca/handle/10219/3342

Neff, K. (2003). Self-compassion: An alternative conceptualization of a healthy attitude toward oneself. *Self and Identity*, 2(2), 85–102. https://doi.org/10.1080/15298860309032

Ortiz, R., & Sibinga, E.M. (2017). The role of mindfulness in reducing the adverse effects of childhood stress and trauma. *Children*, 4(3), 16. https://doi.org/10.3390/children4030016. Medline: 28264496

Pillay, K., & Eagle, G. (2019). The case for mindfulness interventions for traumatic stress in high violence, low resource settings. *Current Psychology*, 1–15. https://doi.org/10.1007/s12144-019-00177-1

Segal, Z.V., Williams, J.M.G., & Teasdale, J.D. (2002). *Mindfulness-based cognitive therapy for depression: A new approach to preventing relapse.* Guilford Press.

Shiyko, M.P., Hallinan, S., & Naito, T. (2017). Effects of mindfulness training on posttraumatic growth: A systematic review and meta-analysis. *Mindfulness*, 8, 848–58. https://doi.org/10.1007/s12671-017-0684-3

Sinding, C., Warren, R., & Paton, C. (2014). Social work and the arts: Images at the intersection. *Qualitative Social Work, 13*(2), 187–202. https:// doi.org/10.1177/1473325012464384

Stephenson, K.R., Simpson, T.L., Martinez, M.E., & Kearney, D.J. (2017). Changes in mindfulness and posttraumatic stress disorder symptoms among veterans enrolled in mindfulness-based stress reduction. *Journal of Clinical Psychology, 73*(3), 201–17. https://doi.org/10.1002/jclp.22323. Medline: 27152480

Tedeschi, R.G., & Calhoun, L.G. (1996). The Posttraumatic Growth Inventory: Measuring the positive legacy of trauma. *Journal of Traumatic Stress, 9*(3), 455–71. https://doi.org/10.1002/jts.2490090305

van der Kolk, B.A. (2014). *The body keeps the score: Brain, mind, and body in the healing of trauma*. Penguin Books.

10 Posttraumatic Growth: Discovery of Identity and Deep-Driving Desire with Mahavakyam Meditation in Clinical Social Work

INDRANI MARGOLIN AND TULSHI SEN

Introduction

The aphorism "every adversity has a seed of equal opportunity, if not greater" exemplifies posttraumatic growth (Hill, 1937/2007). This concept refers to the positive personal transformation that occurs following a traumatic life event. The notion that adversity precedes change is found throughout ancient civilization. Our primordial ancestors conceived lightning as the "wrath of God," and today we have harnessed that power to light up cities and cure disease. Suffering, while never invited, may become an integral part of and metamorphose into personal growth. Trauma specialists have now demonstrated through neuroscience (van der Kolk, 2014) what Vedic teachers understood thousands of years ago: holistic interventions that engage the spirit, body, and mind are required to assist individuals out of posttraumatic stress. Trauma survivors often become cognitively stuck in a flight/fight or freeze response pattern and simultaneously lose their sense of identity and life purpose after a tragic loss or violation. Clients find inspiration to grow beyond their trauma when they have purpose, a deep driving desire to propel them forward after loss. Without an authentic goal, however, trauma overwhelms their entire being. In this chapter, we propose to identify the process and intervention of trauma for posttraumatic growth.

Every experience of trauma is unique to the individual. We utilize the term *trauma* because it has taken root as a useful clinical term across the English-speaking helping profession to describe, assess, and treat the disruptive, invasive, and pervasive after-effects of a harrowing event. We acknowledge, however, that the term *trauma* may be problematic for some clients because not all languages have a word that directly translates with it. Thus, clinical practice that is led by clients' language and metaphors becomes not only client-centred and trauma-informed but also culturally inclusive. We focus on the spiritual-existential aspect of trauma and posttraumatic growth and offer a meditation intervention, Mahavakyam Meditation (MM), to support self-discovery and self-reliance. This intervention can be applied to not only heal but also evolve out of experiences of suffering or trauma for individuals across cultures.

Trauma

Trauma or posttraumatic stress refers to severe mental and physical distress caused by a disturbing life event. Gray (2015) explained that during traumatic exposure, consciousness severs the connection between physical experience and perceptual, emotional, or mental experience when the sensations become too unbearable to tolerate. Tedeschi and Calhoun (2006) highlighted that a physically or psychologically shattering event disrupts a person's entire image of self, which causes great psychological and emotional turmoil because the person's world view, beliefs, and aspirations come into question. After traumatic exposure, individuals try to protect and dissociate themselves from intrusive, emerging memories, and the associated fear and pain. However, this is not possible without dissociating from feeling in general because all emotions and sensations are registered in the same regions of the brain (van der Kolk, 2014). With a disrupted self-image, survivors lose faith in their own capacity to cope with the pain, and daily life after exposure becomes very difficult (Shiyko et al., 2017). In spite of this key experience, most trauma survivors undergo a process of posttraumatic growth.

Combatting Posttraumatic Stress while Fighting for Posttraumatic Growth

A spiritual viewpoint provides a holistic strengths-based perspective from which to view the trajectory of suffering, which suggests that traumatic experience can psychically prepare individuals and groups for psychological and spiritual transformation (Grof & Grof, 1990). Furthermore, Maslow (1971) put forth that the trigger of trauma may be an internal factor such as the psyche's readiness to transform and can include peak experiences. In fact, growth is directly attributed to the toil that goes along with experiencing and facing trauma (Calhoun & Tedeschi, 2004, p. 99). Life cannot grow without metamorphosis. The butterfly emerges directly from the imaginal cells of the cocooned destroyed caterpillar. Consciousness utilizes the psychological trauma as an opportunity to redirect the individual's focus from the outer to the inner world, dissolve current knowledge of self and the world (Grof & Grof, 1990), and feel mental and spiritual liberation.

Posttraumatic growth, coined by Tedeschi and Calhoun (2004), is a process of personal transformation following a traumatic life event in the domains of life appreciation, interpersonal relationships, recognition of personal strength, openness to taking a different life path, and spirituality. Posttraumatic growth and transpersonal researchers highlight, however, that religious, spiritual, or existential exploration lies at the root of individuals' positive growth in the wake of traumatic experience (Cunningham, 2012; Maslow, 1971; Tedeschi et al., 2017). Individuals undertake a massive psychic metamorphosis of selfhood, life priorities, and sense of place in the universe as they seek to make meaning of the loss and destruction in their lives from trauma. Regardless of an individual's personal belief system, the processes of personal narrative reconstruction, re-evaluation, and whole person development are negotiated through spiritual routes. The objective goes beyond symptom removal to help a person surpass previous functioning and learn to not only survive but thrive in the recovery process.

Openness to the involution, evolution, and dissolution of the developing consciousness plays a significant and supportive role in recovery. This is a key factor that leads an individual from posttraumatic stress to posttraumatic growth (Lancaster & Palframan, 2009) because consciousness can reform the personality without interference from the reptilian and intellectual states of mind. Turning inward with curiosity, along with receptivity and patience in the gradual transformative process enables one to move out of reptilian and intellectual states and into a transcendental state of mind where one can feel their essence. Grof and Grof (1990) emphasized, "What feels like total destruction of the ego is a broader, more encompassing sense of self" (p. 62). Without receptivity to the integrating process of the consciousness and adequate social and/or professional support, however, the crisis cognitively and emotionally endures. Thus, awareness, acceptance, and understanding of one's own transforming levels of consciousness is essential to moving out of posttraumatic stress and into posttraumatic growth. MM is an intervention to support this receptivity in treatment. Yogi Ramacharaka (1904) offers the following suggestion while enduring hardship:

> Look for the flower to bloom in the silence that follows the storm … not until the whole personality of the [hu]man is dissolved and melted … not until the whole nature has yielded, and become subject unto its higher self, can the bloom open. (p. 26)

Understanding Consciousness

A world view of unity, where the ultimate reality is spiritual, is shared by Eastern and Western philosophical and spiritual traditions such as universalism, hermetic philosophy, and perennial philosophers of nonduality such Joseph Campbell, Aldous Huxley, and Meister Eckhart (Kelley, 2008). These traditions have been influenced by the Hindu Advaita Vedanta tradition and prominent sages and social reformists such as Krishna, Radha, Shankara, Ramakrishna, his disciple Vivekananda, and Ram Mohan Roy (Huxley, 2009; Prabhavananda & Isherwood, 1975). Advaita is a spiritual pathway or philosophy rather than a religion because followers can still have their own faiths. Advaita Vedanta philosophy is based on the premise that the ultimate reality is spirit or Consciousness and liberation (moksha) from illusion, separation, and suffering is achievable by realizing our omnipresent unity with Consciousness. Unity is not union; it is one. Consciousness is both the awareness that creates in this world and the substance with which all matter is moulded into form, from the imagination (Sen, 2016). The ego self that we identify with in daily reality is part of the relative world, Maya, which is an illusion we have come to believe through the perception of superimposition of the sense-impressions (Prabhavananda & Isherwood, 1975). The nondual Supreme Self, or Atman, is an individualized Consciousness, contracted and concretized Universal Consciousness.

We incorporate the term Universal Consciousness to refer to the "life force of all matter," which resides within us as Individualized Consciousness (Sen, 2016, p. 104). Universal Consciousness is not a blind mechanical system but a creative intelligence and substance that serves as a reliable source to rely from within oneself as oneself. Sen (2016) explained that, "individualized consciousness … takes form in thought and word" (p. 103). This awareness guides individuals to recognize their inherent self-worth and in-born creative power.

Mahavakyam Meditation: A Path to Self-Identity and Self-Reliance

Meditation is the most practised tool for self and spiritual understanding across nearly all contemplative and spiritual customs. The Eastern philosophical traditions have most clearly described and systematically laid it out as a path to cultivate insight and awareness into the self (Shapiro, 2009). Meditation reveals that human awareness or consciousness is an all-knowing intelligence designed to integrate the total personhood of an individual and actualize one's potentialities. Meditation is an ideal treatment for trauma because the heightened awareness of impermanency that occurs with loss or threat creates an increased receptivity to know and experience the fundamental self (Shiyko et. al., 2017). It enables one to recognize a superior perception of reality where one both feels an integrated beauty and harmony and understand the impermanence of the material world. The adept meditator experiences mental, emotional, and spiritual liberation.

MM is rooted in ancient Vedic philosophy and shares foundational principles about the creative capacity of human thought with Western metaphysics (Herbert, 1985) and Maslow's (1971) Being-Psychology. This meditation practice includes diligent repetition of four proclamations, known as the Mahavakyam (in Sanskrit *maha* means great and *vak*-means word; Sen, 2016). The four Mahavakyam are confirmed by quantum realities from the quantum physics Copenhagen interpretation (Herbert, 1985).[1] The first Mahavakyam identifies that Consciousness creates, which corresponds to Quantum Reality #7, consciousness creates reality (Herbert, 1985). The second Mahavakyam proclaims Consciousness is both the substance that creates as well as the material form of everything from a grain of sand to every universe. This corresponds to Quantum Reality #3, reality is an undivided wholeness. Matter is consciousness that takes specific shape and form in time and space but matter is not a thing. Multiplicity is generated from one Universal Consciousness. The third Mahavakyam declares that individualized consciousness is the creative force that creates our individual worlds according to our awareness. The fourth Mahavakyam is a recognition, "I Am the Creative force or I Am That" (Sen, 2016, p. 113).[2] The final proclamations correspond with Quantum Reality #2: reality is created by observation; there is no reality in the absence of observation. Copenhagen school physicists do not believe in deep reality, only phenomenal reality. Phenomena we see are real but they do not exist in the absence of our observation. Consciousness-created reality physicists emphasize that, "the quantum consciousness assumption asserts, that consciousness is an integral part of the physical world … conscious human decision is what brings one vibratory possibility into reality above others" (Heisenberg, 1958; Margolin et al., 2011, p. 238). Proponents of MM, Copenhagen school physicists, and being-psychologists all stress a consciousness creating reality where the human act of observation dissolves dichotomies and the boundary between observer and observed.

Every thought has a corresponding subconscious image.[3] The continual contemplation of identifying oneself as interconnected with universal consciousness and being a creator in one's own life invites receptivity and acceptance of these ideas by the intellectual mind. This process greatly impacts core beliefs and narratives about the self as having the power to shape one's life. MM facilitates a unitive consciousness which ignites the entire bio-spiritual-psycho-social sphere of the individual. The Mahavakyam provide tools to strengthen concentration and tune into imaginative intelligence where the mind submerges in pure awareness so that individuals can deliberately choose their thoughts rather than automatically ruminate upon negative or disturbing images of previous trauma.

Ancient Vedic teachers formulated MM to condition the mind to experience the relationship between the individual and the universe; and, to empower their students to realize their own self-worth. Sen (2016) explained, the "mind intellectually rejects any thought of Unity or being one with the Universe" (p. 92). Clinicians can apply it similarly with clients. By providing a route to tap into their imaginative power, individuals understand their relationship with the creative process and are inspired to harness that power to create their own thoughts, feelings, ambitions, and circumstances with the Mahavakyam.

This system is the culmination of thousands of years of distillation of the Vedas, the sacred texts of India, by great sages (for a complete discourse, refer to the *Principal Upanishads* by Radhakrishnan, 1953/2011; and Sen, 2016). Sen (2016) studied this system of thought from a Himalayan sage and dedicated his life to teaching leadership based on spiritual principles to inspire educators, entrepreneurs, business leaders, social workers, and Aboriginal communities (Tulshi Sen Consulting, 2018).

Mahavakyam Meditation for Trauma Recovery

MM is well suited to individuals in recovery from trauma. It facilitates PTG by encouraging the tuning into a spiritual creative mode of being. For those overwhelmed by feelings of grief, anxiety, guilt, remorse, or other painful feelings, MM offers a grounding and integrating solution. The proclamations provide a rhythmic point of concentration that serve four protective important functions for a person coping with the after-effects of trauma: (1) the process interrupts the intrusive attack of unwanted thoughts by chanting, whispering, or silently repeating a mantra, called *japa* in Sanskrit (Easwaran, 2007), (2) it dissipates and transforms unbearable sensations into feelings of calm by resonating with a particular nerve centre in the body and raising the frequency or vibration towards mind body balance, (3) it enables one to transcend beyond five-sense perception. From this unity awareness, this meditation can then both instil the idea and strengthen the resolve in the face of adverse conditions that a person has the authority and capacity to choose what to think, feel, and act, (4) and this all-encompassing experience of oneself as balanced, renewed, and connected to the universe frees one to create goals and aspirations from a deeply integrated frictionless understanding of self. Simply put, MM "makes you free to vision your heart's desire" (Sen, 2016, p. 125).

Inventing New Thoughts, Inventing New Habits as Creator and a Compassionate Being

A trauma-informed approach requires interventions that foster self-compassion in recovery. MM, applied as a therapeutic practice, can facilitate this. The second step of meditation is dharana, which means to hold with the purpose of accepting and internalizing the object of focus and simultaneously accepting the process (Sen, 2016). Dharana is similar to mindfulness and an essential component of MM, which enables an individual to stay holistically focused on self-healing. This nonjudgmental and accepting approach helps trauma sufferers perceive their pain within a spectrum of experience rather than wholly identify with it. In addition, they learn a different habit of self-understanding. This pattern grows stronger than the self-criticism as they acquire a new way to relate to their mind: "Professor Elmer Gates, of Washington, has demonstrated this physiologically in his studies of brain formation. He stated that every thought produces a slight molecular change in the substance of the brain, and the repetition of the same sort of thought causes a repetition of the same molecular action until at last a veritable channel is formed in the brain substance, which can only be eradicated by a reverse process of thought" (cited in Troward, 2011, pp. 92–3).

Thus, according to Gates, thoughts create grooves through which the potent electrical currents of intention flow, make an impression upon the mind, and form habits. That neural pathways are established in this manner signifies the importance of guarding thought against undesirable ideas. Furthermore, this reveals why *japa*, repetition of the Mahavakyam, is such a potent practice to transform identity. With prolonged concentration on the Mahavakyam, one's meaning becomes an integral part of the individual's understanding of herself as powerful and creative. Replacing remorse, regret, guilt, shame, embarrassment, and anger grooves of thought with elation, understanding, and forgiving grooves of thought then become viable options.

Intertwinement of Identity and Desire

Finding purpose is one of the most difficult tasks of one's lifelong pursuit of happiness. An individual's capacity is directly relative to the aspirations they set for themselves. The after-effects of trauma often severely disrupt an individual's capacity to remain focused on their aspirations; in fact, their entire life priorities become (distorted) shattered. In trauma treatment, clients often first set goals to move out of their traumatized state and end intolerable sensations, thoughts, and feelings. These reasonable responses to the unbearable pain, however, do not propel them forward enough to transcend their current shattered self-narratives. After they have moved out of crisis and stabilized, how do they find direction for a new life? The key factor that enables a person to eventually move out of persistent distressing states is a vision for one's life beyond the trauma. Victor Frankl (1963), a Nazi holocaust survivor and psychologist, emphasized that having and assiduously dwelling in a reason, a purpose, to live beyond the trauma enabled himself, and those around him, to survive. He observed that those that lost sight of a vision beyond the current nightmare, that is, stopped imagining a possible positive life afterward, and instead dwelled in the torture, were unable to survive. The brain does not distinguish between imagery that comes from imaginal or phenomenal reality.

People need a method to discover their identity after the loss, which is where their authentic desires reside. Discovery of identity is key to posttraumatic growth. Maslow (1971) highlighted that discovery of identity essentially means unearthing genuine desires and characteristics and then spontaneously speaking and behaving in ways that express congruent thoughts and feelings. We discover our authentic selves when we discover our identity, our purpose, which is our deepest desire. No living entity can ever be devoid of desire. In the Brihadaranyaka Upanishad, the same is described more poetically: "You are what your deep, driving desire is. As your desire is, so is your will. As your will is, so is your deed. As your deed is, so is your destiny" (Easwaran, 2007, p. 114). The message is that discovering deep driving desire enables us to discover identity so that we can genuinely be and express ourselves. The second part of MM is envisioning one's desires from a state of cleared mind, where one is attuned to Consciousness. Once an individual is soaked in this awareness, one has the courage, concentration, and perseverance to think and maintain a goal or vision she truly desires. This type of goal holds enough import for an individual to want to contemplate it continuously and in this contemplation, she creates first with her intention and imagination, which then becomes reflected in the manifest world. MM helps individuals recognize their uttermost self, where their deep driving desires reside and for individuals that do not know their goals, this meditation helps bring them to the fore of their consciousness, along with life purpose and direction. Goal setting may appear future oriented but a discovery of authentic goals is a discovery of our deep-seated self, which is connected to Universal Consciousness and resides in a state of timelessness. In fact, all meditations have as their ultimate goal for the student to enter the Absolute, where one can feel and taste infinity. The quality of desire referred to in the Brihadaranyaka Upanishad, is not speculative desire, or *Vasana* in Sanskrit, an uncertain hope for a future outcome in the relative world of Maya, but rather an assured expectation cultivated and created in the depths of one's Consciousness, beyond time and space, which is then reflected like in the mirror of our environment. Genuine self-discovery requires a holistic intervention that bypasses reptilian and intellectual mind states, where awareness is consumed with self-protection from further physical and emotional pain and enters a transcendent state, where Consciousness is free to feel the depths of one's deepest desires and imagine in assured expectation.

Social Work Practice

The Mahavakyam practice soothes and calms the mind so that clients can feel their unity, and then identify themselves with that as a source of unshakable inner strength. In the process, like in other expressive arts or integrative therapies that engage body, mind, and spirit, the emotional content can be digested and integrated indirectly. We have witnessed individuals transform their self-narrative over time from identifying wholly with overwhelming suffering to identifying with inner silence and stillness. From that metamorphosed state, individuals set larger life goals that enable them to further transcend the traumas they endured. As long as they are overcome by intrusive, automatic rumination of the trauma, larger aspirational goal setting cannot occur. This meditation, applied as a therapeutic practice, adds to the clinicians' toolkit to increase holistic self-awareness in treatment so that clients are enabled to integrate emotions, cognitions, and sensations without reliving them. This practice does not require contact with the traumatic material. A trauma-informed approach means that precaution must be taken to avoid re-traumatization. As with any mind-body-spirit intervention, tuning into one's own breath and body can quickly bring to light previously dissociated pain and requires proceeding gently at the client's pace. With an express focus on the Mahavakyam practice and reflection about the meditation rather than the trauma experience, risk of re-traumatization is significantly reduced. Self-disclosure about the process deepens catharsis, validation, and meaning making about the resulting cognitive, emotional, and somatic states. Self-disclosure about the trauma, of course, may arise, but ideally this is client-directed.

We have observed this system work for those that believe in a transcendent God as well as atheists that hold ideals of truth and social justice to improve their own and others' lives. When individuals imbue themselves in the Mahavakyam, faith in the goodness of people and an intelligent growth-promoting principle of the world is reportedly restored. The proclamation, *Tat Tavm Asi* (everything is consciousness, everything is one) helps trauma victims move out of isolation and feel connected to others and the world.

Mahavakyam Meditation Research

Margolin (2017) explored the effects of MM as a strategy to support awareness, resilience, and holistic wellness with fourth year undergraduate social work students in the classroom. Findings indicated that this practice greatly reduced anxiety and trauma symptoms. For example, one student suffered from test anxiety. She reported that regular practice of centring herself with the meditation and focus on envisioning the outcome she wanted directly before the exam greatly reduced her pre-test anxiety symptoms of shaking hands, sweating, and shortness of breath. Her ability to recall knowledge during the exam greatly improved and, subsequently, so did her test scores. Another student noticed, after one month of practising the meditations, she felt significantly calmer while driving than prior to the MM practice. She reported that she no longer felt the extreme agitation and anxiety as she navigated sharing the road with other drivers. She concentrated on her own driving rather than others. An immigrant student reported that during meditations, her perspective shifted. Previously, her mind was consumed with regret and torment about moving to Canada. Engaging with the Mahavakyam empowered her to focus on acceptance and gratitude for her new life. All students reported a new-found connection to the divine and their authentic selves. Other participants reported feeling spiritually connected to the world around them in a novel way, which stabilized and uplifted their overall mood. They made clear connections between their thoughts and the accompanying imagery and how this impacted their feelings, choices, and relationships on a daily basis. Their new-found self-awareness reportedly enabled some participants to "think on a deeper level and actually make a choice to recognize uncomfortable visions ... remedy it and replace those visions with images [they] want." Participants disclosed that they did not criticize others internally anymore and felt an emotional weight lifted. One participant spoke about enhanced relationships in a social service agency with women who are schizophrenic or bipolar. Lila explained, "At work, I see a lot of my coworkers get frustrated easily because a lot of the conversations we have with them are repetitive ... I'm much calmer and patient. I find I'm a better listener now to what is said and more attuned to the person's feelings."

I (Indrani) personally experienced tremendous healing and transformation from practising this system as a trauma survivor myself. After a deep sense of despondency, I was driven and destined to find a more reliable and sustainable world view then the one I was carrying. In that pursuit I met Sen and learned about MM, a system devised to empower and cultivate a person to reclaim Selfhood as a creator. The practice took me out of isolation and re-established my relationship with my spirit to feel the goodness in people and the world again. I found a solid foundation from which to rely within myself as myself.

Clients can gain sufficient knowledge, confidence, and self-reliance to formulate an authentic goal, a vision that expands their sense of self beyond the onslaught of invasive thoughts and feelings with MM. Existential questions about identity, sense of place or home, and life purpose can be reflexively discovered by contemplating these proclamations. They receive directions for their life from deep within themselves uninfluenced by external impositions. These answers can only come from inside-out: from the awareness of self.

The purpose of MM is to bring the conscious awareness from the reptilian or intellectual mode of operation to a transcendent state where one's field of perception and receptivity is open to their creativity beyond past memories and pain. Thus, the goal setting becomes a vision of discovery from deep within the Absolute-an end state unlimited by 5 sense perception in this time-space world. Consciousness, with its unfettered creativity, then brings the necessary resources together by an orderly sequence of events in time and space as a reflection of the creation that already occurred in Consciousness.

MM cultivates identity formation and supports goal development. This philosophy and practice can be brought into treatment for those suffering from posttraumatic stress and seek a spiritual means to heal. Life aspiration, a definite intention with which one is committed, transforms trauma into growth. Adversity is most often a precursor to personal transformation. Practice of the Mahavakyam and their meaning creates a new groove of thought, and with prolonged concentration, a habit of identifying oneself as an individualized form of Universal Consciousness. Absorbed in this identity as one with the invisible creative force of the world, clients then can believe they possess an inherent capacity to create with intentional imagination. By harnessing that power to think, feel, and create from Consciousness, a person can set purposeful treatment goals and dream what once seemed impossible.

NOTES

1 For further detailed explanation of the quantum physics theory, see Margolin et al. 2011.
2 Further explication is provided by Radhakrishnan 1953/2011 (see pp. 458, 523, 695, 168).
3 Cognitive behavioural therapists share this idea and hold that metamorphosing thought is key in intervention. Imagery rescripting, for example, guides clients to replace unwanted negative mental imagery with new positive imagery. Holmes et al. (2007) highlighted that cognitive behavioural techniques have the most potent impact on positive emotion when they include imagery.

REFERENCES

Calhoun, L.G., & Tedeschi, R.G. (2004). Authors' response: The foundations of posttraumatic growth: New considerations. *Psychological Inquiry, 15*(1), 93–102. https://doi.org/10.1207/s15327965pli1501_03

Cunningham, M. (2012). *Integrating spirituality in clinical social work practice: Walking the labyrinth*. Pearson.

Easwaran, E. (2007). *The Upanishads: A classic of Indian spirituality* (2nd ed.). Nilgiri Press.

Frankl, V.E. (1963). *Man's search for meaning*. Washington Square Space.

Gray, A.E. (2015). The broken body: Somatic perspectives on surviving torture. In S.L. Brooke & C.E. Myers (Eds.), *Therapists creating a cultural tapestry: Using the creative therapies across cultures* (pp. 170–90). Charles C. Thomas.

Grof, C., & Grof, S. (1990). *The stormy search for self: A guide to personal growth through transformational crisis*. Tarcher.

Heisenberg, W. (1958). *Physics and philosophy*. Harper & Brothers.

Herbert, N. (1985). *Quantum reality: Beyond the new physics: An excursion into metaphysics and the meaning of reality*. Anchor Books.

Hill, N. (2007). *Think and grow rich*. Arc Manor. (Original work published 1937). http://think-and-grow-rich-ebook.com/

Holmes, E.A., Arntz, A., & Smucker, M.R. (2007). Imagery rescripting in cognitive behaviour therapy: Images, treatment techniques and outcomes. *Journal of Behavior Therapy and Experimental Psychiatry, 38*(4), 297–305. https://doi.org/10.1016/j.jbtep.2007.10.007. Medline: 18035331

Huxley, A. (2009). *The perennial philosophy*. Harper Collins.

Kelley, C.F. (2008). *Meister Eckhart on divine knowledge*. Frog Books.

Lancaster, B.L., & Palframan, J.T. (2009). Coping with major life events: The role of spirituality and self-transformation. *Mental Health, Religion & Culture, 12*(3), 257–76. https://doi.org/10.1080/13674670802500684

Margolin, I. (2017, 13–15 March). *Exploring proclamation meditation and visualization with undergraduate social work students in the classroom: A qualitative arts-based inquiry to support awareness, resilience, and self-care* [Presentation]. International Spirituality and Psychology Conference, Bangkok, Thailand.

Margolin, I., Pierce, J. & Wiley, A. (2011). Wellness through a creative lens: Meditation and visualization. *Journal of Religion & Spirituality in Social Work: Social Thought, 30*(3), 234–52. https://doi.org/10.1080/15426432.2011.587385

Maslow, A.H. (1971). *The farther reaches of human nature*. Penguin Books.

Prabhavananda, S., & Isherwood, C. (Eds.). (1975). *Shankara's crest-jewel of discrimination (Viveka-chudamani)*. Vedanta Press.

Radhakrishnan, S. (2011). *The principal upanishads* (H.D. Lewis, Ed.). George Allen & Unwin Ltd. (Original work published 1953).

Ramacharaka, Y. (1904). *Advanced course in yogi philosophy and oriental occultism*. Yogi Publication Society.

Sen, T. (2016). *Ancient secrets of success: The four eternal truths revealed*. Omnisun Systems.

Shapiro, S.L. (2009). Meditation and positive psychology. In S.J. Lopez & C.R. Snyder (Eds.), *Oxford handbook of positive psychology* (2nd ed., pp. 601–10). Oxford University Press.

Shiyko, M.P., Hallinan, S., & Naito, T. (2017). Effects of mindfulness training on posttraumatic growth: A systematic review and meta-analysis. *Mindfulness, 8*, 848–58. https://doi.org/10.1007/s12671-017-0684-3

Tedeschi, R.G., & Calhoun, L.G. (2004). A clinical approach to posttraumatic growth. In P.A. Linley & S. Joseph (Eds.), *Positive psychology in practice* (pp. 405–19). John Wiley & Sons. https://doi.org/10.1002/9780470939338

– (2006). Time of change? The spiritual challenges of bereavement and loss. *OMEGA: Journal of Death and Dying, 53*(1), 105–16. https://doi.org/10.2190/7mbu-ufv9-6tj6-dp83

Tedeschi, R.G., Cann, A., Taku, K., Senol-Durak, E., & Calhoun, L.G. (2017). The posttraumatic growth inventory: A revision integrating existential and spiritual change. *Journal of Traumatic Stress, 30*(1), 11–18. https://doi.org/10.1002/jts.22155. Medline: 28099764

Troward, T. (2011). *The Edinburgh lectures on mental science: 1904–1909.* YogeBooks. http://www.yogebooks.com/english/troward/1904edinburgh.pdf

Tulshi Sen Consulting. (2018, 18 March). *The man who transforms lives.* https://tulshisen.com/tulshi-sen/

van der Kolk, B.A. (2014). *The body keeps the score: Brain, mind, and body in the healing of trauma.* Penguin Books.

11 Spirituality and Faith Communities Relative to Developmental Disability and Health Issues: Considerations in Disability, Illness, and End-of-Life Care

DAVID NICHOLAS AND CHRISTOPHER KILMER

Introduction

For many individuals, spirituality and faith are important contributors to wellbeing despite or amid adversity in their lives. Accordingly, post traumatic growth based on spirituality appears to be an important notion despite relatively little literature in this field. Hardin et al. (2003) describe spirituality as an "awareness of who and what we are now and what we are becoming" (p. 43). Spirituality encompasses a broad collection of beliefs (Edwards et al., 2010), including formal religion as well as meaningful relationships with self, a higher being and/or elements such as nature, art or music. In this chapter, we seek to convey our contention that in the context of disability and illness, spirituality and faith communities can nurture individual and family well-being, and this contribution often reflects a range of facilitative approaches, practices, and sensitivities. The chapter initially focuses on the potential role of spirituality and faith communities in the developmental disability community, including an example of a faith community that intentionally has aimed to be integrative relative to the engagement of individuals with developmental disabilities. We then turn to elements of spirituality in the context of health and addressing illness and end-of-life care, drawing on examples in paediatrics.

The chapter provides a selected review of literature variably suggesting that faith and spirituality offer, for some, a source of hope and guidance, and sometimes additionally involve integrated support from a faith-based community. The chapter concludes with practice implications for social workers. We integrate notions of spirituality and faith communities yet realize that these two notions are not necessarily synonymous or intertwined. Spirituality may be a unique notion and experience from person-to-person, family-to-family, and community-to-community. However, these elements of lived experience are viewed to have the potential to be a helpful resource that may be desired, relevant, and meaningful. In the context of developmental disability and illness, ensuring access to such opportunities seems worthy of resource/organizational support.

Developmental Disability Relative to Spirituality and Faith Communities

Engagement in spirituality and faith communities is valued by a proportion of the population, including individuals with intellectual and/or developmental disabilities (Liu et al., 2014; Shogren & Rye, 2005); however, a scoping review by Hills et al. (2016) noted an overall dearth of literature relative to the role of faith or spirituality in the lives of people with disabilities. Furthermore, there is a gap in the study of posttraumatic growth for individuals with intellectual and/or developmental disabilities, yet there may be potential for posttraumatic growth given noted social and emotional growth in this population. In a study of young people with autism spectrum disorder (ASD) or intellectual disability (ID), participants positively reported faith and spiritual engagement as important in such areas as demonstrating a commitment to their beliefs, nurturing spiritual growth, and gaining meaning (Liu et al., 2014). Positive aspects of engagement included being a part of a community in which participants felt they belonged and were treated well, and participating in faith practices as a source of personal support and healing (Liu et al., 2014). Liu et al. (2014) noted social and emotional growth as a result of spiritual and faith engagement, suggesting that there is potential for posttraumatic growth.

In contrast, Shogren and Rye (2005) noted that, despite engagement in worship services, participants with ID were minimally involved in additional faith-community activities. In a study of participants who largely reported physical disabilities, Möller (2012) identified the following potential barriers to inclusion and engagement: (1) environmental considerations, including physical space and transportation issues, (2) certain healing practices that may be negatively experienced by individuals with disabilities (e.g., prayers to "heal" the disability which can be construed as problematizing the person with a disability), (3) congregating people on the basis of having a disability with limited consideration of each individual's uniqueness, (4) a lack of understanding about disability by faith community leaders and community members, and (5) "support" provided in a condescending manner. In a survey of caregivers of individuals with developmental disabilities

(Ault et al., 2013), nearly 65 per cent of respondents reported a lack of needed accommodations for their child in the faith community. Participants reported their children being placed in programs that did not suit their needs and/or did not match their abilities, denial of access into programming, lack of understanding on the part of leadership as well as the community, lack of recognition for the value of contributions offered by individuals with disabilities, and families being left with the responsibility for providing supports (Ault et al., 2013).

Considerations in Moving Forward

In redressing the challenges associated with engagement in a faith community, Goldstein and Ault (2015) developed a framework for inclusion of individuals with disabilities in faith communities, which consists of the following steps: "1) assess the needs, 2) develop recommendations based on the assessment and involve religious leaders, 3) implement the program, and 4) evaluate and follow up" (p. 4). In the initial step, information is gathered from a range of stakeholders regarding the strengths and needs of the individual, their family, the faith community, and the faith community's leadership. Based on this information, a plan is developed that includes goals, priorities, and needed modifications. Following this, the plan is implemented and then evaluated, and recommendations are provided. In a case example involving a child with ASD, Goldstein and Ault (2015) noted the following as keys to the success of their inclusive framework: buy-in from faith leaders, involvement and support from skilled experts already in the faith community, familial involvement in developing a plan specific to their loved one, and the development of a program that allows the individual to participate in developmentally appropriate activities.

Participants in a survey by Ault et al. (2013) reported promising practices in their communities, such as one church that had developed an inventory of needs for each child, peer mentors engaging with individuals with disabilities, and inclusion and adaptation of additional programming (e.g., Bible school, vocational opportunities). A small number remarked about the important benefit of support to family caregivers, including during services but also outside of services such as the provision of respite for parents.

Carter (2016) identified elements related to inclusion in a faith community, noted as "Dimensions of Belonging": "To be present, invited, welcomed, known, accepted, supported, cared for, befriended, needed, and loved" (p. 169). "Being present" addresses the engagement, involvement, and attendance of individuals. "Being invited" encompasses how individuals and families are informed about and encouraged to attend faith community activities. Carter (2016) noted that broad-based announcements are typically less effective than personal invitations for this population. "Being welcomed" includes authentic engagement and warmth towards newcomers. "Being known" involves taking the time to get to know individuals and considering them beyond labels attached to them or their disability. "Being accepted" involves aspects of the previous elements such that an individual is known, welcomed, and engaged. "Being supported" includes steps taken to support the individual and their family in faith community participation, including accommodations made to activities based on individual needs. "Being cared for" addresses both disability-specific and general supports provided to individuals and families, which may go beyond the organization and into the larger community. "Being befriended" considers the importance of faith community relationships existing beyond times of congregational activity. "Being needed" recognizes and considers that along with the individual with a disability and their family benefitting from the faith community, so too does the faith community simultaneously benefit from the involvement of this individual and family; thus, a mutually beneficial relationship is recognized. Finally, "being loved" is noted as difficult to encapsulate yet reflective of feelings about how one is treated in the faith community, including aspects of the aforementioned elements of integration and inclusion. Carter (2016) suggested that faith communities could delineate these elements, and record what they are currently doing to address respective elements as well as determining what could be improved.

In another study, Carter et al. (2017) engaged in community conversations regarding inclusion with faith communities. Multiple stakeholder groups were involved, including family members of an individual with a disability, disability service providers, and individuals with disabilities, along with faith community leaders, staff, and others. Participants raised numerous strategies for engagement, divided into "disability-specific efforts," "internal activities," "external activities," "influencers (things that shape the attitudes, beliefs, and activities of the community)," and "resources in the community" (Carter et al., 2017, pp. 582–3). In addition to activities that resonated with Carter's (2016) previously identified elements of inclusion, key points included increasing disability awareness in the community, continued evaluation of efforts made by the community, and forging partnerships with other community organizations and faith communities. However, participants reported varying views regarding the ongoing commitment of their faith community to these aims and actions.

One framework is illustrated in the work of L'Arche® Canada (2020a), an international organization that, "creates communities where the members, with and without intellectual disabilities, share life together. Each member receives support to grow, attain their goals, and contribute their gifts and abilities" (para. 1). Thulberry and Thyer (2014) note that community membership can extend beyond those with intellectual disabilities, and can also include, as examples, those with developmental and/or physical disabilities. Individuals with and without disabilities live together and support one another in a variety of ways, including activities of daily living, work, celebrations, personal growth, and finding meaning, as well as engage in their larger ecosystem; mutuality and reciprocity are key. Members with disabilities are seen as having gifts that can be shared with the entire community, and all individuals grow from the relationships they develop with one another (Thulberry & Thyer, 2014).

L'Arche® Canada (2020b) reports that their communities are: "rooted in a Christian tradition, but its members belong to a variety of faith traditions or follow other spiritual or personal pathways. There is a shared spirituality in L'Arche® that includes finding mystery in the ordinary things of daily life, celebrating the unique gift of each person, and seeing our need for one another as a pathway to inner freedom, mutual care, unity, and communion" (para. 1). Thulberry and Thyer (2014) note that a L'Arche® community is often founded based on a singular religious institution and then becomes more interfaith in nature over time. This can reportedly cause some community members to feel like outsiders if they do not belong to the dominant faith group. McCrary (2017) identifies other potential areas of concern, including potential paternalistic views of community members who do not have disabilities, and those without disabilities viewing community members with disabilities as a means "to facilitate their own spiritual transformations" (p. 389). Notwithstanding these considerations and concerns, this approach illustrates a model that exists in multiple sites across the world.

Leadership as a Facilitator of Engagement and Inclusion

The literature has noted that attitudes, beliefs, and practices of faith community leaders have the potential to substantially influence community members. Buy-in from leadership is noted to be a critical step to successful inclusion (Ault et al., 2013; Goldstein & Ault, 2015). As an example, from the literature, successful programs were cancelled after an individual left a faith community due to that individual solely managing the programs (Ault et al., 2013). Attitudes and beliefs of faith leaders were noted to influence perceptions about inclusion or exclusion, and the views of community members around individuals with various disabilities. For instance, in a study of one group of religious leaders (Patka & McDonald, 2015), deficit-based views about individuals with an ID were reported: "Generally, the 'Close to God' narrative suggests that people with intellectual disability have a relationship to God that is closer than others. The 'Conformity' narrative holds that people with intellectual disability need to conform and adjust to parish environments. The 'Unfortunate Innocent Children' narrative posits that individuals with intellectual disability are children in adult bodies, and the 'Deficient' narrative puts forth that people with intellectual disability are incomplete and require fixing through means such as religious healings" (p. 1253). Despite some negatively held views, it was noted that some faith leaders in this study disagreed with such beliefs, and instead actively promoted and engaged inclusivity and diversity.

Finn and Utting (2017) conducted a qualitative study exploring the experiences of future pastors who spent a year living with individuals with ID in "The Inclusion House." Participants reported that unique challenges arose with their roommates with ID that required them to problem solve in novel ways – an important skill for future leaders of faith communities. Engagement with family members and caregivers was also noted to be integral for success, including communication about the inclusiveness and participatory nature of one's faith-based organization, program, or way of being.

As illustrated in this literature, welcoming and engaging faith communities and spaces of spirituality indeed are achievable – including various means of accommodation as needed. Yet to date, variable uptake has been achieved in creating such accessible opportunities within faith community culture, structure, and practice. This unfortunately, can result in gaps in opportunity for some with developmental disabilities to meaningfully engage in faith or spiritual communities. Yet this literature also offers instructive guidance in potentially changing the tide. In the following section, as one of multiple such examples, a Canadian-based faith community is briefly described in exemplifying a welcoming program of participation and wayfinding within a faith community context.

Circle of Friends: A Faith Community in Development

Edmonton Circle of Friends (in Edmonton, Canada) is a resource that has emerged within a faith community context. It espouses inclusion, acceptance, meaningful community connection and access to spirituality. Meeting within a church, it offers multiple programs such as youth activities, worship opportunities, family navigation support, transitional programming, and vocational support. Individuals across all ages with or without disability are welcome, with supports tailored to individuals' needs and desires. Children, youth, and adults, and their unique experience and presentation are integral in the design of programming that in turn focuses on equity and engagement. Various "stations" of activity are offered based on interests and foci of partici-pants relative to needs and areas of skill and challenge, all contributing to the central aim of connectivity and belongingness to, and within, the group. Resources for the transition to adulthood, and vocation are focused on aims of quality and community engagement. Key elements include leadership that is committed to programming commensurate with the needs of community participants, and advocacy and support are central to supporting individuals to thrive in their community. Accordingly, respectful engagement is sought, and intra-group engage-ment entails communication styles and learning/sharing that accom-modate diversities within the context of the faith community.

Role of Spirituality and Faith Communities in Paediatric Health/Illness

For families in which a child has a chronic or acute illness, asking spiri-tuality and faith-based questions may be an important resource and illuminate spiritual needs. In a study examining adolescent cancer patients largely in an Islamic context and country (Iran), Zeighamy and Sadeghi (2016) noted that some children stated that prayer offered a sense of peace and solace during treatment (e.g., "I pray at the time of radiation" [p. 10]), yet this work cited the lack of a peaceful area to pray as an unmet need in the treating hospital.

Navigating communication about spirituality with ill children's needs was noted as needing to be done with care and intentionality (Kassam et al., 2013). Reflecting on the literature in applying these notions to life-threatening illness, Foster et al. (2012) developed a model of child development in relation to understanding the concept of death. A child's cognitive ability to comprehend an abstract concept like death may be limited, but the concept may be thought about and is relevant to children, who have reported spirituality and death as "taboo" subjects and potentially isolating (Boynton, 2016). This must be carefully considered relative to supporting children in their spiri-tual understanding. Potential questions may include: "Once you are dead are you always dead [?]" and "Why did God let me get cancer?" (Foster et al., 2012, pp. 111–12).

Grappling the spiritual and medical needs of children may be seen in the context of more complex spiritual questions and possible discomfort with this issue. Nurses in particular, "at the bedside, who typically have well-established relationships with ill children and their families," may provide helpful assessment (Foster et al., 2012, p. 113), yet support from chaplains, imams, priests, pastors, and other spiritual leaders can assist in applying a spiritual and theological lens that is complementary and/or nurturing to child and/or family understandings and values. Open communication seems integrally important and is often cited as a helpful element of care offered to those experiencing fear and uncertainty due to illness (Mack et al., 2009). Accordingly, a member of the interdisciplinary health care team or others in a child and family's circle of care need to consider potential spiritual needs of the individual and family, including how a child's belief system may differ from their parents'. In an increasingly non-homogenous culture, this task is increasingly complex as more arenas of spiritual belief may need to be considered.

Peace and Hope Offered by Spirituality

In situations usually marked by confusion and despair, much of the literature describing the spiritual coping of patients and their families in palliative or intensive care suggests spirituality as offering peace and hope. Peace of mind was noted by Mack et al. (2009) as a potential challenge for parents of a child with cancer. Such a lack of peace may stem from uncertainty or despair due to the child's unknown or poor prognosis. In another study, Zeighamy and Sadeghi (2016) noted that within the religious beliefs of Islam, "disease and death is a part of God's plan, and this situation is an opportunity for prayer" (p. 3). In this case, the experience of childhood cancer was not viewed to be external to the scope of the faith community's beliefs. Moreover, the illness was not viewed as divine disfavour, but instead spiritual beliefs offer a perspective suggesting that this trying time should be accepted and worked through with the help of the religious community.

In the Christian community, the presence of God during times of difficulty is often viewed to provide comfort in infirmity (Nicholas et al., 2017). Canadian parents in Nicholas et al.'s (2017) study, who primarily self-identified as Christian, reported that their faith provided a sense of hope and guidance, fostered acceptance of difficult circumstances (i.e., the child's illness), and facilitated support from other community members. Christian teachings, including scriptural guidance, speak of God's presence and help in times of trouble, offering solace and the potential for a deeper purpose.

From an Islamic perspective, Sadeghi et al. (2016) explored spiritual coping among parents whose infant had died within her/his first month of life. Factors nurturing healthy grieving practices included "acceptance" and "surrendering" to the ultimate plan of God (Sadeghi et al., 2016, p. 41). This gave context to the loss, and the family's religious beliefs offered direction to parents without labelling their grief as inappropriate or a lack of faith. It appears that particular theological concepts pertaining to illness and death in a religion/faith teaching may play a part in adherents' ability to cope and potentially move them towards healing. Acceptance of loss seems to be reflected as part of some religious traditions and, as such, creates an alternate story for individuals such that rather than being merely a patient or victim without hope, they seemingly are playing a role in a larger plan (Purcell et al., 2015).

Reviewing this phenomenon from a longitudinal view, Grossoehme et al. (2011) interviewed parents twice over the two years after their child was diagnosed with cystic fibrosis. An emergent theme was that parents moved from statements reflective of their ability to handle the situation to an external locus of control in which they were a part of a larger plan, and more readily described their situation as a vocation or calling of being a caretaker for a child with cystic fibrosis.

Along with peace as a prominent benefit of spiritual health, hope is purportedly offered, for instance, with the idea of possibly being healed and/or being comforted by a belief in an afterlife. In a literature review by Edwards et al. (2010) on spiritual coping in adult palliative care, hope emerged in a majority of articles, both in ideas of recovery and imagining a future for those who have died. This phenomenon was not restricted to the traditionally spiritual; "even affirmed atheists spoke of their beliefs in the afterlife, in the anticipation of a spiritual existence after death and being able to meet loved ones again" (p. 759). Evidence of this perspective may be reflected in Tamburro et al.'s (2011) sample, where families who indicated that spirituality was important to them were more likely to opt for less intervention in the palliative setting than the families that did not indicate the same.

For some, spirituality provides activities in which patients and their loved ones can actively participate via rituals and ceremonies. This engagement may not only increase a sense of connection to a higher power but also offer a sense of greater efficacy. For example, adolescent patients were observed engaging in prayer and worship before treatment (Zeighamy & Sadeghi, 2016). Schneider and Mannell (2006) noted that while interviewing parents of children with cancer, the act of praying was mentioned many times and was seen as beneficial because it was something active – "something concrete that [parents] could *do* for their child in an otherwise uncontrollable situation" (p. 13).

Faith Community Support: Contribution to Adaptation

For patients and families whose beliefs typically include regular gatherings with attendees/congregations, assistance from peers from within the faith community was noted, including phone calls, electronic greetings, and prayers for the family (Hexem et al., 2011). These acts of care contributed to creating what was described as a *network* of support – a system that helped lighten the burden of day-to-day tasks and long-term stress related to illness (Hexem et al., 2011).

These faith community connections also provided protection against isolation. Notably, it was found that families who felt most isolated were often those with family members who due to their condition, were bound to home or the hospital (Purcell et al., 2015). In a qualitative study on the experiences of 73 parents of children receiving paediatric palliative care, Hexem et al. (2011) asked open-ended questions regarding any "religion, spirituality, or life philosophy" (p. 40) that had provided support to them while caring for their child. Recurring comforts were the prayers of friends, community recognition of their suffering, and the perceived promise of eventual peace for their child in an afterlife. These provided substantial encouragement as they faced an unknown future.

In a qualitative study on spirituality and coping among parents of children with cystic fibrosis, the proposition of venturing out and engaging with community came with substantial costs both in tasks of preparation and risks of the child's condition worsening (Grossoehme et al., 2011). Yet to combat disconnection and isolation, some caregivers were described to nonetheless engage in church activities, with some reportedly disinfecting areas where the child would sit, including the pews and books used by the child during the service (Grossoehme et al., 2011). Connection and solidarity in one's faith community emerge as generative even though extra work and mitigation were deemed to be required of parents to render worship engagement palatable.

Potential Difficulties and Risks of Spirituality in Health Issues

Despite the reported support and benefits of spirituality and faith community engagement, negative experiences have been described by those who have encountered a serious diagnosis in themselves or a loved one, including despair and anger. For instance, Hexem et al. (2011) identified reports of parental blame directed towards a higher power for "allowing" health deterioration (Hexem et al., 2011, p. 41). The literature describes such feelings as "negative religious coping strategies," and notes how such strategies can decrease family cohesion (Brelsford et al., 2016, p. 320). A parent of a child in critical care expressed anxiety about how prayer could be "a potential liability" if one went from *hoping* for something miraculous to *expecting* its occurrence. In contrast, a parent described being fearful of prayers not being answered (Schneider & Mannell, 2006), and in some instances, parents reportedly chose to disconnect from their faith (Hexem et al., 2011).

A skill was identified by Zelcer et al. (2010) that allowed parents of children with a brain tumour to both gain strength from spiritual exercises while avoiding disappointment. This was described as the "ability to hold on to 2 dichotomous beliefs" (Zelcer et al., 2010, p. 228) at once: first, the prognosis from the health care professionals is serious and real, and second, miraculous healing is possible. Others in similar situations reportedly found solace in believing that a higher power cannot be commanded to heal their child, and interventions from such a power sometimes come in a "more-subtle or nuanced way" (Purcell et al., 2015, p. 32). In a study of families of children with cystic fibrosis, parents described viewing the diagnosis as a part of God's plan, and in this way "normalized" the diagnosis whereby parents reportedly did not feel guilty about potentially passing on genes related to their child's disease (Grossoehme et al., 2011).

Many parents have identified faith as difficult to maintain in a child's illness journey (Schneider & Mannell, 2006; Woodgate & Degner, 2003). A qualitative study suggested a link between the diagnosis and the nature of spiritual struggle as experienced by family members (Purcell et al., 2015). In an example of a rare but treatable paediatric lung disease in which there is a lengthy diagnostic process that often appears to lead to other lung diseases with a comparatively less hopeful prognosis, parents reported spiritual growth as a result of the illness (Purcell et al., 2015). Likewise, researchers have speculated that parental hope may relate to the extent of hope they receive from the doctor's prognosis (Schneider & Mannell, 2006).

In another study, parents described difficulty maintaining direct connection to their faith community due to care requirements of their ill child that restricted attendance at scheduled rituals or gatherings (Nicholas et al., 2017). Despite this, parents reported appreciating the continued support from their faith community, such as prayers for the family (Nicholas et al., 2017).

Spiritually Imbued Pathways Forward

While individuals and families convey a range of responses to and levels of affinity for spirituality, spiritual practices and/or faith community engagement appear to offer, for some, important resources in times of adversity. Calibrating life circumstances within a spiritual lens appears to draw on core elements of meaning-making and moving forward amid variable challenges, including grief and loss.

These findings invite spiritual and faith community supports, as desired by individuals and families. Ensuring accessible spiritual support, on terms that are relevant and desired by individuals and families, reflects broader tenets of person and family-centred care in disability and health care as well as complimenting the established notions of community engagement and anti-oppressive practice. Accordingly, we argue for the integration of accessible spirituality-based resources within both community and clinical contexts.

Organizational and systemic barriers to one's ability to engage in their desire for spirituality and faith communities, invite critical reflection and transformation. Accordingly, capacity and resource development and discursive reflection are invited in the aim of increasing options for life pathways and generative experiences.

Some Implications for Integrating Spirituality in Social Work Practice

Mullaly (2006) locates social workers as ideally positioned in seeking societal and community shifts, thereby linking social workers to this endeavour of improved access to spiritually imbued pathways, as desired by individuals and families touched by disability and illness. In seeking such structural and experiential change, Mullaly (2006) asserts: "Given social work's belief that people have a right to develop fully and freely their inherent human potential and to live productive and satisfying lives free from domination and exploitation by others, those in social work must ask what social arrangements best accommodate those values" (p. 50).

Social workers and others such as faith community/spiritual leaders are invited to look critically at elements of imposed restriction and "discursive assumption" in pushing against potentially limiting thinking, practices, and processes. This may invite deep thinking about what spirituality and faith community means to an individual and a community. Moreover, considering key messaging and opportunity (or lack thereof) are important. For instance, definitions of disability or illness in a faith community will reflect how individuals and families with disability or illness are viewed and potentially treated. Social work and other care professions are well positioned to advocate for individuals who face adversity and system-level barriers. Viewing what might otherwise be seen as largely personal challenges from a broader environmental and discursive perspective offers a helpful framework in moving forward.

Supporting individuals in finding their spiritual mooring and meaning-making, as illustrated in this chapter, can be instrumental in their journey of navigating life challenges. Accordingly, spirituality is conveyed as foundational for some individuals and families as they grapple with a history of trauma related to illness and disability as well as potentially facing episodically heightened symptoms, stigma, isolation, and/or other challenges. This journey may entail finding/ shifting meanings, grappling with loss and uncertainty, yet potentially moving forward given spiritually imbued meanings including divine and human connections – indeed, drawing on one's spiritual moorings. Spirituality in this context serves a potentially generative role, particularly when it represents affinity with the values of the individual and family. Accordingly, working with individuals and families to create accessible paths that support their spiritual quest, if relevant, represents an area that is indeed worthy of pursuit.

Recommendations

Towards a heightened orientation to spirituality, the following recommendations are proposed:

- Greater attention to spirituality in clinical and community settings, with a particular focus on how it intersects and resonates for an individual or family
- Integration of spiritual care in the compendium of available "holistic" supports
- Dialogue with persons living with disability and illness and their families about how, if desired, spirituality and spiritual resources could be provided
- Training for health care and community service providers in spiritual care considerations
- Training for spiritual leaders and faith communities in ways to more effectively engage individuals with disabilities and health conditions

- Development of health and disability resources that address the spiritual needs of individuals across the lifespan
- Evaluation of spiritual/faith-based interventions
- Direct inclusion of child and adolescent voices in research as their perspectives otherwise could be glossed over by caregivers' perspectives or others' interpretations
- Research that addresses spirituality in this population relative to posttraumatic growth, including systematic inquiry across the lifespan and inclusive of ethnocultural, faith community and other diversities
- Advocacy for heightened policy development that enshrouds respect for one's spirituality and spiritual conventions/practices at mezzo (e.g., program support, space in facilities for ceremony) and macro (e.g., regulation that upholds opportunity for faith observance) levels of society

Summary

This chapter has demonstrated that spirituality can play an important role in the lives of individuals and families affected by disability and/or illness. Spirituality and faith communities offer meaning, hope, social support, and other potential benefits. Ensuring opportunity for engagement in one's community emerges as a need and indeed a human right which must not be usurped by organizational or programmatic restrictions impeding meaningful engagement. Accordingly, finding ways to bridge access and increase community understanding may be pivotal to better supporting individuals and families in their quest for meaningful engagement in spirituality and a faith community. This may involve resources in the community and in clinical settings (e.g., hospitals) that build capacity and nurture authentic "welcoming" environments. It seems intuitive and imperative that individuals and families are welcomed in environments in which they can engage in their spiritual practices regardless of life circumstances.

Social workers, faith leaders, and others in both clinical and community settings can bridge individual needs with spiritual and other resources. Viewing spirituality as potentially a part of one's "ecosystem" invites integrative practice, relational authenticity, and inclusivity. Partnering with children and their families around their spiritual perspectives and needs, and ensuring complementary resources and opportunities, invite reflection and action. To the extent that such resources are garnered, spirituality and growth can be nurtured.

REFERENCES

Ault, M.J., Collins, B.C., & Carter, E.W. (2013). Factors associated with participation in faith communities for individuals with developmental disabilities and their families. *Journal of Religion, Disability & Health*, 17(2), 184–211. https://doi.org/10.1080/15228967.2013.781777

Boynton, H.M. (2016). *Navigating in seclusion: The complicated terrain of children's spirituality in trauma, grief, and loss* [Unpublished doctoral thesis]. Department of Social Work, University of Calgary. https://doi.org/10.11575/PRISM /27063

Brelsford, G.M., Ramirez, J., Veneman, K., & Doheny, K.K. (2016). Religious and secular coping and family relationships in the neonatal intensive care unit. *Advances in Neonatal Care*, 16(4), 315–22. https://doi.org/10.1097 /anc.0000000000000263. Medline: 27391569

Carter, E.W. (2016). A place of belonging: Research at the intersection of faith and disability. *Review and Expositor*, 113(2), 167–80. https://doi.org /10.1177/0034637316637861

Carter, E.W., Bumble, J.L., Griffin, B. & Curcio, M.P. (2017). Community conversations on faith and disability: Identifying new practices, postures, and partners for congregations. *Pastoral Psychology*, 66, 575–94. https:// doi.org/10.1007/s11089-017-0770-4

Edwards, A., Pang, N., Shiu, V., & Chan, C. (2010). Review: The understanding of spirituality and the potential role of spiritual care in end-of-life and palliative care: A meta-study of qualitative research. *Palliative Medicine*, 24(8), 753–70. https://doi.org/10.1177/0269216310375860. Medline: 20659977

Finn, J., & Utting, A. (2017). The Inclusion House: Where pastors learn to minister to individuals with disabilities. *Journal of Research on Christian Education*, 26(2), 172–88. https://doi.org/10.1080/10656219.2017.1331777

Foster, T.L., Bell, C.J., & Gilmer, M.J. (2012). Symptom management of spiritual suffering in pediatric palliative care. *Journal of Hospice & Palliative Nursing*, 14(2), 109–15. https://doi.org/10.1097/njh.0b013e3182491f4b

Goldstein, P., & Ault, M.J.(2015). Including individuals with disabilities in a faith community: A framework and example. *Journal of Disability and Religion*, 19(1), 1–14. https://doi.org/10.1080/23312521.2015.992601

Grossoehme, D.H., Ragsdale, J.R., Snow, A., & Seid, M. (2011). We were chosen as a family: Parents' evolving use of religion when their child has cystic fibrosis. *Journal of Religion and Health*, 51(4), 1347–58. https://doi.org/10.1007/s10943 -011-9477-5. Medline: 21409481

Hardin, S.R., Hussey, L., & Steele, L. (2003). Spirituality as integrality among chronic heart failure patients: A pilot study. Visions: *The Journal of Rogerian Nursing Science*, 11(1), 43–53. https://www.societyofrogerianscholars.org /visions.html

Hexem, K.R., Mollen, C.J., Carroll, K., Lanctot, D.A., & Feudtner, C. (2011). How parents of children receiving pediatric palliative care use religion, spirituality, or life philosophy in tough times. *Journal of Palliative Medicine*, *14*(1), 39–44. https://doi.org/10.1089/jpm.2010.0256. Medline: 21244252

Hills, K., Clapton, J., & Dorsett, P. (2016). Towards an understanding of spirituality in the context of nonverbal autism: A scoping review. *Journal of Disability & Religion*, *20*(4), 265–90. https://doi.org/10.1080/23312521.2016.1244501

Kassam, A., Skiadaresis, J., Habib, S., Alexander, S., & Wolfe, J. (2013). Moving toward quality palliative cancer care: Parent and clinician perspectives on gaps between what matters and what is accessible. *Journal of Clinical Oncology: An American Society of Clinical Oncology Journal*, *31*(7), 910–15. https://doi.org/10.1200/jco.2012.44.8936. Medline: 23182989

L'Arche® Canada. (2020a). *The L'Arche relational model.* https://www.larche.ca/the-l-arche-relational-model

– (2020b). *Spirituality.* https://www.larche.ca/spirituality

Liu, E.X., Carter, E.W., Boehm, T.L., Annandale, N.H., & Taylor, C.E. (2014). In their own words: The place of faith in the lives of young people with autism and intellectual disability. *Intellectual and Developmental Disabilities*, *52*(5), 388–404. https://doi.org/10.1352/1934-9556-52.5.388. Medline: 25247730

Mack, J.W., Wolfe, J., Cook, E.F., Grier, H.E., Cleary, P.D., & Weeks, J.C. (2009). Peace of mind and sense of purpose as core existential issues among parents of children with cancer. *Archives of Pediatrics & Adolescent Medicine*, *163*(6), 519–24. https://doi.org/10.1001/archpediatrics.2009.57. Medline: 19487607

McCrary, L.K. (2017). Re-envisioning independence and community: Critiques from the independent living movement and L'Arche. *Journal of Social Philosophy*, *48*(3), 377–93. https://doi.org/10.1111/josp.12195

Möller, E. (2012). Experiences of people with disability in faith communities: A journey. *Journal of Religion, Disability & Health*, *16*(2), 154–71. https://doi.org/10.1080/15228967.2012.673082

Mullaly, B. (2006). The new structural social work: Ideology, theory, practice (3rd ed.). Oxford University Press.

Nicholas, D.B., Barrera, M., Granek, L., D'Agostino, N.M., Shaheed, J., Beaune, L., Bouffet, E., & Antle, B. (2017). Parental spirituality in life-threatening pediatric cancer. *Journal of Psychosocial Oncology*, *35*(3), 323–34. https://doi.org/10.1080/07347332.2017.1292573. Medline: 28300487

Patka, M., & McDonald, K.E. (2015). Intellectual disability and faith communities: Perspectives of Catholic religious leaders. *Disability & Society*, *30*(8), 1241–58. https://doi.org/10.1080/09687599.2015.1090953

Purcell, H.N., Whisenhunt, A., Cheng, J., Dimitriou, S., Young, L.R., & Grossoehme, D.H. (2015). "A remarkable experience of god, shaping us as a family": Parents' use of faith following child's rare disease diagnosis.

Journal of Health Care Chaplaincy, 21(1), 25–38. https://doi.org/10.1080/08854726.2014.988525. Medline: 25569780

Sadeghi, N., Hasanpour, M., Heidarzadeh, M., Alamolhoda, A., & Waldman, E. (2016). Spiritual needs of families with bereavement and loss of an infant in the neonatal intensive care unit: A qualitative study. *Journal of Pain and Symptom Management, 52*(1), 35–42. https://doi.org/10.1016/j.jpainsymman.2015.12.344. Medline: 27233143

Schneider, M.A., & Mannell, R.C. (2006). Beacon in the storm: An exploration of the spirituality and faith of parents whose children have cancer. *Issues in Comprehensive Pediatric Nursing, 29*(1), 3–24. https://doi.org/10.1080/01460860500523731. Medline: 16537278

Shogren, K.A., & Rye, M.S. (2005). Religion and individuals with intellectual disabilities. *Journal of Religion, Disability & Health, 9*(1), 29–53. https://doi.org/10.1300/j095v09n01_03

Tamburro, R.F., Shaffer, M.L., Hahnlen, N.C., Felker, P., & Ceneviva, G.D. (2011). Care goals and decisions for children referred to a pediatric palliative care program. *Journal of Palliative Medicine, 14*(5), 607–13. https://doi.org/10.1089/jpm.2010.0450. Medline: 21438709

Thulberry, S.C., & Thyer, B.A. (2014). The L'Arche program for persons with disabilities. *Journal of Human Behavior in the Social Environment, 24*(3), 348–57. https://doi.org/10.1080/10911359.2013.831012

Woodgate, R.L., & Degner, L.F. (2003). A substantive theory of keeping the spirit alive: The spirit within children with cancer and their families. *Journal of Pediatric Oncology Nursing, 20*(3), 103–19. https://doi.org/10.1053/jpon.2003.75. Medline: 12776259

Zeighamy, H., & Sadeghi, N. (2016). Spiritual/religious needs of adolescents with cancer. *Religions, 7*(7), 91. https://doi.org/10.3390/rel7070091

Zelcer, S., Cataudella, D., Cairney, A.E.L., & Bannister, S.L. (2010). Palliative care of children with brain tumors: A parental perspective. *Archives of Pediatrics & Adolescent Medicine, 164*(3), 225–30. https://doi.org/10.1001/archpediatrics.2009.284. Medline: 20194254

Conclusion

JO-ANN VIS AND HEATHER BOYNTON

Trauma, Spirituality, and Posttraumatic Growth in Clinical Social Work Practice is a book that offers diversity in spiritually sensitive approaches that can be used and adapted to encourage PTG in various contexts and across the lifespan. This book is about transformation and hope, as it challenges social workers to begin to more fully and intentionally incorporate the spiritual dimension for supporting PTG into their practice. The chapters discuss ways in which spirituality can offer a choice to individuals to move them beyond rumination, struggle, and resilience to greater levels of functioning. Spirituality can offer a sense of purpose and belief in a positive future through a spiritual vision. As reflected in the earlier chapters of this book, there is commonality in spiritual concepts and overlapping information from various experts in the area of trauma, spirituality, and PTG. The characteristics of PTG are resonant with spirituality. Overall, the authors share a perspective that the essence of spirituality is about intrapersonal, interpersonal, and transpersonal connectivity. The common thread is that PTG can occur and remain strong through spiritual activities, practices, and connections found in relationships including those beyond the human realm, and through balance and harmony with the universe. These chapters are filled with examples of PTG, which include awareness of new possibilities, transformation, strengths, hope, and engagement with self and others, reinforcing definitions of PTG that exist in the literature. It is clear that despite the diversity of issues presented in these chapters, all of the authors agree that PTG requires components of spirituality.

Moreover, the authors discuss that inclusion of spirituality is a complement to commonly known psychotherapeutic interventions which can expand the client's connectivity to self, others and one's world, linking to the core domains of PTG. Calhoun and Tedeschi (1999) outlined five core domains of PTG: personal strengths and a renewed self-perception; changes to relationships with others and a sense of more significant connections with others, and feeling compassion and a greater understanding for others who are suffering; appreciating life more fully, and changes to priorities and meaningful activities; new possibilities, new interests and activities; and existential and spiritual change. Furthermore, PTG involves emerging from trauma feeling stronger, enriched, and better equipped to deal with future challenges (Thompson & Walsh, 2010). These areas are evident in each chapter and really all are interconnected with spirituality in its broad sense.

Many chapters discuss the importance of family, community, and spiritual relationships as the foundation through which spiritual connections can be made and maintained. Themes that highlight the significance of meaning-making and spiritual strength as part of spiritual exploration are frequent. Other chapters emphasize the relationship between the individual and finding one's balance in the universe and the significance of the spiritual connection to one's culture, or identity and belonging in the world. Examples of bodywork, meditation, and mindfulness are offered with central details, reinforcing connectivity with self, others, and existence. The chapters also cover the spirituality across the lifespan and with diverse populations.

Each chapter offers a diverse lens on the characteristics of spirituality. This reflects the uniqueness of spirituality for all individuals. As such, social workers may find themselves drawn to help clients in a number of distinct yet interconnected areas of spirituality. First is the exploration of one's sense of self and identity, and one's unique strengths, abilities, and capacities. They may focus on strengthening connectedness to others such as family, peers, and community which can buffer the effects of trauma. They may seek to further develop any relationships that the client feels are supportive and considered sacred such as a belief in a higher power, spiritual entities, or other relationships including connections to those who have died. In addition, connecting with and spending time in nature can elicit feelings of peace and joy, it allows for contemplation, reflection, clarity, and a deepening of spirituality. Feeling the presence of animals, trees, flowers, rocks, water, landscapes, mother earth, as well as the sky, stars, planets, and the cosmos can not only bring gratitude, tranquillity, and a sense of mystery or belonging in the world but can also foster personal transformation. Furthermore, mindfulness and meditative practice can expand the sense of self, create calm, groundedness, and the capacity for self-regulation. These practices can foster acceptance, non-judgment, self-compassion, appreciation, and empathy which can be incredibly helpful in moving beyond trauma. They also can stimulate creativity and visioning which can spark excitement, renewal, or one's contribution in life.

Social workers can facilitate meaning making and integrate trauma within an expanded spiritual world view. Meaning making processes can involve many spiritual and existential aspects such as grappling with existential and spiritual questions and struggles, changes to perceptions and beliefs of events and oneself, and accepting realities. It also may involve re-evaluating values, morals, and goals. Social workers can assist clients in recognizing the unique qualities of one's identity and purpose, or embedding the purpose of the event into a new spiritual world view. Confronting and transcending barriers and limitations, or limiting beliefs can be important spiritual processes social workers can support. Furthermore, social workers may facilitate a client's connectedness to religious or faith-based supports, or focus on hope, faith, and transformation as pathways to PTG. So as one can see, there is great diversity in the pathways that a social worker may support clients spiritually through trauma, grief, and loss, while fostering PTG.

Canda, Furman, McCann and Pearlman, Seleebey, Tedeschi and Calhoun, and VanderKolk are some of the authors that appear consistently throughout the chapters, reinforcing the commonalities concerning trauma, spirituality, and PTG. For those new to the area of trauma, spirituality and PTG, readers can easily reference some of the familiar authors and researchers as beginning sources for further study. Many chapter authors are specialists in their own right, citing their own research and the works of others supporting their chapter's thesis. Social workers will find that regardless of the clinical issue, the importance of spiritual connections and its link to PTG supports the need for spiritual assessment, intervention, and reflection.

The importance of integrating spiritual exploration within existing psychotherapeutic strategies and approaches is evident in each of the chapters. Expanding assessment questions to include spiritual beliefs and practices, and resources and supports, past and present, open up options for change and healing. Engagement in positive spiritual activities as part of treatment can support clients in their healing journey. Treatment strategies can include seeking spiritual connection and spiritual relationships, spiritual support and direction, practising compassion and forgiveness, mindfulness, and spending time in nature or engaging in meaningful activities that bring peace, joy, compassion, and connection. Spiritual practices, actions, supports, and resources can be evaluated as pillars of strength for individuals going through the effects of the aftermath of trauma and can support and facilitate PTG and further spiritual development. Social workers can support positive spiritual coping to enhance mental and overall health outcomes and PTG. Linking objects including statues, talismans, crystals, prayer beads, photographs, and mementos often have spiritual significance for individuals which bring them peace, comfort, and connection, and as such, Boynton (2016) considered these to be spiritually symbolic objects. Listening for and asking clients about spiritually symbolic objects could offer spiritual connectedness. There is a vast array of activities and coping strategies that practitioners can include in treatment that can promote PTG. Therefore, it is critical for social workers to inquire about a client's current spiritual activities and practices, and to explore the ways to incorporate these in treatment as well as an expansion of a repertoire of these healing spiritual avenues in fostering PTG.

This book also highlights the challenges to including spirituality within our work with clients. Social workers are well aligned to assist trauma survivors, however, their comfort and ability to engage in conversations about spirituality can create unintended healing barriers. Cadell reminds us that we live in a grief-denying society and that social workers receive limited education concerning grief or trauma and the linkages to spirituality. Social workers appreciate strengths-based principles and the importance of promoting PTG. Yet, many are ill-equipped to include spirituality as part of this intricate process. Social workers may not be trained to assess, discuss, or build on a client's spiritual strengths and practices. Given the nature of our work, social workers must strive to increase one's knowledge about trauma and spirituality to facilitate PTG. Development of a spiritually sensitive practice is of utmost importance and gaining competence in this area and is critical for practice, and should be focused upon in academia.

This book contends that the lack of research and literature concerning the importance of spirituality in addressing trauma and healing needs much greater attention. Children, Indigenous peoples, front line workers, and those with disabilities are four of the core areas requiring further research. Research historically focuses on adults and adolescents, and children appear to fall through the cracks since they are not asked about their experience of spirituality in trauma and how it contributes to PTG. For children there is a great need to explore spiritual development, including how it is experienced through gender. There is a lack of comprehensive theoretical frameworks on development that embed spirituality in them, and the inclusion of spirituality in treatment and PTG. Schools are a large part of a child's community and contribute to spiritual development as well. Schools can foster spirituality through resilience, sense of mastery and competence, however, more research concerning trauma informed outcomes with the inclusion of spirituality are needed.

Spirituality is a large part of Indigenous culture, yet research and knowledge concerning spirituality, informed by Indigenous research

is negligible. While research has demonstrated the spiritual devasta-
tion of Indigenous culture through colonialism, little is written about
how Indigenous culture is linked to spirituality and PTG. There is a
need to include research that explores the role of Indigenous knowledge keepers in cultural continuity and holistic care. There is a need
for strength-based assessment tools that can incorporate the diversity
of Indigenous spiritual beliefs, traditions, customs, rituals, and ways of
being. Indigenous clients who have been exposed to trauma deserve a
culturally trauma-informed approach based on spiritual practices that
have been transmitted through Indigenous knowledge. We welcome
the voice of Indigenous scholars to fill this void and offer direction in
this important area.

Research for front line workers has also been limited in the area of
spirituality. Much has been researched and written about the psychological, behavioural and physiological impact concerning trauma exposure. Although this is important, the lack of research concerning the
spiritual impact has implications for healing and growth. Research in
the area of spirituality and PTG for front line workers who are continuously exposed to critical incidents is imperative to support and sustain
professionals in these vital roles.

The fourth core area identified as a gap in the literature concerns
research into spirituality and PTG for individuals with intellectual and
developmental disabilities. Further research exploring the potential
for spiritual practices and faith community engagement, as a means
to assist individuals and families to move forward as they experience
challenges, grief and loss is valuable and needed.

We are hopeful that this book contributes to the quest of adding to
the literature and important discourse in this area. The chapters in this
book offer a response to a need to increase social workers' spiritual
competency and offer diverse solutions to garner a spiritually sensitive practice. We hope this book will provide a significant contribution
and resource to social workers seeking to invite spirituality into their
practice, research, and academic approaches when seeking change for
others.

REFERENCES

Boynton, H.M. (2016). *Navigating in seclusion: The complicated terrain of children's spirituality in trauma, grief, and loss* [Unpublished doctoral thesis]. Department of Social Work, University of Calgary. https://doi.org/10.11575/PRISM/27063

Calhoun, L.G., & Tedeschi, R.G. (1999). *Facilitating posttraumatic growth: A clinician's guide* (I.B. Weiner, Ed.). Lawrence Erlbaum Associates.
Thompson, N., & Walsh, M. (2010). The existential basis of trauma. *Journal of Social Work Practice, 24*(4), 377–89. https://doi.org/10.1080/02650531003638163

Index

www.ingramcontent.com/pod-product-compliance
Lightning Source LLC
Chambersburg PA
CBHW030244030426
42336CB00009B/248